LET LOVE SERVE

A Memoir Celebrating
Tennis and Life

By Steve Wilkinson, Ph.D.

With love and gratitude,
Steve Wilkinson

ADVICE THAT MATTERED

It was May of 2003, and I sat on the sideline in the NCAA Division III singles semifinal against top-seeded Amir Marandy of Cal Lutheran. He was up 6-4, 5-4 and serving for the match. He had not lost a match or even a set all year and was seeded first in the tournament. I had achieved a successful year myself, undefeated at #2 singles for Gustavus and the third seed in this event, but I was feeling more or less defeated as my opponent readied himself to serve for the match.

Wilkinson and Butorac at the 2010 Minnesota Tennis Challenge, a fund-raising event benefiting Northern Tennis Association youth

As I had done many times in the past, I looked to Wilk for advice. Just the day before, he had helped me plot my way through my quarterfinal match against a tough opponent from MIT, in which I fought back from 6-4, 4-2 down to win. This was different. Amir was a superior player and a mere tactical change wasn't going to cut it. I needed something more.

Wilk shared with me the following advice: "Eric, you've given everything you've had to give this year. You have prepared as best you can. You are playing great tennis, and you are playing in front of your family and friends, potentially for the last time. Go out there and enjoy whatever is left." I believe that in that situation, 99% of coaches would have told me to "fight hard" and "believe I could win." But Wilk took a different approach. He helped me understand that I had already achieved success, because it hinged not on the outcome of the match, but on effort and preparation.

As I prepared to return at 4-5, about to play maybe the last game of my college career, I became totally relaxed. I accepted that I might lose the match, and I was at peace with that. For the first time in my life, I played completely free tennis...free from worry about losing and what people might think if I did lose.

I broke Amir's serve, won the tie-breaker and took the third set 6-1. As you will read later, this three set victory only set the stage for drama that came that afternoon.

I realized something after that. Coach had a point. If I could put in full effort leading up to and during the match, there was no reason to worry. For me, less worry meant less pressure, and less pressure meant better and more enjoyable tennis.

I am only one of many who have been affected by Wilk's teachings through his team and his camps. For those who haven't had the opportunity to be coached personally by Wilk, this book is the next best option. For those who were coached by him, it will serve as a necessary reminder of what is important, both on and off the court.

Eric Butorac

CONTENTS

WITH APPRECIATION

Thank you to my wife, Barb. I could speak to her at all times about this memoir. When I was ready to share my drafts, she made practical suggestions on every page. Most importantly, she told me every day that she loved me.

Thank you to our daughters, Stephanie and Deb. They first encouraged me to write this memoir. Our daughters, their husbands Scott and Jon, and our grandchildren—Caroline, Eloise, Stephen, and Audrey—bring us great joy.

Thank you to my parents, Byron and Delpha Wilkinson, Arthur Ashe Jr., Karen Gibbs, and Dr. Don Klotz. They were instrumental in helping me formulate my approach to tennis and life.

Thank you to Neal Hagberg, Dan McLaughlin, David Lachman, Tommy Valentini, and Kevin Whipple. They carry forward my commitments to Tennis and Life Camps, Gustavus tennis, and sport ethics.

Thank you to Paul Brosnahan, Eric Butorac, Neal Hagberg, Dennis Johnson, Nicole LaVoi, Charles Loprinzi, Bruce McKinnon, Dan McLaughlin, Daniel Slager, Deb Sundal, Tommy Valentini, Kevin Whipple, Ann Wilkinson, Barb Wilkinson, John Wilkinson, Stephanie Wilkinson and Bob Young. They have read my entire manuscript and made many helpful suggestions.

Thank you to Marc Miller, Mike Helgeson, Dave Bruggeman, Dennis Johnson, Jen Johansen and Loralea Baldwin. They have helped immensely with the publication process.

Thank you to Jack Ohle, Ken Westphal, Warren Wunderlich, Tom Young, Tim Kennedy, Tom Brown, Steve Kjelgren, Heidi Carlson, and many other staff members at Gustavus Adolphus College. They have leadership positions that greatly enhance the Tennis and Life mission.

Thank you to Billie Jean King, Nicole LaVoi, Dennis Johnson, Eric Butorac, and Charles Loprinzi for their generous words of praise.

Thank you to Dr. Manish Kohli, Dr. Nadia Laack, Dr. Charles Loprinzi, and Dr. Tom Shives. They are the oncology team at Mayo Clinic that has helped me exceed the anticipated life expectancy for a patient with Stage 4 kidney cancer.

FOREWORD

"Thirty-some years ago, when you started working at Tennis and Life Camps, did you ever think that we would be at the place we are now?" That's what Steve Wilkinson asked me on a beautiful summer afternoon a couple years ago.

He and I were standing on the Gustavus Adolphus College campus outside the Swanson Indoor Tennis Center, a facility to match any in the country. We were looking at the Brown Outdoor Tennis Complex, which contained twelve courts and a tower viewing area for spectators.

He was musing over his life and the dream he had built. But the tennis structures were not the crux of his dream.

Steve wanted to create a philosophy that took the pressure off winning; and that put the focus on trying hard, remaining positive, and treating your opponents and yourself with the utmost respect, even in difficult circumstances.

Steve's approach was "character driven." He opposed the "win at all cost" mentality that led coaches to accost players verbally (and sometimes physically), and that caused parents to live their own dreams through their children, at the expense of their wellbeing and happiness.

His Tennis and Life Camps have offered a radical, yet disarmingly simple, approach that has transformed the lives of 50,000 campers. World ranked players to beginners, coaches, families, tennis officials, and parents of all races and religions are implementing his simple system of the Three Crowns and the Serenity Prayer, and are finding that both their tennis games and their interpersonal relationships have positively changed in profound ways.

But people want proof. People want to know if you can WIN with this approach.

Yes, you can. Steve Wilkinson has coached more winning matches than any other coach in NCAA tennis history.

But take away this fact. Take away, also, the fact that as a competitor, he ranked at or near the top in the U.S. and the world in his age division from his 30s until his 60s. Take away the fact that he taught simple tennis methods that helped thousands of tennis students improve. Take away the fact that he was inducted into both the NCAA/ITA Tennis Hall of Fame and the USPTA Hall of Fame, and received the Tennis Educational Merit Award from the International Tennis Hall of Fame.

Take all of this away. What do you have? One of the most successful people I know; not because of his winning, but because of his servant approach to life.

Neal Hagberg

Director, Tennis and Life Camps at Gustavus Adolphus College

Neal Hagberg leading the 2011
TLC staff in a final program song

PROLOGUE

To my shock, I was peeing bright red blood!

It was July 2nd, 2008—another beautiful day at Tennis and Life Camps (TLC) on the Gustavus Adolphus College campus in St. Peter, Minnesota. One hundred young tennis players were halfway through their last full day of camp before the 4th of July vacation break. For me, it was a day like many other days over the past 32 summers, centered on teaching tennis skills and a healthy, sportsmanship-oriented approach to athletic competition and life.

I saw myself, as did others, as a shining example of disciplined living. At 67 years of age, I was the apparent epitome of health. I exercised daily, lifted weights, practiced meditation, ate properly, never smoked, and competed internationally in tennis. Because I had been healthy my entire life and relatively injury free, I anticipated playing into my 90s. After so many years of healthy lifestyle choices and the resulting benefits, I could passionately advocate to camp participants the advantages of my approach to life.

Every day I worked into my busy teaching schedule a vigorous game of tennis. I preferred singles to doubles because of the activity involved. I loved to run and to get an intense workout in a short period of time. Even more, I liked to make my opponent run. My ball control and knowledge of court strategy often made that possible.

My opponent that day was Neal Hagberg, TLC instructor since 1981. We ran, struck the ball confidently, and enjoyed our 75 minutes of tennis before lunch. So did some of the kids, who stopped to watch as they moved to and from camper video analysis sessions. I always played better when I had an audience, so this was a bonus. I think they were surprised that an old guy like me could play so well.

When I left the court and headed to the locker room, I was feeling strong and confident. I had not continued to play tournaments in the 60 and 65-and-over age divisions because of my wife, Barb's battle with multiple myeloma, an incurable cancer of the blood and immune system. However, she had miraculously recovered after a bone marrow transplant. It was time for me to go after a national title. I expected to have more time for competing the following spring after my retirement as men's tennis coach at Gustavus.

When I went to the urinal to relieve myself, I looked down. To my shock I was peeing bright red blood. "What is happening?" I thought to myself. "What does this mean?" I knew it wasn't good, but I refused to face reality.

Instead, I wiped the bloodstains off the urinal and tried to pretend that it hadn't happened.

I went back to my regular teaching schedule for the afternoon, hoping it would not happen again. Of course, it did. I struggled to wrap my mind around it. Even though I felt great, there was something seriously wrong with me. I had avoided hospitals, doctors, and sickness for my entire life. This I suddenly feared would be different. The dreaded word "CANCER" entered my mind, but why me? I reluctantly told my wife, Barb, what had happened. Next, I drove to the emergency room at the St. Peter Hospital, expecting bad news but still hoping for a less threatening assessment.

A CT-scan determined my problem. "You have a large tumor on your right kidney, and it is probably cancerous," the doctor told me. The compassionate look on his face and the gentle way that he communicated the verdict did little to lessen the impact of the devastating news. I had cancer. What did this mean? I was tempted to let my mind move toward fear and immobilization. Instead, I closed my eyes and repeated the Serenity Prayer: "God, grant me the Serenity to accept the things I cannot change; the Courage to change the things I can; and the Wisdom to know the difference."

I knew that I did not need to be overwhelmed by the knowledge that I had cancer. It was outside my control. However, cancer is a threat that produces fear in the hearts of the bravest individuals. I anguished for a while, but soon the transformational power of the Serenity Prayer took hold, just as it had for me in other occasions many times before.

INTRODUCTION

Theologian Reinhold Niebuhr wrote the Serenity Prayer in the 1930s. Since then, it has become a widely used prayer by millions of people—both religious and non-religious. By letting go of things we do not control and focusing on the things that we can control, we prepare ourselves to be more loving and able to serve others.

When I developed the Tennis and Life Philosophy (TLP) in 1977, I was strongly influenced by the Serenity Prayer. I had witnessed it being lived by the people whom I admired the most. One was my friend Arthur Ashe Jr., who modeled the ideal way of playing tennis. He simply ignored opponents' bad line calls or other inappropriate behavior. These he could not control. Instead, he competed hard in a composed manner, no matter what his opponents did.

Another influential person was Karen Gibbs, a Gustavus player who fought bone cancer courageously. She did not worry about the cancer, which was outside her control. Instead, she learned to play left-handed after an operation took part of her right arm. A year later, she again made the team and won her doubles match against the University of Minnesota.

When I created Tennis and Life Camps (TLC) in 1977, I wished to do more than teach tennis. I wanted to create a learning environment that emphasized values and relationships. The ideals for tennis were the same as the rest of life. Good tennis games and fulfilled lives can be complimentary. The close connection between tennis and life explained my decision to choose the name "Tennis and Life Camps." More than 37 years and 50,000 students later, the name remains appropriate.

The Tennis and Life Philosophy (TLP) describes a philosophy that has guided me as a tennis coach, international tennis competitor, ethics teacher, youth motivator, and parental advisor. Skilled players in the Gustavus men's tennis program, inhibited by anger and an over-emphasis on winning, have been freed by the philosophy to become national champions. Other players, influenced by TLP, put the team first; one even sacrificed the chance for a national singles title.

My greatest satisfactions at TLC have come when I have helped doubles partners to relate harmoniously on the tennis court; aided youth to successfully navigate abusive coaching situations; assisted parents to support their children in athletics in positive ways; helped campers improve their tennis games and attitudes toward life; led varsity players toward a life-enhancing philosophy; and assisted TLC instructors to gain teaching and relational skills that helped them professionally.

Tennis is well suited to teaching sportsmanship. Correctly played, it is based on mutual trust. *The Code*, the ethical rules for tennis, requires tennis players to call our opponent's shots in or out. If there is any doubt, *The Code* stipulates that the call be made in favor of our opponent. Contrast this with most sports, where officials are required and players try to get away with anything that officials cannot detect.

The Serenity Prayer facilitates our ability to enact the expectations of *The Code*. We must be able to let go of inappropriate behavior by opponents. It is outside our control. If we grow angry and retaliate, we violate *The Code*. Even questioning our opponent is prohibited. It is difficult for many players to achieve the equanimity that *The Code* requires, but the Serenity Prayer helps.

Similarly, TLP depends on the Serenity Prayer, which helps us "turn the other cheek." The philosophy is based on love, nonviolence and forgiveness, the same religious ideals that inspired Mahatma Gandhi, Nelson Mandela, and Martin Luther King Jr. as they tried to transform the violence and racial injustice that dominated socially stratified colonial India, segregated South Africa, and the Jim Crow culture in the southern United States.

While TLP addresses the unsportsmanlike behaviors that ruin sporting environments, it does not stop there. It embraces our responsibility to serve others out of love in all human endeavors. Dr. Don Klotz, my collegiate coach at the University of Iowa, modeled this for me. I first met him as he gave one of his many free tennis clinics. In his 80s, Dr. Klotz still dispensed tennis and life wisdom for no charge to players at the University of Iowa Recreation Center.

Consequently, at TLC we have emphasized service, and even created a camp T-shirt that reads "Let Love Serve." This message cuts to the core of what is most important in life. When we serve others out of love, it doesn't feel like a burden; it energizes us. When we do get tired or discouraged, we roll up our sleeves. We believe in what we are doing apart from outside accolades or financial rewards, leaving us with the feeling that our lives truly count.

On the other hand, serving primarily for financial compensation feels different. When we have put in the required hours, we are ready to go home. If the project demands more time or harder work than we anticipated, we often "burn out." This may be service but in this situation, we are not serving out of love.

LET LOVE SERVE, A Memoir Celebrating Tennis and Life describes how I formulated TLP, applied it to tennis camp participants, communities, varsity tennis players, and my own tennis playing. Other chapters explain the surprising history of tennis facilities at Gustavus, the people to whom I feel deep gratitude, and the beliefs that have sustained me as a husband, father, grandfather, camp director, professor, coach, cancer patient, worshipper, and public servant.

My hope is that this book will help people better understand and appreciate a clear alternative to the "win-at-all-costs" mentality that has undermined the potential for tennis and all competitive sports to enrich our lives.

My family first urged me to write this memoir. I hope it helps them remember, understand, and appreciate my life's mission.

Deb, Steve, Stephanie, and Barb Wilkinson at the
1992 Swanson Indoor Tennis Center dedication

Section I

MY PASSION
FOR TENNIS

Being the top tennis player in the state, or the region,
or the country is often a misplaced priority. Too often it
feeds the belief that the world centers on me, rather than
I am here to serve my family, my community, and the world.

I grew up in northwest Iowa in a city that had no tennis lessons, high school tennis teams, or indoor tennis courts. Still, a Big 10 coach whose team had just finished third in the NCAA tournament recruited me. Under his tutelage I developed the skills to play number one for three years at the University of Iowa. At the Big 10 Championships in my senior year, I came within two points of defeating Marty Riessen, an NCAA singles finalist for three consecutive years. Eventually, I became a player who was fortunate enough to face the world's best—including Poncho Gonzales, Arthur Ashe Jr., Alex Olmedo, Chuck McKinley and Rafael Osuna.

Today, my story is counter-intuitive to many aspiring players and their parents. Talented youth often specialize in tennis at an early age, travel across the country playing national tournaments, attend away-from-home tennis academies, and experience the continuing pressure of meeting performance expectations created by zealous parents and coaches.

In the process normal childhoods are sacrificed. Family lives are disrupted as special attention is showered on talented children. Winning-at-all-costs and other damaging beliefs are implanted at a young age, and the fun of the game is stripped away.

Today's talented tennis youth are disadvantaged if they grow up without working at a job, are pampered with special opportunities, and follow non-academic priorities. When I am asked by parents if they should send their teenager away to a tennis academy, my answer is always "no." Don't part with them during their formative years. Hold them close to you, and instill in them the values that will truly make their lives count.

Being the top tennis player in the state, or the region, or the country is often a misplaced priority. Too often it feeds the belief that the world centers on me, rather than I am here to serve my family, my community, and the world. Selfish, prima donna behavior is way too common among gifted athletes who prioritize winning.

More important goals center on wisdom, values clarification, healthy lifestyle habits, self-reliance, and ways of serving others. I was blessed with parents, a university coach, religious ideals, and other important influences that kept these goals front and center for me.

Sioux City tennis champions: Steve and his father, Byron Wilkinson, are 3rd and 4th in the back row.

1

CHILDHOOD TENNIS DREAMS

*My father kept things fun. He never corrected me or
told me how I could have played better. Instead,
both he and my mother proudly watched me
compete and praised all my efforts, win or lose.*

When I was only four years old, I had tennis dreams. They were shaped by who my parents were, what they loved to do together, and how they shared that love with our family. My mother and father started playing tennis together when they were in college. Their love for the game continued into their marriage. They loved playing mixed doubles, primarily with a couple that became so close to us that they and their children seemed like family to me.

Even before my father could buy our first family car in 1947, our family would walk two miles together to the Smith Elementary School playground on the west side of Sioux City, Iowa. I rode my scooter and my sister, Ann, her tricycle. My parents pulled my younger brother, John, in a wagon. We were a curious troupe, walking down the steep 17th Street hill on which we lived, across Perry Creek and through the black section of a highly segregated city that depended on stockyards and meat processing for its economic vitality.

When we reached the school, my siblings and I ran immediately for the jungle gym and sand box, while our parents headed to the tennis courts. Before long, I would grow tired of the playground and would gaze over to the courts, where my parents seemed to be having a great time. I would wander over and watch intently, intrigued by the ball that was being struck back and forth over the net.

For a while, I was content to chase out-of-play balls and retrieve them for my parents. However, that stage did not last long. I would be a pest until they tossed balls to me. Taking an adult racket in both hands and hitting the balls baseball style, I dreamed of the day when I could beat my parents. That day eventually came. I defeated my mother when I was 10-years-old and my father when I was 12. Looking back, those defining moments remain indelibly printed in my mind. Most importantly, they show the critical role that my parents played in my growing love for the sport.

However, my most memorable gift as a child was not a tennis racket, but the full sized bicycle that I received on my 8th birthday. It would give me the freedom to ride wherever I wished to go. Even though I was big for my age, I was barely able to reach the pedals. Getting on and off was a challenge, requiring my father's patient assistance for the first couple of weeks. Yet, I was determined.

My primary destination in the following years was the Bryant Grade School playground, more than three miles away, where I used a school wall to play tennis games against imaginary opponents. With chalk I marked a net line and target boxes. I won points if I hit the boxes with my serves and kept the ball above the net line for a certain number of consecutive hits.

I kept hitting against the wall interesting. Moving close into the wall, I developed a consistent volley and a strong forearm with rapid-fire blocks, never allowing the ball to touch the ground. Also, I worked on my overhead. Standing close to the wall, I hit the ball upward so that it would glance off the wall and go back and up over my head. Then, I would move quickly backwards for an overhead smash. I also practiced using different spins, drop shots, and serve-and-volley sequences. By hitting against the wall and reading instructional books on tennis technique, I was able to develop a well-rounded game.

Without other tennis playing youth in my community, I depended on my father for actual matches. He played with me on weekdays after work, took our whole family to Riverside Park on weekends for picnics and afternoon tennis, and led the tennis club in organizing citywide tennis tournaments and inter-city tennis matches with Sioux Falls, Omaha, and Storm Lake. When I was 10, he took me to the South Dakota Open in Sioux Falls, where I won my first trophy. For many years, he drove me to out-of-town tournaments.

Though my father loved playing tennis with me and arranging competitive opportunities for me, he never tried to be my coach. Perhaps his restraint was related to his own lack of professional training, but I think it had more to do with his philosophy of child rearing. My father kept things fun. He never corrected me or told me how I could have played better. Instead, both he and my mother proudly watched me compete and praised all my efforts, win or lose.

2

DR. KLOTZ, MY TENNIS COACH
AND ROLE MODEL

Dr. Klotz was more than a master tactician. He was
a minister disguised in tennis clothing. He encouraged
me to marvel at my natural talents and to trust the
computer that had been placed on my shoulders.

Dr. Don Klotz, varsity coach at the University of Iowa, was the only tennis coach I ever had. He was a gifted and innovative tennis teacher whose team finished third at the NCAA tournament in 1958. His most successful student was NCAA semifinalist Art Andrews, an Iowa City native whom Dr. Klotz coached from childhood through his university years.

Inspired at a young age by Dr. Klotz

When I was nine years old, Dr. Klotz, Art Andrews, and several others from Iowa City journeyed to Sioux City, Iowa, to give a free tennis clinic. I can still remember how excited I was. I did not realize that tennis could be played so well. Dr. Klotz spent the afternoon helping everyone. Then, near the end of the day, when only the most dedicated still remained, THE Dr. Klotz told me that I had potential. Was I elated! That encouragement kept me inspired into my high school years.

We had no tennis team at Sioux City Central High School. However, my biology teacher submitted an application to the Iowa State High School Association that permitted me to compete individually in the state high school tournament. I reached the finals twice, but Dr. Klotz was the only Division I coach who recruited me. I was flattered but also concerned that I was not good enough to play Big 10 tennis. However, Dr. Klotz's belief in me won me over, and I decided to enroll at the University of Iowa.

Sitting in Dr. Klotz's office, I soaked up insights on tennis and life as he strung rackets for the team. On his wall was a framed pearl of wisdom by Robert Schuller that read, "Any fool can see the seeds in the apple. Only God can count all the apples in one seed." The apple seed analogy to life occasionally crept into his advice. There was little doubt in my mind that he possessed some super-human qualities. He was the one who had perceived my tennis potential.

Learning tennis from Dr. Klotz

My tennis skills and knowledge developed quickly under Dr. Klotz's watchful eye. He charted my matches and praised me for my resourcefulness—using my head, trying something different when my opponent was hot or I was cold, and never giving up. I learned quickly that there was a way to beat everyone.

Dr. Klotz taught me that no points were awarded for form. Classic textbook strokes were not necessary for success. If I had focused too much on changing my limited backhand, I might not have learned how competitive I could be. Instead, I learned how to protect my backhand and pursue strategies that exploited my opponents' weaknesses,

Dr. Klotz was more than a master tactician. He was a minister disguised in tennis clothing. He encouraged me to respect my natural talents and to trust the computer that had been placed on my shoulders.

Also, I learned how to teach tennis by watching Dr. Klotz. I could see the looks of surprise and then delight in beginners. First, he won their confidence with praise, and then he skillfully slipped in tips. I was amazed at how quickly his suggestions produced improvements. Teaching was easy, rewarding, and so much fun.

Dr. Klotz designed the Volley Method of teaching tennis. He started students near the net practicing volleys. As soon as they could do that, he had them hitting ground strokes from the service line. In their first lesson, Dr. Klotz had them playing short court games, learning the basics of strategy, and keeping score. Much could be accomplished in a short time by using the natural athletic skills of his students and simple progressions.

Dr. Klotz as an innovator and role model

Dr. Klotz was an innovator—so far ahead of his time that few understood or agreed with him. To many it was preposterous that he would suggest table tennis scoring, tiebreakers, and other modifications in the scoring system. Many of his innovations were introduced years later as "new" developments.

Dr. Klotz's recommendations made sense, yet most players resisted. In practice, why not start rallies with a serve instead of a groundstroke? After all, 65% of all tennis strokes hit in matches are serves and service returns. When rallying, why allow the ball to bounce twice? The opportunity to practice adjusting to the ball is lost. Why hit the ball to each other in the middle of the court? We would not do this in a match. These and many other questions prodded us to question the conventional ways of practicing when they were challenged by Dr. Klotz's perceptive observations.

Dr. Klotz's teaching approach influenced me profoundly. However, his commitment to serving others affected me even more. Dr. Klotz was still teaching tennis and life skills in his late 80s, without any expectation of compensation. This remarkable man died in 1999 at the age of 93.

Dr. Don and Vivien Klotz, watching a 1956 University of Iowa basketball game in the Iowa Fieldhouse.

3

FACING TOP COLLEGIATE PLAYERS

My best chance to beat Marty Riessen came during my
senior year in a 1963, Big Ten semifinal match. I led 6-5
in the third set, and had him down love-thirty on his serve.

My tennis competition became more challenging after I arrived at the University of Iowa. Unable to play on the varsity as a freshman—it was against NCAA rules at the time—I instead practiced frequently against All-American Art Andrews, who had graduated from Iowa two years before. He was back in town before going to Oxford to pursue a Rhodes scholarship.

In the 1961 season, I was thrust as a sophomore into the #1 singles and doubles positions. My season highlight was playing in the NCAA tournament at Iowa State University in Ames. It came in June, after my classes were finished. I could sandwich NCAA participation between tennis teaching obligations in Iowa City, which was only 100 miles from Ames.

My most memorable match came in doubles. Mike Schrier and I played U.S.C's Ramsey Earnhart and Rafael Osuna, the top seeded team. The agility, foot speed, and touch of Osuna were breathtaking. We lost 6-2, 6-2, but they did not break my serve. I was serving rockets into the corners, and Mike was knocking off their returns. Earnhart/Osuna went on to win the NCAA 1961 doubles title, the first of three consecutive doubles titles for Osuna.

To play against Osuna was a dream come true. He and Dennis Ralston were the reigning Wimbledon doubles champions. Osuna went on to win the U.S. National Doubles title in 1962 and the Wimbledon title again in 1963, both with Antonio Palafox. At the end of 1963, the International Tennis Federation (ITF) gave him the top amateur world ranking. In 1969, playing Davis Cup for Mexico, he won two singles matches and the doubles against heavily favored Australia, the winner of 17 world titles. Just two weeks later, on June 4, 1969, Osuna died at the age of 30 in a Mexican Airlines plane crash.

**Wilkinson competing in the Big 10 Championship
at Northwestern University in 1963**

In my junior and senior seasons, Marty Riessen from Northwestern University was the top player in the Big 10 Conference. He held that honor for three years, including the one after I graduated. He went on to reach the NCAA singles final each season—losing to Rafael Osuna in 1962 and Dennis Ralston in 1963 and 1964. After graduation, Marty won six professional titles in singles, 53 in doubles, and seven in mixed doubles.

My best chance to beat Riessen came during my senior year in a 1963, Big 10 semifinal match. I led 6-5 in the third set and had him down love-30 on his serve. Riessen served and came to the net. I hit a great return, but he made a lunging, stab volley off his racket frame for a winner. If I had won that point and one of the following three, I would have achieved the biggest upset of my collegiate career. Instead, I lost the third set 9-7.

The new, outstanding player in the Big 10 Conference during my senior season was Clark Graebner, a Northwestern University teammate of Riessen. He was tall, well built, and hard-hitting, with one of the game's fastest serves. Clark kept his body super erect, and his walk seemed like a strut. Often, his ego seemed as big as his body. His first name was the same as Clark Kent's, the comic book character who transformed himself into Superman. Opponents frequently referred to Graebner as "Superman," a persona that he liked to cultivate.

Graebner's self-righteous and intimidating personality was on full display in our 1963 dual match with Northwestern University. My doubles partner Dave Strauss and I were playing well against Riessen/Graebner. We won the first set 7-5. At 2-2 in the second set, Strauss hit a volley that Graebner thought was a "carry."(an illegal continuous swing where the ball stays on the strings too long.) Without an umpire, the infraction had to be called on oneself. Graebner was furious when Strauss did not call the "carry." For the rest of the match, Graebner hit every ball as hard as he could, directly at Strauss. The tactic worked, and they won in three sets. When we played them again in the finals of the Big 10 tournament, there was no need for intimidation. Riessen/Graebner won in straight sets.

Graebner went on to win the French Open doubles with Dennis Ralston in 1966. In 1968, Arthur Ashe Jr. and Graebner led the 1968 Davis Cup team to victory, the first time in five years.

Graebner's 1968 U.S. Open semifinal match against Ashe became the subject of John McPhee's *Levels of the Game*. The book alternates between descriptions of the match and an analysis of their sociological backgrounds. Graebner was the privileged, wealthy, upper class white competing against Ashe, the poor, lower class black. McPhee even correlated their styles of play and their shot selections with their personalities and societal influences. In the 1960s, racial prejudice and violence had reached a high point in recent American history. McPhee brilliantly transposed this conflict into the context of an important tennis match. Robert Lipsyte of *The New York Times* wrote that the book "may be the high point of American sports journalism."

4

PLAYING THE NATIONAL CIRCUIT

After sitting at the counter for several minutes, we soon
recognized that the waitress did not intend to serve us.
I looked around the room and saw people glaring at us.
I told Lance, "We better get out of here!" We moved
quickly to the door, dashed to my Volkswagen, and drove
out of town, hoping that no one was following us.

The summer of 1964

After completing the first year of my MBA program at the University of
Iowa, I played tournaments throughout the United States with Lance
Lumsden. He was a black, Commonwealth Caribbean Davis Cup player,
who had played #1 for Southern Illinois University for the previous two
years. I met and played him during my senior year at the University of Iowa.

In 1966, Lance would become a Jamaican tennis celebrity. He and his
partner Richard Russell defeated Venezuela 3-2, the first time in history that
the Commonwealth Caribbean had won a Davis Cup contest. In their
following match against the United Sates, Lance and Richard scored another
historical first. In doubles, they beat Arthur Ashe Jr. and Charlie Pasarell in
five sets, 6-4, 7-9, 14-12, 4-6, 6-4. Although the United States won 4-1, this
doubles victory is still considered a highlight in Jamaican tennis history.

Lance and I were evenly matched, and we enjoyed each other's company. A
1964 summer playing tennis together seemed ideal to both of us. Our mode
of transportation was my 1962, green-colored, Volkswagen "bug." First, we
headed south to Corpus Christi for the Texas Sectional Championship, one
of the toughest regional tournaments in the country. Neither of us was top
seeded, but fortunately we were placed in opposite halves of the singles draw.

We both worked our way through the tournament, setting up a final on the
stadium court. The temperature was in the high 90s, and the wind blew
strongly in an unpredictable, circular pattern. There were no tie-breakers.
Every set went to extra games. At the 10-minute break after the third set, I

was down two sets to one and wondering if I had the energy to continue. However, I dug deep and pulled out the final two sets in a match that lasted over five hours. After that, the two of us went on the court again for the doubles final. Fortunately, it was only two out of three sets, and we emerged victorious.

Our next tournament was the Tri-State Tournament in Cincinnati, Ohio. A direct route took us through Mississippi. We were naively unaware of the potential dangers. This was 1964, a year when racial tensions were building. That summer, civil rights workers headed south to register blacks. A black and two white civil rights workers, James Chaney, Andrew Goodman, and Michael Schwerner, were murdered by the Ku Klux Klan and dumped into a pond. In spite of an FBI investigation and arrests, local juries did not convict anyone.

We came within 50 miles of where those murders occurred, two days before they happened. Our trip took us through Jackson and Tupelo, Mississippi. We stopped for gas in Sandhill, but the station attendant refused to help us. We went on, got gas at another station in Louisville, and decided to go into a nearby restaurant. After sitting at the counter for several minutes, we soon recognized that the waitress did not intend to serve us. I looked around the room and saw people glaring at us. I told Lance, "We better get out of here!" We moved quickly to the door, dashed to my Volkswagen, and drove out of town, hoping that no one was following us. Later, I realized that we had been viewed as civil rights workers, not tennis players on the way to a tournament.

Our travels that summer took us west to Denver for the Colorado State Open, north to Minneapolis for the Minikahda Invitational, and east to New York. We ended our tour at the U.S. Nationals. It was still an amateur tournament, although all of the top stars received generous expense allowances and appearance fees. I was not in that group, but anyone admitted to the tournament was given housing and meals. Professional tennis with prize money did not begin until 1968.

Upon arrival at the West Side Tennis Club, we checked into the tournament. Next, we went to the housing desk. There was no problem for me. I was given the name and address of my host family and directions on how to get there. When Lance asked for his housing, there was none for him. "Why?" I asked. "Everyone else in the tournament that requested housing has been accommodated. This is not right. Then he can have my place!" The housing official said that such a switch was not possible, but she offered to make some calls. Both of us waited until she found a host who would accommodate a black person.

My first round opponent was Tim Sturdsa from Switzerland. While winning the first set, I started having breathing difficulties. I felt myself wheezing and gasping for breath. I loafed for a set and a half, hoping that my breath would return. When it did not, I was forced to default. On the courts near me,

Wilkinson and Wendell Ottum, the top two seeds at the
1964 South Dakota State Open

others were leading but then defaulted. Press releases blamed it on the heat, but I knew that was not the reason.

What was the explanation? In the summer of 1973, I figured it out. While doing research on my Ph.D. dissertation, I experienced several smog alerts in the Los Angeles area. On those days, residents were advised to stay inside. As I sat and tried to write, I gasped for breath. Then, I realized that it was smog in New York City in 1964 that had taken away my breath and forced me to default.

The summer of 1965

In the summer of 1965, I played the national grass court circuit. At the Newport Casino tournament in Newport, Rhode Island, I met James Van Alen, who founded the International Tennis Hall of Fame. He also invented tie-breaks and no-ad scoring, which are still used in professional tennis doubles. As tournament director, he experimented with one-serve tennis, which minimized the impact of a big serve on a fast, grass court surface. In a consolation tournament that used the one-serve rule, I achieved my best win of the summer, beating Ray Moore, a South African Davis Cup player.

The summer ended with another trip to the U.S. National tournament at Forest Hills. I drew Chuck McKinley, #1 ranked singles player in the world in 1963. That year, he had won Wimbledon and the U.S. Clay Court Championship and had led the United States to victory in the Davis Cup.

Bill Talbert described him in a *Sports Illustrated* article: "There is nothing he can't do on the court. He has all the strokes. He's fast. He's strong. He has marvelous reflexes. He has the eyes of a hawk—sees the ball as well as anyone in the game." McKinley was too much for me. He dove, leaped, and rolled on the grass on his way to a convincing, serve-and-volley victory. The score was 6-2, 6-2, 6-2.

After losing, I hopped into my Volkswagen "bug" and began a long, cross-country journey to Washington, stopping briefly in Sioux City, Iowa, for the wedding of my sister, Ann. My destination was Western Washington State, located in the coastal town of Bellingham. There I would spend the following school year teaching in the economics department. Also, tennis adventures on the 1966 Pacific Northwest Circuit were in store.

5

PACIFIC NORTHWEST CIRCUIT EXPERIENCES

After reaching the singles final, I was awarded the
privilege of playing Arthur Ashe Jr. in an exhibition set.

During the 1965-66 school year that I spent teaching at Western Washington State, I did not find any experienced tennis players in the city of Bellingham. For competition I traveled to the University of British Columbia campus in Vancouver, 50 miles to the north. However, a severe sprain to my right wrist, suffered during an intramural basketball game in early February, kept me from playing again until late May.

Fortunately, my injury healed before the 1966 Pacific Northwest Circuit began. I reached the finals in my first three tournaments and won two of them. I made my mark in the Pacific Western Tennis Championship at the Eugene, Oregon, Swim and Tennis Club. In the semifinals I beat top seeded Emery Neale 6-4, 11-13, 6-4 in a three-hour battle that club pro Vernon Ball described as "the best match ever played at ESTC."

My early results sent me into the Pacific Northwest Open in Tacoma, Washington, as the top seed. There, I became an advocate for Larry Hall and Bob Shephard, California junior college champions and future NCAA All-Americans. Even though the Tacoma Lawn Tennis Club officials had housed most players, Larry and Bob were left out, probably because they entered the tournament late. They had no money for a motel, so I asked the tournament officials to reconsider. When they did not, I drove back to Bellingham, picked up my camping tent, returned to Tacoma, and helped them erect it in Garfield Park, which was adjacent to the club. The local press covered the story, showing a picture of Larry, Bob, and me in front of the tent.

My highlight experience on the circuit came the following week in Seattle at the Washington State Open. The tournament was held at the Seattle Tennis Club, which overlooks Lake Washington and offers breathtaking views of majestic Mount Rainier. Since 1890, the club had played host to the state's most prestigious tournaments.

After reaching the singles final, I was awarded the privilege of playing Arthur Ashe Jr. in an exhibition set. He was stationed at Fort Lewis, Washington, fulfilling his military obligation. I admired Arthur for both his playing skill and sportsmanship. His tennis was beautiful to watch—booming serve, stinging volleys, fluid ground strokes, graceful movement, and calm disposition. I was fortunate to be on the same court with him. I kept the score close but lost the set 7-5.

Wilkinson practicing on the Pacific Northwest Circuit in 1966

6

FACING RICHARD "PONCHO" GONZALES

*The man that I played in Omaha in 1967 was amazing. I was
struck by the graceful footwork of Gonzales and how easily he got
to every ball. I tried to be aggressive and to knock him out of his
smooth rhythm, but it never worked. He was the one who set the
tempo, the maestro who was directing our performance.*

During my Ph.D. graduate school years between 1966 and 1970, my most
memorable match was against Richard "Poncho" Gonzales, arguably the best
tennis player of all time. The Omaha Tennis Association picked me to play
him in an exhibition match on August 8, 1967, at the dedication of the
Hanscom Park Indoor Tennis Center. Omaha officials touted my
credentials, mentioning two Missouri Valley Sectional Championships and a
national ranking two years before. They wanted potential spectators to
believe that a competitive match was in store. Sports writer Bill Last of the
Omaha Herald ended a pre-match article about Gonzales writing, "Age has
eroded his playing skill, which could make it advantage, Mr. Wilkinson."

I chuckled to myself when I read that, knowing whom I was facing. At 6'3"
and 183 pounds, his vital statistics were identical to mine. But there the
similarities ended. By 1949, Gonzales had already won the U.S. singles
championship at Forest Hills twice. By 1953, Gonzales had established
himself as the best player in the world. His dominance continued until 1960,
with convincing records against the best tennis players in the world, which
included Tony Trabert, Lew Hoad, Ken Rosewall, Poncho Segura, and Frank
Sedgman. His seven-year reign as the world's top player was unparalleled.

The man that I played in Omaha in 1967 was amazing. I was struck by the
graceful footwork of Gonzales and how easily he got to every ball. I tried to
be aggressive and to knock him out of his smooth rhythm, but it never
worked. He was the one who set the tempo, the maestro who was directing
our performance. The score was 6-4, 6-4, but I doubt that the match was
really that close. Gonzales alternated between baseline play and his preferred

serve-and-volley approach. Whenever he needed a point, he seemed to achieve it effortlessly. The description of Gonzales offered by Tony Trabert in an interview with the *Los Angeles Times* rang true: "Gonzales is the greatest natural athlete tennis has ever known. The way he can move that 6-foot-3-inch frame of his around the court is almost unbelievable. He's just like a big cat."

When I played 39-year-old Gonzales in 1967, prognosticators thought his professional career was over. They miscalculated. What he accomplished after he was 40 years old is mind-boggling. Gonzales beat Roy Emerson (12 times), John Newcombe, Ken Rosewall, Stan Smith, Arthur Ashe Jr., Rod Laver, and Jimmy Connors—the best players in the world at that time. In 1969, at the age of 41, Gonzales beat Charlie Pasarell at Wimbledon in an epic 5-hour, 12-minute battle, then the longest match ever played.

However, there was a tragic side to Gonzales' life that was caused in part by American prejudice against Mexican Americans. Growing up, he could not play at the Los Angeles Tennis Club, where most of the top players in the area practiced. Perry Jones, the autocratic director of tennis in southern California, banned him from the club and the tournaments played there. Jones and others called him "Poncho," a derogatory term for all Mexican Americans. Instead, Gonzales asked to be called "Richard," his given name. After both truancy from school and brushes with the law, Gonzales joined the navy at the age of 17.

In 1947, Gonzales left the service with a dishonorable discharge and again took up tennis. He soon burst onto the national tennis scene, earning the top American amateur ranking within two years. Promoter Bobby Riggs offered Gonzales a pro contract for a series of exhibition matches against Jack Kramer, the top professional player. After Kramer throttled him, Riggs did not renew his contract. Gonzales quickly learned that he needed to win or he would be abandoned. His rough introduction to professional tennis contributed to his becoming a difficult and arrogant loner. He found it hard to maintain personal relationships for the rest of his life. Gonzales was married six times, the last time to Rita Agassi. In 1995, Gonzales died of cancer, impoverished, at the age of 67. Andre Agassi, the famous, world-ranked brother of Rita, paid for the funeral.

Section II

ROOTS OF
TENNIS AND LIFE
PHILOSOPHY

*My contact with Arthur Ashe Jr. gave me an orientation
to competitive tennis that kept it fun. I learned
how to focus only on the things within my control.*

A number of important influences became important contributors to the development of my Tennis and Life Philosophy (TLP), which crystallized in 1977 when I created Tennis and Life Camps (TLC).

My contact with Arthur Ashe Jr. gave me an orientation to competitive tennis that kept it fun. I learned how to focus only on the things within my control. In the process, I became a player that prioritized sportsmanship and a calm, focused approach to competition.

Next, my exposure to Dr. Klotz provided crucial lessons that would aid my effectiveness as a teacher and coach. I had learned tennis strategy from a master tactician, been exposed to the teaching methods of a pedagogical genius, and been mentored by a tennis and life minister who modeled service to others.

Another important influence that would shape TLP was my educational journey, which took some sharp turns during my 10 years at the University of Iowa. I pursued an undergraduate degree majoring in accounting, an MBA centering on international finance, and a Ph.D. emphasizing ethics, world religions, and Japanese studies. Between my MBA and Ph.D. programs, I taught accounting and humanities at Western Washington State.

During my educational journey, my views on religion changed significantly. My genuine appreciation of all major world religions allowed parents from many religious traditions, or none at all, to feel safe sending their children to a camp where values and reflection would be emphasized.

Finally, other important influences helped form the complete TLP. They included, but were not limited to, my exposure to Karen Gibbs, Tim Gallwey, Reinhold Niebuhr's Serenity Prayer, and Eric Fromm's understanding of love.

7

MY TEACHING JOURNEY

I urged students to suspend initial judgments and
to see the world through the eyes of the people we
were studying. Empathetic understanding was not
possible until "we walked a mile in their shoes."

Exploring undergraduate interests

I admired my father. In the early 1960s, he was president of the Iowa Society of Certified Public Accountants (CPAs). My decision to be an undergraduate accounting major at the University of Iowa was predictable. I loved mathematical precision and business applications. I knew there was a job in my father's CPA-law office waiting for me in Sioux City after I graduated in 1963.

However, halfway through my senior year, I decided against this path. Instead, I prepared for either a master's in business administration (MBA) or law school at the University of Iowa. When the accounting department offered me a teaching assistantship while I worked on my MBA, my decision became easy. I had begun to realize that my true passions were teaching and coaching. Neither practicing accounting nor law would offer me those opportunities.

Moving from business to humanities

Two professors played an important role in my transition from business to the humanities. The first was Dr. George Forell, who directed the "Religion in Human Culture" course that I took as a freshman. I was fascinated to learn how religious values were present in literature, economics, art, and music. Also, I appreciated Dr. Forell's approach to ethics, which led me to take more courses from him.

The second professor was Dr. Harvey Bunke, the economics department chairman. As I worked on my MBA, I took his course on economic theory.

His book, *The Liberal Dilemma*, confronted the need for a dynamic force that would combine a sound economy with ideal human goals.

Both Dr. Bunke's and my ethical concerns helped forge a personal relationship that led to a job offer. He was leaving the University of Iowa to become president of Western Washington State. The school had an innovative humanities program that intrigued me. When Dr. Bunke saw my interest, he offered and I accepted a position in the business/economics department teaching accounting and humanities at Western Washington State.

My humanities responsibility was teaching two honors discussion sections in a large, western civilization core course that comprised half of all freshmen's course load. The course was interdisciplinary, with faculty members from many departments participating as lecturers and discussion leaders. Historical periods were analyzed from the perspectives of philosophy, art, music, economics, literature, and sociology.

The challenge was invigorating. No longer was I teaching only accounting classes, where debits always equaled credits. Instead, I was encouraging students to think critically, integrate knowledge, and discover the philosophic assumptions that influenced all aspects of culture in a particular time period. The contrast between the two fields could not have been greater.

Themes in the humanities course brought back memories of my undergraduate "Religion in Human Culture" class. I was hooked. I decided to pursue a Ph.D. in either religion or economic theory. My two teaching mentors laid out divergent, potential pathways for my future. Dr. Forell proposed a graduate program in ethics at the University of Iowa, and Dr. Bunke recommended a plan in economics at the University of Colorado. Both matched my interests and goals.

Deciding to teach religion

Once again, a teaching opportunity at the University of Iowa cemented my choice. Dr. Forell asked me to coordinate the "Religion in Human Culture" core course, which had 1,400 students and 35 teaching assistants. I was surprised and honored that he offered me this important leadership role. I immediately accepted both the position and admittance to the Ph.D. program in ethics.

During my first year in the Ph.D. program, I struggled with a pressing ethical dilemma—the war in Vietnam. Students were being drafted, and I was asked by some to write letters supporting conscientious objection. I was concerned that the United States was being pulled into a conflict in a country that we knew little about. At that time, there were no graduate programs in the United States teaching the Vietnamese language or culture. With the escalation of the war, I tried to learn as much about Vietnam and its cultural values as I could.

Vietnam: Lotus in a Sea of Fire, a book by Thich Nhat Hanh, a Vietnamese Buddhist monk, had a profound effect on me. It intensified my opposition to the war and influenced me to study Asian religions. A Ph.D. concentration in this area required an Asian language proficiency. Because Vietnamese was not an option, I considered other Asian languages. A National Defense Foreign Language grant in Japanese helped me decide to concentrate on ethical issues in modern Japan.

I completed my coursework and comprehensive Ph.D. exams in the spring of 1970. My background in world religions, religion in human culture, ethics, and Japanese studies proved to be marketable. The University of North Carolina-Chapel Hill hired me for the summer, and Gustavus Adolphus College offered me a position starting in the fall.

Following a parallel journey in tennis teaching

While attending the University of Iowa, I gave tennis lessons to Iowa City players. I needed the income as I worked my way through my undergraduate years. It was a lot more fun than my other job, scrubbing pots and pans for the university dining service. The tennis lessons eventually became a summer job, and for two years I ran a citywide tennis program. In 1963, I even missed my graduation from Iowa to assume summer tennis pro duties at the Homestead Country Club in Kansas City.

During my MBA and Ph.D. graduate programs between 1963 and 1970, I also gained coaching experience with the Iowa varsity tennis team. First, I was an assistant to Dr. Klotz. When he retired in 1968, I worked under John Winnie until 1970.

From 1961 to 1970, my appreciation for the teaching and coaching techniques of Dr. Klotz continued to grow. Ten aspects of his mentoring strongly influenced my teaching journey.

1) **Keep it simple by teaching one thing at a time.** The KISS approach is well known. Traditionally it has stood for "Keep it simple, stupid," but Dr. Klotz changed it to "Keep it simple, smarty." An instructor may notice several things in a tennis stroke that need to be corrected. The challenge is to identify the single, most important correction and to focus the student on it alone.
2) **Do not over-teach.** Use the applicable knowledge that people already have. For example, realize that the serve is a throwing motion. Build upon the student's prior knowledge of throwing when teaching the serve.
3) **Allow your students to play games and have fun.** The games need to be adjusted to the skill level of the participants. Dr. Klotz always included playing games and keeping score in a student's first lesson. He disagreed with the idea that beginner students needed to take a series of lessons on strokes before they could play games.
4) **Praise your students first and help them relax.** Compliment the things they are doing right. Gain their confidence before pointing out

corrections. Always maintain a ratio of at least three compliments for every constructive criticism.

5) **Teach your students to practice the way that they intend to play.** Get to the ball on one bounce. Start rallies with a serve. Make the practice partner move. Work on transition shots. Play out the patterns that are used in matches.

6) **Encourage your students to aim for high percentage targets.** Seventy per cent of your opponent's points come from your errors. Conversely, 70% of your points come from opponent's errors. Pick high percentage targets and avoid errors. Seventy per cent of all errors go into the net, so aim high. Winning tennis is a game of percentages.

7) **Respect individual differences.** All strokes do not need to be hit the same way. Strategies can vary according to personality differences and physical attributes.

8) **Emphasize strengths more than weaknesses.** In my case, I had a strong serve, a good forehand, and effective volleys, but my backhand was relatively weak. Dr. Klotz showed me how to maximize my strengths and keep opponents from attacking my backhand.

9) **Before correcting a mistake, be certain that it is a persistent one.** Otherwise, ignore the mistake and praise the successful actions. Praise is the more effective tool for molding good habits and desirable behavior.

10) **Urge their students to trust their instincts.** Believe in your ability to do things right instinctively, without detailed explanations.

Coming to Gustavus to teach world religions and ethics

I came to Gustavus in the fall of 1970 as a member of the religion department. In my courses I emphasized people's core beliefs—the basic values that made their lives count. For many, belief in God was a critical component, but for some it was not.

I communicated essential information through books, handouts, and movies, instead of lectures. Spacious dormitory lounges were my classrooms. We gathered as one group in the center of the lounge for part of the class and then split into smaller discussion groups. I challenged students to compare their own attitudes and beliefs to the ones being studied. Required journal entries pushed my students to come prepared and to be engaged.

Also, experiences outside the classroom were essential to my teaching approach. Students studying Zen meditated at the temple in Minneapolis or practiced judo under a Zen master. Students studying Hinduism learned directly from Hindu swamis or practiced traditional religious dances at the Minneapolis Hindu temple.

In 1972, Gustavus worked with me to establish an exchange program with Kansai Gaidai University near Kyoto, Japan, and 21 students participated in the first year. The following fall, 22 students accompanied my family and me to Japan, where they lived in Japanese homes, spoke Japanese, and attended classes at the university.

January terms at Gustavus provided other opportunities for travel and complete immersion in other religions and cultures. Highlights included a trip in 1976 to India to study popular worship and several trips to Hawaii to understand both Japanese and ancient Hawaiian religion and culture. In every situation I urged students to suspend initial judgments and to see the world through the eyes of the people we were studying. Empathetic understanding was not possible until "we walked a mile in their shoes."

Gustavus supported me. I could teach world religions, ethics, and religion in human culture. I initiated a Bread for the World chapter on campus and finished my Ph.D. dissertation on Nichiren Shoshu Soka Gakkai, a fast growing, "new religion" in Japan. In addition, President Frank Barth asked me to coach men's tennis on a volunteer basis, and I gladly accepted. I loved teaching, coaching, and travel. I felt energized and empowered.

Nevertheless, a 1976 faculty review committee decided that my approach to education was incompatible with their preferred approach. I was faulted for my non-historical and non-lecture approach to education. Also, my lack of scholarly publications was an issue. In spite of strong student recommendations, they denied me tenure.

While a great disappointment, their decision would become a springboard for me into an endeavor that would change my life. Tennis and Life Camps (TLC) became the new medium through which I developed my philosophies of education, religion, ethics, and tennis competition.

CREATION OF TENNIS AND LIFE CAMPS (TLC)

*My vision included Eastern influences, but my philosophy was
rooted in universalistic Christian principles. I envisioned an
approach to tennis and life that integrated mind, body and spirit.*

I was fascinated by the potential relationship between tennis and life. While
in Japan in 1973, I had observed unique relationships between Zen masters
and students as they practiced judo. "Ju" means gentle and "do" translates as
"the way." I was intrigued by the idea of combining tennis with the "do,"
and so I coined the word "tendo," or the "way of tennis."

While in India in 1976, I visited two Mahatma Gandhi ashrams and met
spiritual leaders who had worked with him on nonviolent causes. Gandhi
had influenced Martin Luther King Jr., who, in turn, had applied
nonviolence to his quest for racial equality and economic justice. I wished to
apply Gandhi's principles of nonviolence to tennis participation.

My vision included Eastern influences, but my philosophy was rooted in
universalistic Christian principles. I envisioned an approach to tennis and life
that integrated mind, body and spirit.

In the 1970s, tennis was exploding as a participant sport in the United States.
In the upper Midwest, National Tennis Schools was pulling in record
numbers at the Shattuck Academy in Faribault, Minnesota. Also, Joan
Ramey had run a tennis camp at Gustavus for two years. For me to establish
a competing camp would be challenging.

Nevertheless, starting my own camp was the right decision. I saw the
opportunity to create a camp that combined tennis instruction, a holistic
lifestyle, and an ethics-based approach to tennis and life. The inspirational
life of Karen Gibbs personified the most important values that I would be
teaching at the camp. She was a Gustavus varsity player who lost part of her
right arm to bone cancer in 1975. This marked the beginning of her
courageous journey.

In the winter of 1976, I informed the College of my plans to create a tennis camp. As the varsity coach, I was given priority over the Ramey Tennis Camps. Next, I wrote the words and prepared the layout for the camp brochure. The central concept was *Total Tennis*, which emphasized the five dimensions of the complete tennis player. They included the *Inner You*, which focused on methods that improved concentration, relaxation, and confidence; the *Relating You*, which covered sportsmanship; the *Thinking You*, which explained tennis strategy; the *Mechanical You*, which featured stroke corrections and video analysis; and the *Physical You*, which stressed conditioning, injury prevention and nutrition.

However, the most important task was selecting the right name for the camps. Given my appreciation for Zen, meditation, and yoga, I could have picked an Eastern name. However, I wanted a simple, Western title that communicated my unique approach. TLC seemed perfect. Explaining tennis and life, I wrote:

> To us, you are more than a tennis player. Yes, we refine your strokes, emphasize strategy, and provide action-oriented drills. But we also heighten your confidence, concentration, and motivation. All these areas help you reach the next level of tennis play.

> Improving and having fun go together. We encourage you to praise each other's successes with words, smiles, and high fives. We are enthusiastic teachers, giving you constant feedback as you master new skills. Humor, laughter, and acting are always present in our teaching.

> Principles learned for tennis do apply to school challenges, office tasks, and relationships with family and friends. Learning to focus on controllable elements and to be serene with things outside your influence is valuable wisdom for both tennis and life.

When I realized that the initials for Tennis and Life Camps were TLC, I was thrilled. Yes, my mission for the camp tied in beautifully with its universal meaning of "tender loving care." Before long, we developed t-shirts that read, *"Tennis Begins with Love,"* and *"Let Love Serve."* The link between TLC and a loving, service-oriented approach to others was essential.

Just as I began to advertise the camps in January of 1977, Bob Larsen published his first edition of *Tennis Midwest*, a tennis newspaper that soon became the primary source of tennis related information in the upper Midwest. The cover article featured TLC and my philosophy of tennis and life. Subsequent issues of the newspaper frequently contained articles that explained my approach to concentration, relaxation, sportsmanship, strategy, strokes, and other topics. *Tennis Midwest* could not have arrived at a better moment. The free, positive publicity helped jumpstart TLC.

Other factors also played a role. Starting in 1974, I had run coaching clinics for the state high school coaches. Their support helped immensely. Also, my position as the top ranked male player in the upper Midwest added instant credibility. So did the national titles achieved by Gustavus tennis players.

In 1977, TLC's first summer, 400 campers attended 10 junior, adult, tournament, and family camps, as well as a coaching clinic. Dave Kubes, the first Gustavus All-American, returned to be my assistant director. Teri Morton, my sports information student assistant, assumed business manager responsibilities. Six Gustavus team members rounded out the full time teaching staff. Instruction took place on four indoor courts, which were an ice arena during the winter, four outdoor courts on the north end of campus, and three more outdoor courts on the south end. The layout was not ideal, but we were on our way toward a future that would prove to be life changing for both campers and staff!

Wilkinson family with the 1979 TLC staff

9

KAREN GIBBS AND THE THREE CROWNS

After competition, win or lose, we can build up our
opponents. Wins over worthy opponents bring credit
to us. Conversely, losses are no reason for shame.

The Karen Gibbs story

Karen Gibbs entered Gustavus in the fall of 1974. During her freshman year, she was one of the top tennis players in the upper Midwest until cancer ended her season. Part of her right arm was amputated, so she decided to play tennis left-handed. After hours of practice hitting the ball against the wall, she came out for the team again in her sophomore year. Surprisingly, she made the team and even won her match against the University of Minnesota at #3 doubles.

As her cancer spread, radiation and chemotherapy treatments caused Karen to lose her hair and almost 50 pounds. In her weakened condition, she had a shoulder separation that ended her competitive tennis career. Even so, she was there at practice, leading the women through conditioning drills and assisting in every way possible. The team elected her captain for her senior year, but she died on August 8, 1977, at the age of 21.

Karen's story is displayed on the college tennis courts named in her honor, in the lounge of the dormitory that is named after her, and within every TLC brochure. Scholarships to the college and summer tennis camps bear her name. No other Gustavus student has been recognized with so many honors. Her continued effort and positive attitude in the face of adversity is reflected beautifully in a journal entry that Karen wrote a few months before she died.

> I must be thankful for the rough spots too, because that is when I
> seem to really grow and discover not only new things about myself,
> but also others around me as well. I must remember to always be
> thankful for what I have because there are so many people who are

worse off than me, and I really have no reason not to be thankful…
LOOK AT MY ABUNDANCE!

The Three Crowns

Karen Gibbs's story inspired the Three Crowns (positive attitude, full effort, and good sportsmanship), which became part of the foundation for the Tennis and Life Philosophy (TLP). These three priorities lie within everyone's control. If we prioritize them, we can be successful every time. If instead, we emphasize winning or playing well, both things outside our control, we will not succeed many times. This often produces fear of failure, which causes nervousness, anger, and lack of confidence. Ironically, the Three Crowns give us the best chance of winning and playing well, even though that is not the focus.

1) Positive Attitude: Karen is still remembered for her ability to find the bright side of everything no matter what happened to her. Losing the use of her right arm brought the challenge of playing left handed. Frequent stays in the hospital were fun because of all the visitors. She felt comfortable sharing her feelings and ideas on cancer, handicaps, and the prospect of early death. However, if anybody started feeling sorry for her, she quickly changed the subject to a more pleasant topic.

Each of us, in every situation, has a choice. Our cup can either be "half full" or "half empty," depending on how we choose to view it. Charles Swindoll aptly described the crucial role of attitude.

> The longer I live the more I realize the impact of attitude on my life. Attitude, to me, is more important than facts. It is more important than the past, than education, than money, than circumstances, than failures, than what other people say or do. It is more important than appearance, giftedness or skill. It will make or break a company…a church…a home.

> The remarkable thing is that we have a choice everyday regarding the attitude we will embrace for that day. We cannot change our past… we cannot change the fact that people will act in a certain way. We cannot change the inevitable. Instead, I am convinced that life is 10% what happens to me and 90% how I react to it. And so it is with you… We are in charge of our attitude.

2) Full Effort: Having one arm and playing left handed put Karen in a position where she could not play as well as before or win as many matches. However, her predicament did not keep her from giving full effort. In the process she accomplished a win over the University of Minnesota and other amazing victories that no one could have anticipated.

Karen strove for excellence through daily discipline and an undaunted spirit that saw each new setback as a creative opportunity to accomplish more. She wanted to win but was not afraid to lose. She wanted to improve, but starting over again left-handed did not discourage her. She wanted to live, and the threat of death did not deter her. Karen continued to try, in spite of everything.

Gibbs in 1977, the year she died of cancer

If we commit ourselves completely to full effort, we put ourselves in the best possible position to be successful. Instead, many of us find reasons to quit. Three of them are:

The desire and need to win: There is no question that championships, team position, and making the team are determined by wins. The first question that many people ask a competitor is "How'd you do?" or "Did you win?" They want to know the outcome, not how we played or how well we followed the Three Crowns. The emphasis on winning permeates athletics. Yet, so many things outside our control, such as your opponent's playing level or the weather, can determine the outcome. It is easy for us to give up when winning seems impossible, when the opponent is too good, or unfortunate breaks go against us.

The expectation that we should play well: If we have been practicing well going into a match, is it not reasonable to anticipate a similar level of play in the match? However, it often does not work out that way. We are human and subject to mistakes. We may play well for most of the match, but then at a crucial moment we don't. The more that we worry about it, the worse it gets. And soon, we discouragingly conclude there is no point to trying.

The anticipation that things will work out fairly: If an umpire punishes us unjustly, or opponents make mistakes on line calls in their favor, it is easy to become frustrated. If our opponent gets several "let" winners while all our balls hit the tape and fall back, it doesn't seem fair. If the wind and sun seem to affect our shots more than our opponent's, the pressure can build. Soon we can conclude that there is no sense in giving full effort.

If instead, we focus just on full effort, we are prepared to compete. We are focused on a goal completely within our control, one that gives us the best opportunity to play our best and win, but guarantees us neither.

3) Good Sportsmanship: Karen counseled aspects of sportsmanship that I had not considered. I used to offer excuses after I lost to someone whom I considered my inferior. "Excuses," Karen claimed, "detract from the accomplishments of my opponents. So does losing my temper. In effect I'm blaming a loss or poor performance on my own mistakes rather than giving credit to my opponent. I don't want to do that."

Karen modeled good sportsmanship. She genuinely cared about her opponents as well as her teammates. She did not make excuses or lose her temper. Her commitment to sportsmanship was not contingent on the behavior of the opponent. Karen would call the lines fairly and treat her opponents with respect regardless of their actions. Karen made it obvious that good sportsmanship is more than the absence of inappropriate behavior. What distinguishes a truly good sport is more subtle. Karen took into account the feelings of her opponents. As a winner Karen knew that excessive celebration rubbed salt into the wound of a loser. As a loser she believed that successes by an opponent deserved smiles and praise, not self-criticism.

Gibbs competing in 1975

A great test of sportsmanship comes when we lose to people that have never defeated us before. Perhaps they are younger and less experienced. We may have had a poor day, or our opponents may have been lucky. We still have a choice. We can make them feel special by praising the things they did well. Or we can throw cold water on their wins by making excuses and putting ourselves down.

Building up opponents is always the right thing to do. Avoid telling teammates that their next opponent will be an easy match. That puts them in a "no-win" situation. If they win, it's no big accomplishment. But if the match should prove difficult, they may start to think, "I am losing to someone who is no good! What is wrong with me? This is embarrassing!"

After competition, win or lose, we can build up our opponents. Wins over worthy opponents bring credit to us. Conversely, losses are no reason for shame. Putting opponents down make us look worse, no matter what excuses we offer.

10

TENNIS BEGINS WITH LOVE

Roger Federer and Rafael Nadal
epitomized "tennis begins with love"

"Tennis begins with love" has been featured on Tennis and Life Camps (TLC) t-shirts for many years. Advocates of this approach acknowledge that "love" is the term used in tennis to denote zero. More importantly for them, love is the starting point score-wise for every tennis game and the basis for a sportsmanlike, trusting relationship with all opponents.

"In tennis, love means nothing" is another slogan that starts with "love" as the term for zero. However, advocates take this fact in the opposite direction. If zero means nothing, than so does love. Accordingly, an "all about winning" attitude is substituted. In the process, love, sportsmanship, and trust are abandoned.

Rafael Nadal & Roger Federer: "Tennis Begins with Love"

From 2006 to 2011, Roger Federer and Rafael Nadal, the top two players in the world, epitomized *"tennis begins with love."* Their personal conduct was impeccable, win or lose. They always gave full respect to each other and all of their opponents.

For example, in 2009, everyone expected Nadal to win the French Open. Yet, he lost to Robin Soderling, a player whom Nadal had crushed less than a month before. Interviewers encouraged excuses, but Nadal was unwilling to bite. Instead, he gave full credit to Soderling's high level of play.

Equally remarkable was Nadal's outspoken respect for Federer. Nadal praised him as the best male player of all times. From the standpoint of Grand Slam singles titles, this was true. However, Nadal had a superior record over Federer, winning 70% of their matches.

Nadal and Federer always demonstrated a touching fondness for each other. No matter how disappointing a loss might be, each showed the capacity to rejoice in the success of the other. For example, Federer was a heavy favorite to win his sixth consecutive Wimbledon title in 2008. However, he succumbed to Nadal's tenacity and brilliant play. Nevertheless, Federer could embrace Nadal, smile, and cherish the moment.

Off the court, Nadal and Federer committed themselves to serving others. They raised millions of dollars for earthquake and flood victims and helped create a culture among tennis professionals that celebrated sacrifice and giving back. Also, they served the sport of tennis and fellow tennis professionals through their volunteer work on the Association of Tennis Professionals (ATP) Players' Council.

John McEnroe and Jimmy Connors: "Love Means Nothing"

On the other hand, the behavior of John McEnroe and Jimmy Connors, the world's top two players from 1981 to 1986, epitomized "love means nothing." Their mutual disdain and unsportsmanlike behavior are legendary. Connors, forever the loner, usually declined Davis Cup play. Consequently, McEnroe and Connors did not play together, except when the United States met Sweden in the 1984 Davis Cup final in Stockholm.

McEnroe arrived in Sweden looking tired and out of practice. He had been suspended from tournament play for 21 days, following unsportsmanlike behavior in a Stockholm tournament. Following that suspension, he was injured. Now, he returned to the place where he had made a disastrous impression, not having played for seven weeks.

Connors came equally unprepared, not having played any competitive tennis for six weeks. He clearly did not want to be there, even though he was representing his country in a world championship final. Mats Wilander, having just won the Australian Open, made short work of Connors in the opening match. The score was 6-1, 6-3, 6-3. At the end of the first set, Connors cursed both the umpire George Grimes and the referee Alan Mills. Connors was docked a penalty point, and later, a penalty game for obscene outbursts. At the end of the match, he shook the umpire's chair and called Grimes names that were heard on television around the world. Mills was outraged, fined Connors $2,000, and came close to banning him from further competition.

Connors could not have cared less. He did not play the reverse singles, leaving that responsibility to Jimmy Arias. Connors never played Davis Cup again.

The United States could have easily won, even after Connors' opening match loss. Next, John McEnroe faced Henrik Sundstrom, a 20-year-old, clay court specialist who had just earned a spot on the international stage. He had lost 14 matches that year while McEnroe had suffered only two defeats. Few expected that Sundstrom would beat McEnroe, but that is precisely what happened. Sundstrom won in straight sets, 13-11, 6-4, 6-3.

Even though down 0-2, all was not lost. The Americans were still capable of winning. McEnroe and Peter Fleming were undefeated in Davis Cup play doubles. They ended their partnership winning 57 men's doubles titles together, including four Wimbledon and three US Open titles. They were paired against 18-year-old Stefan Edberg and 22-year-old Anders Jarryd, a young and somewhat untested doubles team. Again, few would have expected the Swedes to prevail, but they did. The final score was 7-5, 5-7, 6-2, 7-5, spelling defeat for the Americans. Now, the two reverse singles were only exhibition matches.

McEnroe did not handle his two losses well. In a post match interview, he claimed that Fleming and he had played terribly. During the match, McEnroe's poor conduct did not match Connors' or reach the level that had earned him a 21-day suspension. Nevertheless, it was unacceptable. Ball and racket abuse, obscenities, and condescending behavior toward his opponents embarrassed Coach Arthur Ashe Jr. and American officials.

American outrage toward the unacceptable behavior of McEnroe and Connors was widespread. William Simon, former U.S. Secretary of Treasury, thought that their vulgar displays of poor sportsmanship were the worst that had ever been displayed in a Davis Cup match. A *Washington Post* sportswriter recommended that they be kicked off the team. Louisiana-Pacific Corporation, the sponsor of the American Davis Cup team, threatened to withdraw its financial support. This reaction pushed outgoing USTA President Hunter Delatour to recommend a required sportsmanship pledge for anyone playing Davis Cup in the future. McEnroe's response was predictable. He dismissed the pledge saying, "It's a big joke. He thinks we're embarrassing. He should look in a mirror."

Other American players supported the pledge. Former Davis Cup player Charlie Pasarell said, "Davis Cup is lot more than just winning for your country. It's also how you represent your country." Aaron Krickstein, Davis Cup hopeful, said, "Obviously, if they can't sign it, they're either stubborn or they can't abide within the rules. I don't understand it."

In 1985, new USTA President Randy Gregson, sent out letters to potential Davis Cup team members, notifying them that they would need to sign a Davis Cup contract that required good sportsmanship. Even though McEnroe always prided himself in being ready to play for his country, this was an exception. The pledge to be a good sport was too much. Neither McEnroe nor Connors played for their country in 1985.

Two Approaches to Tennis in Contrast

Tennis players commonly exhibit both "tennis begins with love" and "love means nothing" approaches. People who prioritize love praise their opponents before the match begins, applaud when their opponents hit good shots, and remain calm after easy mistakes. On the other hand, the "love means nothing" advocates put their opponents down with trash talk, put themselves down when opponents hit good shots, and show temper when play falls short of their own expectations.

Love-based players sincerely congratulate their opponents after losses and remain humble after wins. On the other hand, players for whom "love means nothing" make excuses after losses and celebrate excessively after wins, thereby rubbing salt into the loser's wound.

The same contrast can be seen in spectators. Love-based ones applaud excellent shots by both opponents. They avoid becoming improperly involved in matches by showing disapproval of line calls. These spectators even compliment opponents' supporters for their players' accomplishments. On the other hand, "love means nothing" fans only praise their favorites, intimidate opponents by questioning their line calls, and get into confrontations with opposing spectators.

Also, coaches and captains can fall into either category. The love-based ones approach their players with praise and reinforcement, never correct opponents' calls, and show respectful attitudes toward officials, even when they disagree with their decisions. On the other hand, "love means nothing" coaches withhold praise and focus on correcting mistakes first. They challenge mistaken line calls by opposing players and argue with officials in a non-respectful manner.

This memoir celebrates "tennis begins with love" for its emphasis on sportsmanship, trust, and keeping tennis competition fun.

11

LOVE, THE GOLDEN RULE, AND SPORTSMANSHIP

*For tennis players, good sportsmanship is the discipline
that needs to be practiced, not because we are coerced to
do so, but because it is an expression of who we can be.*

Love for one's neighbor is a commonly held ideal. So is the Golden Rule. "Do unto others as you would have them do unto you." Both affirm mutual acceptance, while rejecting an "eye for an eye, tooth for a tooth" mentality often cited to justify revenge. Gandhi claimed, "An eye for an eye only ends up making the whole world blind."

Love and the Golden Rule are emphasized universally.

Love from a Golden Rule perspective is emphasized in all of the world's religions. For example, the Jewish Talmud states, "What is hateful to you, do not to your fellow man. This is the law; all the rest is commentary." Within Islam, Muhammad said, "As you would have people do to you, do to them; and what you dislike to be done to you, don't do to them." Confucius, when asked for a word that summarizes proper conduct, said, "It is the word 'shu' or reciprocity. Do not impose on others what you yourself do not desire." Within Hinduism, the Mahabharata claims, "This is the sum of duty: do not do to others what would cause pain if done to you." The Christian Gospel of Mark quotes Jesus, "Thou shalt love thy neighbor as thyself." Also, within Buddhism, Thich Nhat Hanh writes, "If love is real, it will be evident in our daily life, in the way we relate with people and the world."

All religions agree that love depends on the way that people treat each other. It requires forgiveness, trust, compassion, tolerance and sacrifice. Without these virtues, true love is absent. There must be a willingness to "turn the other cheek." This understanding of love is at the heart of the Golden Rule, which is the opposite of revenge.

Transformational leaders advocate love and forgiveness.

Transformational leaders know that societal change depends on incremental changes in individuals. Consider the situation of Nelson Mandela, imprisoned for 27 years by a brutal, apartheid regime in South Africa. When he became president, he led the country through a process of truth and reconciliation. Mandela amazed everyone by inviting his former, white jailer to his inauguration as a VIP guest. On numerous occasions, victims of the most appalling atrocities embraced their perpetrators in displays of forgiveness during the truth and reconciliation trials.

Or consider Martin Luther King Jr., who consciously applied Gandhi's theory of non-violent resistance to the American civil rights movement. King and his followers were willing to suffer and shed their own blood. The willingness to suffer wrong and forgive is more powerful than violence. Love is central to nonviolent resistance. King's approach, based on Gandhian and Christian principles, helped transform the United States into a more just society.

Good sportsmanship is an expression of who we can be.

Perhaps the most significant book of the 20th century on love by a psychologist/social philosopher is *The Art of Loving* by Erich Fromm. He was certain that the final need of every human being is love, which is a skill that can be taught and developed. Fromm understood love as a practice, discipline, and commitment. It requires patience, concentration, and practice toward all people, not just one's spouse, family, or friends. Love involves one's total personality and requires humility, faith, respect, discipline, and courage.

Fromm's "art of loving" and the Golden Rule's "do unto others as you would have them do to you" are both ways of acting toward others based on respect, forgiveness, and empathy. Neither comes naturally to people, but they can be practiced and learned.

The last chapter of Fromm's book centers on how love should be put into action. Love is an art that can be practiced through self-discipline.

> It is essential, however, that discipline should not be practiced like a rule imposed on oneself from the outside, but that it becomes an expression of one's own will; that it is felt as pleasant, and that one slowly accustoms oneself to a kind of behavior which one would eventually miss, if one stopped practicing it. (*Art of Loving*, p.101)

For tennis players, good sportsmanship is the discipline that needs to be practiced, not because we are coerced to do so, but because it is an expression of who we can be. Competition is fun and rewarding when sportsmanship is prioritized. A feeling of unity and connectedness emerges that surpasses the thrill of individual victory.

2011 TLC instructor Victoria Bravo and a camper share a high-five

12

INNER GAME INSIGHTS

*The Inner Game of Tennis is a brilliant approach to
the mental game. Gallwey's techniques and insights
clearly enhance the Tennis and Life Philosophy (TLP).*

Inner game

The Inner Game of Tennis by Tim Gallwey, first published in 1974, is a classic
that revolutionized tennis teaching and helped set the stage for modern sports
psychology. Billie Jean King called the book her tennis bible. It offered an
approach for overcoming self-criticism and self-doubt.

Gallwey described two parts of our psychology. Self #1 is the conscious mind
that thinks, makes judgments, and consciously controls our bodies. On the
other hand, Self #2 is the intuitive, non-judgmental self that stores knowledge
and retrieves it without conscious effort. When we free Self #2, trusting
completely in our ability to perform the task at hand, we play effortlessly.
When we think our way through an activity, or when we judge how we are
doing, then we rely on Self #1. Unfortunately, Self #1 often inhibits Self #2,
leaving us nervous, angry, frustrated, and unfocused.

The secret for peak tennis performance is to keep Self #1 out of the picture.
Gallwey offers mental tips that quiet Self #1 and keep it still during points so
that it does not interfere with Self #2. For example, he recommends: (1) Say
"bounce" when the ball bounces on our side and "hit" when we strike it. (2)
Determine whether the ball is rising, at the peak, or falling when we strike the
ball. (3) Notice the axis around which the ball spins before it bounces. (4)
See where the ball lands and call out the number of feet it is from the target.
(5) Notice the height of the shot above the net and match that height on the
return shot.

When Self #1 becomes absorbed in activities that gather relevant information,
it prevents positive and negative critiques, and Gallwey's ideal approach
unfolds. Seeing the ball is enhanced, unhelpful thoughts are eliminated, and

reliance on the superior Self #2 is facilitated. Playing "in the zone" is a self #2 activity, where we simply let it happen and cease to make judgments.

How TLP quiets Self #1

TLP quiets Self #1 by making it aware of what it can control and what it cannot. Self #1 invariably wants to control winning and playing well, given the importance that society places on these aspirations. However, these are ends that lie outside the control of Self #1. If Self #1 operates under the illusion that it should be able to achieve these objectives, it can be frustrated, nervous, and angry.

Instead, TLP directs Self #1 to the things within its control. They include positive attitude, full effort, and good sportsmanship. These can be achieved in every situation. When Self #1 values these ambitions and acts upon them, a feeling of self-confidence grows, one that frees Self #1 to trust in the natural capabilities of Self #2.

Self #1, following a commitment to positive attitude, can choose to reflect only on the things it did well, even if the positives are few in number. The willingness to give full effort, no matter how hopeless victory may seem, marks a true champion. The same can be said about good sportsmanship. Self #1 can choose to be a good sport, no matter how outrageous the opponent's behavior may be.

How TLP can be enhanced by inner game techniques

When players, parents, and coaches adopt TLP, players no longer get nervous about losing, parents are proud of their children even when they played poorly, and coaches no longer berate their players with negative condemnations.

However, societal and personal pressures can deter people trying to follow TLP. For example, players on a team may know that attitude, effort, and good sportsmanship are the high standards to which they may aspire. Yet, they feel a strong pressure to win, which can be created by teammates and a coach that prioritize winning.

For them and many others, adding Tim Gallwey's inner game methods can be very beneficial. They keep Self #1 occupied with activities that divert its attention away from winning and playing well. Consequently, Self #1 relaxes and turns play over to Self #2 when otherwise it would not be inclined to do so. *The Inner Game of Tennis* is a brilliant approach to the mental game. Gallwey's techniques and insights clearly enhance TLP.

Kevin Whipple competing in 2003 NCAA III tournament.
As a tennis pro in 2014, he emphasizes inner game
techniques

Section III

TLP APPLIED TO
CAMPERS
AND
COMMUNITIES

Since 1977, more than 50,000 tennis players have attended Tennis and Life Camps (TLC). Many write back describing significant improvements in their playing skills and their love for competition. People laud the positive, fun attitude that permeated their camp experience. Most importantly, they describe transformed relationships on and off the tennis court with doubles partners, opponents, teammates, parents, children, and coaches.

Compare TLP with the ideas and practices that frequently dominate many competitive environments. Parents criticize their children when they do not perform well, intimidate their children's opponents, berate the referees, and complain about the coaches. Coaches stress winning too much, chastise their players for mistakes, encourage them to cheat and retaliate, and show favoritism to the more talented players. Also, players put down their opponents, make excuses, intimidate opponents, criticize their teammates, and put themselves first.

Many tennis players and coaches have accepted lack of sportsmanship as a necessary part of competition. This was the case for a high school tennis coach who brought his two young daughters to TLC, where they learned a trusting, non-confrontational approach to competition. His girls loved TLC, and so each year he sent them back.

However, the coach doubted that TLP could be used with his high school team if they were going to remain competitive. Line-call challenges and other confrontational behavior were practices that he had associated with competitive success. When his daughters became old enough to play for his team, he was faced with a dilemma. Would he insist that they renounce TLP, or would he change his team's approach? He chose the latter. To his surprise, his team remained equally competitive while being more happy and upbeat. Also, he discovered that coaching became more fun.

2010 TLC instructor Courtney Lynne with smiling campers

Another case involved Amy. She came to TLC for four years, where she learned the Three Crowns and an approach to doubles that included smiles, positive words, touching, and eye contact between partners after every point. When Amy became older and good enough to make her varsity team, she discovered an environment that troubled her. The coach stressed that she never smile. Instead, she was expected to project a deadpan, "game" face, which showed that she was serious about winning. The overemphasis on winning by the coach and many of Amy's teammates took the fun out of the game for Amy and drove her to the point where she considered quitting.

Near the end of her season, Amy poured her heart out to her mother. They decided that she would call me for assistance. I agreed to meet with her, and we came up with a plan. In two weeks, after the season was over, Amy would share with her coach a couple of articles that explained the TLC approach to competition. If the coach were comfortable with having Amy follow that approach next year, she would come out for the team during her senior year. Otherwise, she would not. Also, Amy proposed that she bring her whole team to TLC and that her coach might attend as well. It remains to be seen how Amy's initiative will work out, but I suspect that it could change the culture of an entire tennis program.

The effects of the TLC camp experience go further than some might expect. A professor at a nearby medical school wrote a letter describing the impact of his first visit to camp. It was the Serenity Prayer, which we emphasize through talks and a musical version sung together, that affected him profoundly. The professor returned from camp to face new residents that were beginning their rotations in the intensive care unit. He wrote:

> The ICU is a very tough first rotation. I copied the Serenity prayer, printed it off and walked up to the ICU to meet my

team of young doctors. I always give a 10-minute discussion the first day on how things should operate, what everyone's responsibilities are, and my expectations of them. I then said I had this life changing experience this past weekend at TLC and held up the prayer and read it to them. It is a perfect prayer to help with all the emotional turmoil within them as they start their new careers in this very stressful part of the hospital. I taped the prayer on the wall and encouraged them to look at it every day. I reminded them that the beauty of the Serenity Prayer is its relevance to all aspects of life outside of the ICU.

The ripple effects of TLC can be surprising.

TLC instructor Jen Johansen with adult campers in 2010

13

TLC TEACHING PRIORITIES

We use tennis to promote civility, compassion, and mutual acceptance. We start with the teaching of concrete actions: learning names, saying thank you when complimented, making eye contact, complimenting your opponent's shots, and remaining positive even during a lopsided defeat. These are the tools that allow campers to turn the theoretical into the practical and to see results in their game, their schoolwork, and their lives.

TLC was created in 1977 with a two-fold objective. One was to teach a philosophy that would enrich campers' lives and enhance their tennis games. The other was to offer superior tennis instruction, presented in a dynamic format that would energize and challenge every camper at his or her level. I was not satisfied unless every participant emerged from camp motivated by their experience and willing to apply at home what they had learned.

We have outstanding tennis facilities and a superbly trained staff that has coached thousands of students from the beginner level to world ranked professionals. Our approach to teaching focuses on the positive things players are doing already and then building upon those strengths. Instead of pointing out what they do wrong, we emphasize what they do well and what we want to see next. This accelerates the learning process, builds confidence, and improves motivation.

We use tennis to promote civility, compassion, and mutual acceptance. We start with the teaching of concrete actions: learning names, saying "thank you" when complimented, making eye contact, complimenting opponents' shots, being fair with our line calls while not questioning others, making the decision as a team to reach out to the other team, encouraging parents to cheer for both their children's and their opponents' good shots, and remaining positive even during a lopsided defeat. These are the tools that allow campers to turn the theoretical into the practical and to see results in their game, their schoolwork, and their lives.

Wilkinson recognizing TLC campers for outstanding sportsmanship in 2010

We challenge campers to continue using these tools at home. How are you treating your teachers, coaches, parents, children, spouses, and siblings? How are you treating those with whom you disagree? How can you build bridges to those who believe differently from you by putting yourself in their shoes? Also, we encourage campers to affirm service to others as the key to a fulfilled life. Conversely, focus on the self is ultimately unsatisfying.

TLC knows that maintaining a positive attitude through tragedy, difficulty, and losses is challenging. Both tennis and life are full of unfairness and disappointment. Yet, obstacles can be overcome by focusing on the things within our control (attitude, effort, and sportsmanship) and letting go of the things outside our control (winning, playing well, and opponents' actions).

Ten of TLC's most important strategies for conveying its values are summarized below.

1) **Communicate a personal interest in the students.** Learn their names immediately…on the first day of class…and then continue to use them. Show an interest in who they are and what they have done. Ask students questions and share personal experiences whenever possible— at

mealtime, between lessons, or in dormitory counseling times before bed in the evening. Eye contact, smiles, positive messages, and appropriate touch are all important aspects of communication.

2) **Engage students and parents at every level.** Know that greeting campers as they arrive and depart can be very important. So are the conversations between dorm counselors and youth. Time spent talking and playing games with youth may rank in their eyes above all other contacts at camp. The same can be true for rehearsals of a skit for the variety show.

3) **Teach universal values such as fairness, tolerance, empathy, and inclusiveness through stories**. The story I used most often was about Karen Gibbs. Whenever possible, I drew upon personal events in my life. Students, as well as my own children, were always intrigued by what had happened to me.

4) **Use acting and humor to entertain and teach.** One of the most popular class sessions at TLC features sportsmanship issues. Players dressed in funny costumes act out typical problems in an exaggerated manner. An umpire in the skit stops action and asks the class for assistance. What is the proper rule that applies? The class refers to rule sheets and gives the umpire the appropriate rule. The umpire then explains the rule to an incredulous player who can't believe the rules. But the player agrees to get it right, which sets up another acting situation. The costumes, changing characters, and improvised humor make lasting impressions.

5) **Use music to energize, inspire, and teach.** At TLC Neal Hagberg writes and plays songs that cause students to reflect on meaningful values. He also writes lyrics that feature aspects of tennis and the camp. Then he combines the words with the melodies to pop songs or music he has written. The songs are "catchy" and stay in the campers' minds for years. The staff and the campers bond as they sing together.

6) **Model personally the values and lifestyle that TLC teaches.** The validity of what we teach does not rest on the perfection of the messenger. However, if the students do not see the teachers aspiring to the professed goals, the message is diminished and dismissed as hypocritical. It is very important that we "walk the walk," not just "talk the talk."

7) **Build a culture of gratitude in the students and staff.** Every day campers and staff are both encouraged and required to praise each other verbally and in writing. Compliments are always returned with "thank you," eye contact, and a smile.

8) **Emphasize the Three Crowns.** Here the focus is on three important things within our control: (1) positive attitude, (2) full effort, and (3) good sportsmanship. They are achievable every day of our lives, even though at times they may seem difficult. The commitment to a positive attitude is affirmed when both staff and campers put the smiley faces on their racket strings, which we call "happification."

9) Teach the wisdom of the Serenity Prayer. Knowing when and how to let go of things outside our control can do much to reduce stress and anxiety. By contrast, many of us focus on winning, playing well, or other people's behavior. When we do, we become vulnerable to anger, choking, and lack of motivation.

In 2012, Wilkinson draws a "smiley face" on a camper's racket, which signifies her commitment to a positive attitude

10) Stress charitable giving and serving. We make our lives count by giving to causes that serve others. In this spirit, Barb and I gave TLC to Gustavus so that it could function as a nonprofit. Now, TLC cooperates smoothly with other nonprofit organizations emphasizing service. Eventually, TLC hopes to endow 200 permanent scholarships for economically challenged youth.

14

HOW TO SUPPORT YOUR CHILDREN

You can play an important role in selecting the programs that reflect your values and priorities. Help your child avoid competitive environments where winning is emphasized too much, the better kids receive favored treatment, and negative coaches yell at all the children.

You may have spent hours watching a son or daughter perform in athletic contests, musical events, school programs, and a host of other activities. Does your child appreciate having you there? Does he or she request your presence and look happy when you come? Does your child perform well when you watch?

Or is the opposite the case? Has your son or daughter ever told you that you should not come? Does your child look unhappy when you are around? Does he or she get nervous when you are watching but not as much when you are absent?

In my case, I loved to have my parents watch whenever I competed in tennis or basketball. I was a self-driven kid who grew up in Sioux City, Iowa, in the 1950s. I played both sports on my own with no prodding from my parents. I cannot remember even one occasion when they reminded me that I should go and practice. Even though both my parents played tennis with each other and me, I do not remember them trying to teach me. We just had fun playing together.

I was inspired to play my best when they came to watch. They never showed much emotion one way or the other when I competed. After a competition, they always had something complimentary to say—whether I won or lost. My parents did not analyze my game or point out what I should have done. The thought that I might disappoint them with a poor performance never entered my mind. Any nervousness that I might have had was not accentuated by their presence.

My son has rejected me. What should I do?

By contrast, compare my situation with the one described by a concerned father who wrote me for advice. He was an excellent intercollegiate player who continues to compete at a high skill level. His son is also very talented and has experienced much competitive success.

> I need your advice. My son loves playing tennis. He also loved Tennis and Life Camps and would like to play college tennis. He is a very good player and he likes to practice, which he usually does three to four times per week.
>
> I have always supported his tennis and never really put any pressure on him. I just say, "Give it your best, and then you are a winner, no matter what the score." However, he is putting a lot of pressure on himself—blaming me for putting the pressure on him. He does not like playing tournaments where it is one on one.
>
> He prefers team situations and playing tennis doubles because of that. Becoming a teenager does not make it easier, if you know what I mean. He is becoming rebellious (like my parents told me I was). He also does not want anyone watching him— especially me.
>
> Also, I have become angry at his resistance to play tournaments. I know this is not a very wise reaction, but I have done it anyway. Based on your experience, what would be good/not good in such a situation?
>
> Thanks much,
> Concerned father

My response

I responded with the following advice:

> It is clear from what you describe that your son is feeling the pressure to win. If he is asking you not to be there when he competes, then he associates that pressure with you. He probably fears that he will not live up to your hopes and expectations. Forcing him to play tournaments when he does not want to play is going to backfire.
>
> Next, he will not want to practice. You said that he loves to practice and he likes doubles. Be content with what he loves, and do not ask for more. When you back off, you may find that in a year or two he will want to play tournaments. But also he may not. It needs to be what he wants.

If he loves to practice, his skills will continue to improve. When he gets to the point that he does not feel pressured to play tournaments and win, he may want to step back into competition. Refrain from making the argument that he must play tournaments if he wants to play collegiate tennis. Cease any argument or line of reasoning that pressures him to do something in tennis that he does not want to do.

Most importantly, keep tennis fun for him. He needs to be asking you if he can play in a tournament. You will know that you are being properly supportive when he loves to play, and he wants you to watch him.

The concerned father responded, expressing his appreciation for the advice. However, he was still left with a dilemma.

My son tells me that when he is IN the tournament and winning, he loves it. It is hard as a parent to know where to (gently) push your kids for their own good and where to back off… So often you hear from adults that they wish their parents had pushed them.

I responded:

It can be tough to know when to push and when not to push. In this case, your boy feels a strong pressure to win. As long as he is winning, all is well. But when he loses, it is not. He associates the pressure to win with you, his father. There are many factors that can produce this pressure, besides what you say to your son. His fear of not measuring up to your competitive record can be one. What you say to others and your strong interest in competitive results can be other factors as well.

I suspect that your parents never pushed you. You played because you loved it. My parents never pushed me to do anything connected with sports. Parents need to be facilitators and cheerleaders, not pushers. They can expose young children to a variety of experiences, take them to camps that they may not have been inclined to try, curtail the time that they spend sitting in front of the TV, etc., but they should not pressure/force children to continue a sporting activity that they want to quit.

Guidelines for tennis parents

Following are some guidelines to help parents avoid the pitfalls that create pressure on their children and drive them away from tennis and other sports that they would otherwise enjoy.

1) **Be a cheerleader**. Keep track of the best points and describe them in detail after the competition. This is most important when your child

loses. Losers tend to forget the good points, but they need to be celebrated. They are the building blocks for future performances. If you say "nice job" after a poor, losing performance, your child will dismiss your praise as disingenuous. However, every match has positive elements that should be emphasized.

2) **Emphasize full effort.** The child who continues to try, even when defeat is imminent, is a winner. The child who refuses to quit, even when normal performance skills are lacking, is a champion. The child who has practiced faithfully for a contest, especially when sacrifices had to be made, deserves to be praised.

3) **Praise good sportsmanship.** Again, notice *specific* things the child has done or said. If the opponent has been a poor sport, and your child has responded with trust and forgiveness, the accomplishment is noteworthy. Good sportsmanship comes more easily when the opponents are good sports and is more challenging when they are not.

4) **De-emphasize winning and playing well.** These are not within your child's control. Every competitor wants to win and play well, but this is impossible. For every winner, there is a loser. Humans cannot be at their best every time. When your child focuses on winning or playing well, fear surfaces more frequently. He or she will become nervous and tense and not play in a confident, relaxed manner.

5) **Stress the actions your child can control.** When your child comes back from a competition that you did not observe, ask first about his or her success with the Three Crowns. If instead, "Who won?" is your first question, you communicate a primary interest in winning.

6) **Avoid coaching your child.** Do not tell him or her how their play could have been better. If you do, anxiety and fear of not pleasing you is increased. Leave the coaching duties to the coach. Your primary responsibility is cheerleading and continual positive moral support.

7) **Do not brag about your child's wins.** This puts pressure on him or her to win in order to earn your continued pride. If you brag, you model an egotistical approach that is at odds with the humility that should accompany wins.

8) **Cheer for opponents' good shots.** Pay compliments to their parents. Even if they and their children are poor sports, find ways to genuinely praise them. Never make excuses. Always give full credit to opponents, no matter how undeserved you think their victory might be.

9) **Avoid criticizing mistakes.** Opponents, teammates, coaches, tournament directors, officials, other parents, your child, and even you make mistakes. Often, they influence the outcome of competitions. Realize that gracious acceptance of mistakes, including your own, is a necessary part of both competition and life.

10) **Take your child home if he or she is a poor sport.** This is one time that parents should intervene. Bjorn Borg's parents took Bjorn's rackets away for nearly a year when he misbehaved, and he became a great sportsman. John McEnroe's parents did not.

Starting your child in tennis the right way

It is difficult to be a good tennis parent. Even if you follow the previous guidelines, you will face challenging situations. For example, it may not be feasible to put your child in a lesson program, or there may not be a coach or tennis pro in your area. If so, how do you proceed as both a teacher and a parent? Very carefully, being certain that instruction is minimized and playing is stressed. Having fun together is the priority. That is the way I remember tennis with my parents, and I hope that is the way that my daughters remember tennis with me. We used to see how many consecutive shots we could keep in play. They always set records when they played with me, because I focused on getting to their shots and putting the ball back into their comfort zone.

Roger Boyer, former director of the Minneapolis Inner City Tennis Program, observed an ideal parent-child lesson. A father and his five-year-old son, an obvious beginner, came hand-in-hand to a tennis court in the park together. Each carried a racket, and the father, a bucket of balls. The father hit balls softly from the service line to his son on the opposite service line. The son waited in a prepared forehand position. When the ball came, he would usually swing and miss, but the father showed no disappointment. He offered no corrections, and the boy seemed unflustered. Every once in a while, the boy connected and hit the ball over the net. When this occurred, his face broke into a big smile, and he ran around the net to receive a hug from his father. This pattern continued for about 40 minutes, at which time they picked up the balls and left hand-in-hand, smiling and looking forward to another tennis session together.

You can play an important role in selecting the programs that reflect your values and priorities. Help your child avoid competitive environments where winning is emphasized too much, the better kids receive favored treatment, and negative coaches yell at children. Also, teach your child a perspective that prepares him or her for sports. A mother who recently experienced the Three Crowns at Tennis and Life Camps and then taught them to her six-year-old son wrote:

> The other day, we were driving to his basketball game. I said to him, "What are the three important things that we need to focus on?" He said, "Have a good attitude, try my hardest the whole time, be nice to the players, and listen to my coaches." I couldn't believe how he had internalized this message.

The Three Crowns message is powerful. Focus on the things within your control, and let go of the things outside your control. Be the cheerleader, not the coach. Have a smile on your face, and tell your child what you liked about the performance. If you do, your presence will be appreciated.

Dan McLaughlin helping our granddaughter Caroline
learn the volley in 2010

15

HOW TO HANDLE BAD LINE CALLS

Everything in The Code needs to build mutual trust,
respect, and harmony. Challenging, correcting,
or overruling the opponent does the opposite.

Should I challenge?

Many tennis coaches are convinced that challenging bad line calls in non-umpired matches is necessary. *The Code*, the authority on line-calling procedures and sportsmanship in non-refereed matches, used to permit the question, "Are you certain of that call?" By asking the question politely, a player let his opponent know that he disagreed. Putting pressure on the opponent encouraged him to call lines correctly, when otherwise he might feel comfortable making questionable calls.

When I played collegiate tennis for the University of Iowa, I agreed with this line of thinking. However, I had my own special way of letting my opponent know he had made a mistake. While I didn't go ballistic or yell, I would stare at him and smile.

Sometimes, when my opponent made a bad call, I would retaliate. I always waited for a shot close to the line, but some of my friends took retaliation to a more obvious level. On the next point, no matter where the ball landed, they would call it out. This could produce a confrontation, followed by mutual accusations and demands for an umpire.

Challenging bad line calls seemed logical and fair. I did not want points taken away from me that were rightfully mine. I had worked too hard and made too many sacrifices to have it undermined by bad calls.

However, my way of thinking changed dramatically the first summer that I competed on the national Eastern Grass Court Circuit. At the Merion Cricket Club in Philadelphia, I watched Arthur Ashe Jr. play a first round match that was not umpired. I saw him get at least three bad calls, but each time he did not respond. Afterwards I asked him why. Arthur responded, "My father taught me to never challenge line calls."

Given my previous perspective, his answer was unsettling. I had admired Arthur from our first meeting at a junior tournament in Omaha, Nebraska. His tennis skills, graceful movement on the court, humble demeanor, and caring attitude toward others impressed me greatly. Therefore, I decided to try his approach.

Did a trusting or non-trusting approach help me more?

Certainly, many coaches are convinced that a non-trusting approach works best. I thought so until I used Ashe's approach. I continued to compete in national and international tournaments all the way to the 60-and-over division. During my career I encountered players with reputations for bad line calls. Friends would caution me, but virtually every opponent struck me as being honest and fair with his line calls.

How could this be true? How could my experience be so different from my friends? Was it possible that a trusting approach toward supposed cheaters contributed to better line calls? My experience confirmed that opponents made good calls when I communicated trust and poor calls when I challenged them and made close, questionable calls myself.

A trusting approach helped make competitive tennis fun. I did not worry about things outside my control, such as my opponent's line calls or whether I would win. Instead, I prioritized things within my control. This kept me from getting nervous or upset. Consequently, I played better. Deciding to use a trusting approach helped my tennis play more than any other decision I have made.

What specific things can I do to communicate trust?

1) **Never challenge opponents' line calls, either verbally or with body language.** Trust on the tennis court begins with this commitment. If an error is obvious, I still do not question the call. "Are you certain of that call?" even when spoken politely, communicates distrust. So does my question of an opponent's double bounce, an opponent's racket ticking an out ball, or an opponent touching the net with his foot. All of these calls are ones that my opponent needs to make. If he does not, and I question him, I convey distrust.

2) **Start the match with a friendly introduction and handshake.** Also, I learn my opponent's name, and I use it frequently. I pay compliments to my opponent at the beginning and end of the match and whenever he hits a good shot. I avoid putting myself down when I make an error or my opponent hits a winner. Becoming negative communicates self-absorption, which does not foster a trusting relationship.

3) **Call my own balls out on my opponent's side of the net.** I could remain quiet and say nothing, since the rules require my opponent to make these calls. When my opponent experiences me calling my own balls out, he may be surprised and appreciate that I have put accurate line calls above winning. This will encourage him to do the same. However, there is one important exception to calling my own ball out. I cannot do this when I hit a first serve that my opponent returns successfully. By calling my serve out, I am giving myself a second chance to win the point. This is the only situation where this can occur. However, if my first serve is not returned successfully, then I can call it out.

4) **Follow *The Code* on all of my line calls.** Bad calls are one of the biggest deterrents to an atmosphere of trust. *The Code* requires me to call the ball in, even when I am 99% sure that the ball was out. If there is any chance that the ball was good, I must play it. If my opponent makes questionable calls, I may be tempted to do the same thing, even though the rules prohibit it. Retaliation always undermines trust.

5) **Ask my opponent to overrule my call if he has a better view of where the ball landed.** By doing so I increase the chance for an accurate call and communicate trust that my opponent will not try to take advantage of me. I can be 100% certain that my call was correct and still be wrong. A moving head or a bad perspective can badly skew my accuracy. Whoever is looking straight down a line usually can make the best call.

6) **Ask for help in situations when I am not 100% sure.** Do so realizing that I must call the ball good if my opponent cannot help me. Also, if an opponent should challenge my call in a situation where I clearly had the best view, I politely refuse to change my call. However, inappropriate challenges decrease significantly when a clear environment of trust already has been established.

7) **Call the score clearly before every point that I serve.** Some opponents seem to have a strong aversion to calling the score when they serve. In such cases I ask politely if the score is what I believe it to be. If he agrees, all he has to do is nod. Nothing destroys trust more quickly than arguments over the score. When they occur, I must consider that I might be wrong. A pleasant, accommodating manner builds trust, but an insistent "I am right" attitude does the opposite.

8) **Do not correct my opponent.** He may be foot faulting, grunting too loudly, taking too much time between points, talking too much, or not calling "out" soon enough, but I do not say anything or communicate my disapproval through body language. Any criticism destroys an atmosphere of trust.

9) **Do not teach my opponent the rules.** In most cases he will not appreciate being taught, even when it is clear that he does not know a particular rule. My motives will be questioned, unless my suggestions

produce an advantage for him. Keep all comments positive and affirming, and trust will grow.

When challenging line calls becomes cheating

Recently, some tennis coaches have encouraged their players to challenge opponents' calls on any ball that is remotely close to the line. This can be 20 or 30 times a match. It is intended to intimidate the opponent and to make him unwilling to call any ball out, no matter how certain he might be. If a player wilts under the constant barrage of challenges, the line challenger has found an illegal way to win.

This is cheating and poor sportsmanship. "Are you certain of that call?" was supposed to be used politely and infrequently. Nick Powell, the original author of *The Code*, never dreamed that the question would be used to intimidate and cheat. He saw it as part of a plan that would promote honesty, mutual respect, and good sportsmanship.

However, the development of a cheating mentality in other sports may be having its influence on tennis. Basketball players are taught to pretend they were fouled when they were not, thereby tricking the referee into awarding them free throws. Soccer players are counseled to fake injuries near the end of a game to kill time on the clock when their team is ahead. Also, baseball players are coached to fool the umpires.

For example, in 2010, Yankees' baseball star Derek Jeter put on a great act, pretending that a Tampa Bay pitch had hit him. The umpire was duped, earning Jeter a place on base rather than an easy ground out to the pitcher. Tampa Bay manager Joe Maddon argued too vigorously against the call and got thrown out of the game. Jeter ended up scoring while Tampa Bay fans chanted, "Jeter Cheater."

Afterwards, a video showed clearly that the ball had not struck Jeter's hand. He unashamedly admitted that the ball had not hit him. "It's part of the game," he claimed. "I need to do whatever I can to get on base." After Tampa Bay rallied to win the game 4-3, Maddon praised Jeter's acting skills. "There are several thespians throughout baseball. I thought Derek did a great job, and I applaud it, because I wish our guys would do the same thing." He went on to admit that he teaches batters to pretend that pitches have hit them when the balls just missed.

The Code's intent is trust, respect, and integrity.

In contrast, *The Code* expects integrity, not trickery. It elevates competitors who call rule violations on themselves, even when they are unintentional and undetected by others. Mark Kruger, a former All-American doubles player for Gustavus, reached the doubles final of the Midwest Regional tournament. At match point he hit an overhead smash that bounced over his opponents' heads. They came to the net to shake hands, thinking the match was over.

Instead, Mark pointed out that his racket had touched the net accidentally on the final smash. No one had noticed except Mark. Consequently, the closely contested match continued. The outcome could have gone either way. Mark's desire to win was trumped by his honesty, commitment to the rules, and respect for his opponents.

In 2011, *The Code* no longer recommended the question "Are you certain of that call?" Considering the manner in which this question has been abused, this is a welcome development. However, *The Code* needs further modification. Most tennis players and coaches still believe that the question is appropriate when used properly. Therefore, *The Code* needs to specifically prohibit all challenges of opponents in non-officiated matches. That includes double bounces, net touches, line calls, and all judgments that *The Code* delegates to the opponents.

Also, *The Code* needs to eliminate the language that now permits the service receiver or his doubles partner to warn and then call foot faults on an opposing server. This is contrary to the spirit of *The Code*, which relies on the mutual integrity of both opponents. If the receivers can do this, then why should they not be able to overrule an opponent's call when it is obviously wrong? The answer is simple. Everything in *The Code* needs to build mutual trust, respect, and harmony. Challenging, correcting, or overruling an opponent does the opposite.

16

FOUR KEYS TO DOUBLES PARTNERSHIPS

*Picture what this approach looks like. Partners are
moving with energy, praising each other, saying thanks
when complimented, ignoring each other's mistakes,
encouraging but not coaching each other, touching, making
eye contact, and flashing smiles between every point.*

Four key actions can transform relations between tennis doubles partners.
They work best when all four are combined after every point.

The first key is touch. Handshakes, high fives, low fives, knuckle touches,
hip bumps, hugs, and an arm around the shoulder are all appropriate ways for
doubles partners to touch.

Touch establishes connectedness, care, and support. It is the first form of
communication between a newborn baby and its mother. Studies in hospitals
and orphanages have repeatedly shown that infants do not develop properly
without significant touching. Young children instinctively seek to be held
when they need to be comforted. Think of how important a kiss or hug can
be after a cut, bump, or fall. The benefits from touch are just as strong for
adults.

Realizing this, the highly ranked pro doubles team of Eric Butorac and Jules
Rojer touched after every point in a 2011 New Zealand pro tournament in
Auckland. A television interviewer expressed surprise after observing this in a
quarterfinal victory. "Do you touch all the time…even when you are playing
poorly and losing?" she asked. Butorac responded, "Yes, we do, and it is even
more important then."

The second key is eye contact. When we are disappointed in our own
accomplishments, we instinctively look down. Therefore, "Hold your head
high!" is common advice to someone dealing with a setback. Also, when our
partners let us down, we find it hard to look in their eyes. We instinctively
look away.

When we feel confident and proud, eye contact with a tennis partner comes naturally. Required eye contact after every point, even when we do not feel like it, guarantees that we will always project confidence. When we act confidently, we become confident. Partners can help each other. Eye contact with our partners after mistakes communicates our continuing confidence, no matter how easy the mistake was.

TLC doubles partners demonstrating eye contact, smile and touch

The third key is a smile. When we smile, we relax and communicate trust. We let our partners know that we are having fun and that we enjoy the competition. Conversely, when we frown, we tense and communicate doubt, unhappiness, and stress.

When we frown or act upset with ourselves, we may be tempted to think this is supportive behavior. After all, we are taking the blame for a lost point and diverting responsibility from our partner. However, the opposite occurs. Our partners may blame themselves, saying, "If only I had put the overhead away two shots before, we would have won the point." When this happens, both my partner and I focus on mistakes and get trapped in self-directed negativity. Consequently, our team is pulled down, and our energy is sapped.

So why is a smile appropriate after we have played a poor point? Should smiles not be reserved for well played, winning points? Do not smiles after a lost point appear sarcastic and condescending? They can, if the smiles have been preceded by critical comments and negative body language. However, if the emphasis is placed on things within our control, there can be good reasons to smile after lost points. If my partner and I gave full effort and stayed positive, then we were successful at the most important level.

The fourth key is positive verbal communication. We are a cheerleader for our partner, not a coach. We praise the things our partner does well and ignore the mistakes. Most importantly, we do not tell our partner what should have been done. This creates pressure, leading our partner to fear that he or she is not good enough to play with me. Or it may induce resentment. "Why is he criticizing me when he has made more than his share of mistakes?"

If we dwell on our mistakes, we are more likely to make the same ones again. Even though we are thinking, "Don't make that mistake again," we mostly hear "mistake." We tighten, and then we repeat it. Things work far better when we retain a clear vision of a successful shot, and that shot fills our minds as we prepare for the next point.

We undermine our partners and ourselves when we agonize over missed shots by either one of us. Therefore avoid saying, "I am sorry" after a miss. Instead, we aid our positive visualization and the successful execution of future shots when we express excitement over good shots. Therefore, offer praise after successful points and encouragement after poor points.... "No big deal! We will get the next point! Great hustle! Nice try!" These are all good choices of positive messages for a partner. And whenever our partners say something positive to us, we return that praise with a "thanks."

This type of play is possible for every doubles team. It is a joy to watch, and the results are impressive, win or lose. Picture what it looks like. Partners are moving with energy, praising each other, saying "thanks" when complimented, ignoring each other's mistakes, encouraging each other, touching, making eye contact, and flashing smiles between every point.

Why doubles partners struggle

Ironically, doubles partners often struggle because of their genuine desire to help each other. Each wants his/her partner to play better. Therefore, unsolicited coaching advice to one's partner after he/she has made a mistake may seem warranted.

Even though the intention is good, the corrective suggestion is usually counterproductive. The partner may respond defensively, telling the other to quit pointing out mistakes. The partner offering advice may be hurt by the negative response and find it hard to understand.

Another reason that some doubles partners do not fare well on the court together is familiarity. Most people are reluctant to correct a stranger, boss, or minister, but a relative or close friend is different. Suggestions for improvement just seem to flow out effortlessly. And when they do, they cause trouble on the court.

Realizing this, a doubles partner may try to keep quiet, but body language can be very transparent. The criticisms and judgments continue, in spite of efforts to avoid them. Even silence can be interpreted as criticism.

Also, off-court conflicts between doubles partners can resurface on the court when the pressure builds, and either partner is feeling insecure. Ideally, tennis partners leave behind their cares elsewhere and just have fun. Often, it does not work out that way.

TLC instructor Megan Born playing doubles with a camper in 2012

A difficult challenge—committed-couple teams

More difficulties can occur when committed couples (heterosexual and same sex) play with each other in tournaments. This clearly was evident with most couples playing in the 2010 USTA National Husband and Wife Hard Court Championship. However, the exception was Josh Heiden and Christin Tiegs-Heiden, who won the title. Both were NCAA Division III All-Americans who played for colleges in Minnesota. Josh played for Gustavus

Adolphus College and Christin for the College of St. Benedict. They were both teachers at Tennis and Life Camps, where they met and fell in love.

Former TLC instructors Josh and Christin Tiegs Heiden win
2010 USTA Husband - Wife Hardcourt title

Jennifer Johnson, the TENNIS.com writer who covered the 2010 Hard Court Championship, was struck by the contrast between the Heidens and many other husband/wife teams.

> There are no "mixed troubles" with this couple—no glaring, squabbling or under-the-breath muttering that plague a lot of husband-and-wife teams. "We don't worry too much whether we win or lose," says Christin. Adds Josh: "We have a lot of respect for each other. We don't get uptight or grumpy."…

> Both know the tennis court can be a contentious playground, but Josh, a teaching pro at The Tennis Connection in Rochester, Minnesota, has this advice for other married partners: "The most important thing is just to have fun. Keep it a game."

How does one "just have fun?" The four keys to relationships between doubles partners is a tested method for accomplishing this goal, as well as producing a relaxed, confident state of mind in both partners that facilitates optimum performance.

Also, the four keys can be applied to other activities, job settings, the classroom, family settings, friendships, and, of course, marriages. The four keys are relational skills that enrich every area of people's lives.

17

NOT MAKING THE TENNIS TEAM

*Parents and players need to discover the coach's goals.
Testimonies from parents of the least talented players in
the program can be revealing. If it's all about winning,
there will be problems. If there is talk about character
development and life values, that is good, but it does not mean
necessarily that the less talented will share in the benefits.*

Tennis team tryouts can send anxiety levels through the roof. Not making
the team can be a traumatic experience. Also, making the team and being
treated prejudicially can have a devastating effect on a young person's ego.
The stories of Ella and Laura illustrate the possible heartaches. They both
loved tennis at Tennis and Life Camps (TLC), where all players, regardless of
ability, are treated equally. After camp, they practiced with friends and
avoided disappointment. However, that changed when they went out for
their school teams.

The mothers of each daughter contacted me out of desperation. What could
they say or do that would help? Their emails illustrate the problems that
many teenagers and their parents face. My responses point to some possible
solutions. Both the mothers and I frequently refer to the Three Crowns.
They are positive attitude, full effort, and good sportsmanship—three
priorities that lie within the control of every competitor. In contrast, other
priorities—winning, playing well, making the team, and being treated fairly
by the coach—lie outside the player's control.

Ella's heart-breaking experience

Ella's mother sent me the following email:

> I'm writing to ask you how to handle something with our
> daughter Ella. She is going into the 9th grade and just tried out
> for the JV tennis team at her school. It was her goal to make the
> team this year, and she thought she had a chance. She lived the
> Three Crowns all week, constantly reciting them and visualizing

herself playing well and making the team. She really thought she had a chance, as the group of girls was all about the same skill level.

Yesterday, she found out that she didn't make the JV team. Worse for her, all of her friends did. She was devastated. I have never seen her so broken. She played well this week, winning some matches and losing some too, but she played by the Three Crowns always.

As a parent, I am not sure what guidance to give her. I listened in the car as she cried. I sat with her at home as she wept into her pillow. I knew she needed last night to cry and to get it out. She's still sleeping now, mostly from exhaustion.

Any thoughts are appreciated.

I wrote back with words of encouragement and advice, knowing that whatever I said would not be sufficient to eliminate the heartache or solve the problem.

Thanks for writing. I empathize with you and Ella. It would appear that the coaches made a very questionable decision. However, it is one of those things outside her control. This is a situation where the Serenity Prayer really helps.

Winning matches, playing well, and making the JV are all things outside her control. With these she needs to practice serenity.

The Three Crowns are things within her control. I am thrilled to hear that Ella had those in mind as she competed. These all require courage, but they are within Ella's control.

When adversity strikes, which can be a bad loss or not making the JV team, it can be hard to stay positive. But that is a choice that Ella has. It can be hard to keep trying. That is also a choice that she has. In fact, if she is going to follow the Three Crowns, she needs to remain positive and to keep trying.

When I was Ella's age, my school did not have a team, nor did kids my age play tennis. However, that did not stop me from practicing. I rode my bicycle to a playground and practiced hitting against a wall. In the evenings and on weekends, I played against my dad. In the summers, I competed in tournaments. The first time that I played on a team was when I attended the University of Iowa.

Ella has been blessed with the opportunity to play tennis, a wonderful lifetime sport. I hope she continues. Ella is a talented young girl who will get better and better. If you or Ella would like to talk to me about her situation, please call me at this private number.

The next day I received the following response from Ella's mother:

Thank you so much for responding so quickly to my email. I went to talk to Ella again. We discussed what you said. What helped the most was that you gave her your number to call. She was feeling so alone in this sadness. Knowing that someone cared, other than her parents, meant everything to her. She said to me, "Do you really think I could call Steve?" I told her, "Absolutely!" I am not sure if she will call, but just knowing you care was enough for her.

Yesterday, we had a nice day shopping for school supplies, as school starts next week for her. On our drives to various stores, she told me she realized it hurt so much, because tennis means so much to her. She said she is going to practice today with a smile and follow the Three Crowns. She said she isn't going to focus on whether or not they will let her play JV. She is going to focus on what she can control.

We have been using the Three Crowns since Ella first attended TLC. Now, I am adding the Serenity Prayer to our lives. I think that would be a great morning prayer for my family to start the day off right. Thank you.

Laura's encounter with favoritism toward the best players

Not making the team was the challenge that Ella faced. On the other hand, Laura made the team, but she was treated like a second-class citizen. Laura's frustration is reflected in the following email that her mother sent to me.

My daughter, Laura, attended your Tennis and Life Camps last summer. She learned that tennis is something to enjoy and have fun with. Your training approach is a very positive one. Laura loves tennis and spent many hours this summer practicing her serve, etc. to get ready for the tennis team in the fall.

Unfortunately, the coaching is a problem. Our high school coach plays favorites and only spends time with girls who are winning. She is not there to help a girl if she is struggling. She just criticizes her, then moves on to her favorites, and gives them positive reinforcements.

Laura has never felt comfortable with the coach and perceives that the coach does not like her. Also, the coach told them before the first match that "this is varsity tennis and it's now all about winning." As hard as Laura tries when tennis season starts, she is unable to relax enough to do well. And the coach doesn't spend any time at all helping her through the rough spots.

Laura has lost the pleasure of playing and is now stressed every time she enters a match, due to her lack of confidence in herself and the coach. Consequently, she has not done well at all. She is seriously thinking of quitting tennis this season. It breaks my heart to see her so nervous and uptight about being on the team, because I know how much she loves the sport. But we are supporting her in whatever she decides to do.

I wrote back to the mother, emphasizing the Three Crowns perspective. I encouraged Laura to let go of the emphasis on winning, but I knew that would be difficult to achieve in an environment where winning was being emphasized to the exclusion of everything else. I wrote:

We have enjoyed having Laura here at TLC. She has responded well to our teaching, and we are so pleased to hear how she has continued her practicing at home. How well she does here and how stressed she is playing for a coach who says "it is all about winning" illustrates the problem of the latter approach. No, it's not all about winning. Instead we stress the Three Crowns. These are things within your control. Winning or how well you play is not. They are outside your control, and when you focus on them, they cause worry, stress, nervousness, and lack of motivation to play. Focusing on things outside your control takes away the fun.

Through the coach's attitude, Laura is being persuaded to focus on things she cannot change (winning and playing well), which then undermine her ability to focus on the things within her control (positive attitude, full effort, and good sportsmanship). If she pursues the latter, then her experiences on the team can be as enjoyable as TLC or practicing during the summer.

As parents you can help her focus on the Three Crowns...and be unconcerned about her position on the team, how well she plays, and whether she wins. Be proud of her for full effort (which includes practicing diligently), positive attitude, and good sportsmanship. It needs to be fine with you and her that she does not play in one of the varsity positions, that the coach spends more time with others, that she often does not play well, or that she loses frequently. These are all things outside her control. It happens to all of us. Thinking about things outside our control takes the fun out of tennis.

If Laura is not able to keep her focus on the Three Crowns while playing high school tennis, then it's better to play tennis in other environments where she can. Tennis is such a fun game. I hope

that it remains part of Laura's life and that we see her again at
TLC next summer.

Laura's mother sent a return note after the fall season ended, reporting that
Laura had decided to quit the team. Laura's decision and the coach's reaction
were somewhat predictable, given the situation. Laura's mother wrote:

> At the last match Laura played, she was struggling with her serve.
> The coach came over and said, "I don't care what you have to
> do, just get that serve in." Of course, that only made Laura
> more stressed! When she told the coach she was quitting, the
> coach just said, "Oh, bummer." That was the end of it. The
> coach never attempted to talk further or to contact us.

> After quitting, Laura wrote a letter to the coach. We thought it
> was important that she put her thoughts in writing. She told her
> that she enjoyed playing tennis but was not as competitive as she
> needed to be on this team. Then Laura wished the coach and
> the team luck throughout the remainder of the season.

What you can do to ease the effects of favoritism or being cut

Parents and players need to discover the coach's goals. Testimonies from
parents of the least talented players in the program can be revealing. If it's all
about winning, there will be problems. If there is talk about character
development and life values, that is good, but it does not mean necessarily
that the less talented will share in the benefits. If there is a *no-cut* policy, this
is a step in the right direction, but the less talented players who are kept may
be treated like second-class citizens. Favoritism will be avoided only if the
coach has a defined plan for treating everyone equally and a record for
achieving it.

If your research reveals pervasive favoritism, you may wish to keep your
children out of the program, because it is contrary to your values. If this plan
of action is unacceptable, then prepare your children for the challenges that
will likely be faced. The following eight strategies will put your children in
the best possible position to deal positively with favoritism or being cut.

1) **Give your children unconditional support while they grieve**. Tell
   them why you are proud of them—even though they were cut or treated
   like a second-class citizen.
2) **Let go of things outside your control.** That includes winning, playing
   well, and the actions and philosophy of your child's coach. Learn and
   use the Serenity Prayer.
3) **Focus on positive attitude, full effort, and good sportsmanship.**
   They are three things over which your children have control. When they
   come home from a match that you did not see, do not start with the
   standard question, "Did you win?"

4) **Be proud of your children, no matter what position on the team they hold.** Avoid expressing disappointment when your children lose a match they should have won. Instead, keep track of the specific things they did well in each competition that you watch. Share these good points with your children after every match, especially the losses.

5) **Have an alternative activity planned if the team situation does not work out.** When making the team, playing at a certain position, or having a certain amount of playing opportunities is necessary to be satisfied, back-up plans are helpful. Unnecessary pressure builds and undermines performance when players put themselves into "must succeed" situations over which they do not have control.

6) **Praise the coach for the things he/she does well.** Express thanks every day for any help that is offered. Gratitude is far more effective than criticism for gaining assistance and fair treatment.

7) **Reject the idea that "the squeaky wheel gets the grease."** The accompanying loss of respect from the coach, other players, and other parents makes this strategy ineffective. If it does work temporarily, it produces resentment and the tendency for others to do the same. The resulting negative environment is unpleasant for everyone.

8) **Praise all players.** It is the best way to elevate your children. If you reinforce the idea that they are receiving unjust treatment, you cause resentment and a feeling of injustice. A "chip on the shoulder" attitude undermines possible success. There is no shame in playing behind other good players.

TLC instructor Dave Aasen teaches the serve to a
1993 camper

18

FOLLOW YOUR DREAMS

Eric Butorac dared to dream. He accepted the challenge.
It was difficult for him—making ends meet, trying to improve,
and dealing with discouraging, early round losses. For several
years, Eric's future on the circuit depended on the generosity of
donors. He needed to travel all over the world accumulating
ranking points. This was hard when the money earned was
not enough to cover the cost of travel and living expenses.

In June of 2011, two weeks before I would go to Wimbledon to coach world ranked Eric Butorac, I spoke to players, parents, and coaches that had gathered for an awards banquet before the Minnesota State High School finals. I congratulated the players for qualifying for the state tournament. Next, I pointed out that Eric had been in the same position as they, only 12 years before.

Eric was a senior from Rochester Marshall. He had never won state. Earlier in the year, he had lost several times to Kevin Whipple from St. Cloud. Still, Eric dreamed of winning the state championship. In 1999, that dream came true.

Eric went on to college at Gustavus and continued to dream. He wanted to be an NCAA III singles and doubles champion. As he headed into the final tournament of his senior year, he had not accomplished those goals. Yet, after the final ball was struck, he had won the singles and shared the doubles title with Kevin Whipple. Furthermore, he received the national Arthur Ashe Jr. Award, the most prestigious honor in college tennis. It recognizes outstanding play, sportsmanship, academics, and humanitarian concerns.

After college, most players put aside their tennis dreams and pursue other goals. However, Eric was not ready to do that. While he was a junior in college, he had taken my January term, sport ethics class. It was a travel course that journeyed to New Zealand and Australia. For one week, Eric was at the Australian Open, interviewing spectators and watching the action. He knew then that he wanted to be a pro player.

"Coach," he asked me, "do you think I should try to pursue professional tennis?" That was a tough question for me to answer. I told him about other Gustavus players who had tried, but lasted only a few months. Very few collegiate players have been able to make a living as a pro.

"But coach, do you think I can make it?" he persisted. I told him the odds were against him, but former Gustavus player John Mattke had nearly broken into the ATP top 100 singles players list. He even beat #4 ranked Andres Gomez at the Japan Open. "I think your strength lies with doubles. If you focus on it and remain persistent through the discouraging times, then yes, I think you can make it."

Eric dared to dream. He accepted the challenge. It was difficult for him— making ends meet, trying to improve, and dealing with early round losses. For several years, Eric's future on the circuit depended on the generosity of donors. He needed to travel all over the world accumulating ranking points. This was hard when the money earned was not enough to cover the cost of travel and living expenses. However, he continued to dream that he would move up in the rankings. With persistence and hard work, those dreams have come true.

I encouraged the Minnesota State High School participants to follow their dreams while keeping their focus on things within their control. That meant making the Three Crowns their priority. That approach had kept Eric going through many challenging portions of his journey.

Eric has won many championships by staying focused on the things that he could control. He and his doubles partner Jean-Julien Rojer attracted media attention because of their unusual, positive support of each other. Between points, they have said positive things, used physical contact, smiled, and made eye contact. Also, they have treated their opponents with great respect, thereby earning valuable reputations for good sportsmanship. Furthermore, they have practiced hard after losses and between tournaments. Consequently, Eric has gained the respect of his fellow tennis professionals. They selected him to the ATP Player Council, along with Rafael Nadal, Roger Federer, and seven other pro players. Eric's sportsmanlike approach to players, both on and off the court, has earned him a universally acclaimed reputation that is far more important than his win/loss record.

Eric Butorac in 2003

With Eric's example in mind, I encouraged the Minnesota High School players to make sportsmanship a priority. I told them that yelling "yes" and clenching their fists when opponents made easy mistakes was inappropriate. So was the frequent challenging of opponents' line calls. Even self put-downs indirectly told opponents that their success had nothing to do with their good play.

Instead, the Minnesota high school players should make the values of the Arthur Ashe Jr. Award their goal. Those included academic success, good sportsmanship, and humanitarian concerns. They should do the things on court that would lead their fellow players to pick them as their representative. When they did that, they would be prioritizing the most important elements in both tennis and life. Players should dream big while not losing sight of what would bring true greatness.

Eric Butorac participates in 2012
charity event with Michelle Obama.

19

GOAL SETTING STRATEGIES

Three process goals—positive attitude, full effort, and good sportsmanship are the criteria by which I define true success. To remain relaxed and confident when outcome failure seems imminent, to stay in the present moment when victory is almost achieved, and to be unruffled and true to myself when an opponent is not a good sport —these are the behaviors that permit me to maximize my potential.

The importance of winning and other outcome goals

Winning has always motivated me as a player. First, I wanted to defeat my mother and father. Later, I tried to win the Iowa High School singles championship. At the University of Iowa, it was a Big Ten championship. As an adult, I wanted to earn a top U.S. ranking, make the United States international cup team, and win a world championship in each 5-year age category up to the 90-and-over division.

Outcome goals also drove the Gustavus teams that I coached for 39 years. We wanted to win dual matches, conference championships, and national titles. I recruited prospective student athletes by pitching our winning record. Our tennis center features championship trophies and pictures of All-Americans who won at the national level.

Winning clearly matters. To maintain otherwise is to deny the obvious. Sports enthusiasts around the world spend billions of dollars on stadiums, pro players, and coaches. When teams do not win, spectators decrease, revenues drop, and both players and coaches get fired. All businesses need to make a profit or they go bankrupt. Students need to earn A's to make it into college or professional programs. Winning and other outcome goals are driving forces in contemporary society.

The limitations of outcome goals

Nevertheless, outcome goals have two serious, intertwined limitations. First, they are future-oriented. If we focus on them, we are led out of the present moment, the precise place that we need to be to maximize performance. Concentration and relaxation techniques exist to keep us in the moment—away from anxieties about the future and regrets about the past. These techniques help direct our attention to present actions needed for success rather than the future outcome goal toward which we are striving.

Second, outcome goals (which include winning) lie outside our control. Our pursuit of them can leave us frustrated, angry, nervous, or dejected. For example, when officials or opponents make bad calls that go against us, we can get angry. When opponents outperform us, we can become dejected. When we practice at a high level, but then play poorly in competition, we can be frustrated. When the desire to win and the fear of failure becomes too great, we can get so nervous that our muscles tense and freeze. In each case, our desired outcome lies outside our control, thereby eliciting negative emotions that decrease the probability that our outcome goals will ever be accomplished.

We need to know that we are in control. The slogan "inch by inch, success is a cinch," does not acknowledge that many attempts never result in a successful outcome. Because we instinctively know this, it undermines our confidence. So does the following hope, "I don't care if I win. I just want to play my best." Neither is a controllable goal. If they were, everyone would win and play their best. However, everyone winning is a logical impossibility, and playing one's best upon command is beyond human capabilities.

Process goals that keep us in the present and put us in control

Three such process goals for me are positive attitude, full effort, and good sportsmanship (Three Crowns). These are the criteria by which I define true success. Knowing this, I stay relaxed about outcomes such as winning or playing well. To remain relaxed and confident when outcome failure seems imminent, to stay in the present moment when victory is almost achieved, and to be unruffled and true to myself when an opponent is not a good sport—these are the behaviors that permit me to maximize my potential.

Arthur Ashe Jr. and Karen Gibbs helped shape my commitment to the Three Crowns. They modeled compassionate behavior through good sportsmanship. First, it meant never making excuses or putting myself down. If I did, I would be disrespecting my opponent as well. I would be asserting that my poor play—not my opponent's good play—was responsible for his success. Second, it meant being humble in victory and gracious in defeat. Bragging or celebrating in the presence of a defeated opponent was unacceptable. Also, it meant communicating during competition in a positive way—introducing myself to my opponent with a handshake and an interest in him personally, praising his good shots, calling him by name, smiling and looking into his eyes, and congratulating him afterwards, win or lose.

Even though I have prioritized process goals, outcome goals have remained important to me. Presently, celebrating my 50th wedding anniversary in 2016 with my wife Barb is one of those important goals. Given my cancer challenges, I clearly do not have control over this outcome. Yet, I do have the choice to be positive, which gives me the best chance for reaching my 50th wedding anniversary. When people ask me, as they frequently do, "How are you doing?" I try to answer positively. No matter what I might be facing at the moment, there are positives worth sharing. They have included writing this memoir, visiting family and friends, teaching, coaching, and traveling.

The 1982 NCAA III National Championship Team: Per Ekstam, Bill Sternard, Raman Jayapathy, Rich Skanse, Shaun Miller, Marc Miller, Jim Hearn, Coach Steve Wilkinson

20

WALZ FAMILY: SERVING OUT OF LOVE

*Joe and Cindy have given to their children the belief that they
can make a difference in this world. They have shown that
love is more important than money, fame, trophies, or a USTA
ranking. Love is even more powerful than death. The Walzes
are the living embodiment of "tennis begins with love."*

The Joe, Cindy, Carl, Emily, Andy, and Heidi Walz family from Aitkin,
Minnesota was honored as the 2009 United States Tennis Association
(USTA) Family of the Year. The award is made annually to the family who
has done the most in recent years to promote amateur tennis on a volunteer
basis. The story behind this award began with 15-year-old Carl, who started
a boys high school team in Aitkin in 1998. It continues through the
volunteer work of his family in Aitkin, Minnesota, and the Kambi School in
Kenya, Africa. The Walz story demonstrates the power of grief transformed
into loving service of others.

The story of Carl Walz

Carl grew up in Aitkin, a small, northern Minnesota town. He developed a
love for tennis, even before the rest of his family took an interest in the sport.
Carl often signed up for out-of-town tournaments and then informed his
parents that they needed to drive him there. Tennis matches brought Carl
many happy memories, especially when he played with his good friend Peter
Spreitzer of Duluth.

Carl attended Tennis and Life Camps (TLC) in 1998. It was such a life
changing experience that Carl convinced his parents to attend family camp
later that summer and Peter to go to tournament camp with him the
following summer. Carl fell in love with the instructors and the positive
environment that he found there. As his tennis skills improved, he hoped
that someday he would be a TLC instructor.

Carl Walz

For several years, Carl and his father had developed local high school tennis at the club level. In 1998, Carl convinced the Aitkin School Board to add varsity boys tennis. When the Board pointed out that there was no money for a coach, Carl responded, "No problem, my father will volunteer." Carl had an answer for each objection, and the Board relented. Both Carl and his older brother Andy played on the first team, which was coached by their father with assistance from their mother.

Off the tennis court, Carl also helped others. He organized a fundraiser for a homeless shelter, served in soup kitchens, helped with Operation Christmas Child, became a peer helper, and sang in his high school choir.

Carl loved to practice tennis. Often, he ended a practice session begging to be fed "just a few more" tennis balls so he could work on his stroke of the day. Sometimes another 30 to 60 minutes would go by while he was taking his "last few shots." Even then, Carl usually had to be forced off the court at darkness by a parent taking him home for supper and homework.

All of his hard work paid off. In the spring of 1999, Carl won the high school subsection tennis tournament. Shortly afterwards, on May 28, driving alone, Carl was killed instantly in a head-on collision. Life had been so good, and then, without warning, it was over at the beginning of his 16th year.

Grief transformed into loving service of others

Carl's family was devastated. How could someone so good die so young? His enthusiasm for tennis and life, his contagious smile, and his emphasis on friendships and service were now gone. How could this wonderful life be remembered and honored? In the midst of their grief, the family decided to carry forward the mission that Carl had fostered. With the memorial money they received, a backboard was constructed at the Aitkin tennis courts. On it, the family put a plaque that read, "Tennis begins with love, in memory of Carl Walz."

This was just the beginning. Even though Joe had no sons still involved in the high school program, he continued to coach the boys. Meanwhile, Cindy agreed to coach the girls program with Joe as her assistant. They employed a *no-cut* policy, and the team rosters jumped to 40 for the girls and 30 for the boys. In the summer, Joe and Cindy organized instructional programs, team tennis, and adult programs. They brought in a half-week tennis camp to Aitkin and started the "Carl Walz Memorial Tennis Tournaments." Also, they took extra time to help any player, young or old, who wanted to learn the game.

Behind the scenes the Walzes poured extra effort into becoming better-qualified coaches. Remember, Joe and Cindy came into tennis as adults after Carl started playing. They read books, watched videos, went to coaching clinics, and attended TLC to improve their playing skills.

The Walz family relationship with TLC has been special in many ways. Ever since Carl persuaded them to attend in 1998, the Walzes have felt a close tie. After Carl's death, Joe, Cindy, and TLC decided to establish together a full scholarship at TLC in Carl's name. It would go to a high school junior or senior who had promoted tennis in his/her community in a unique and outstanding way, thereby mirroring what Carl had accomplished in Aitkin. The recipient's picture is permanently displayed in the Swanson Tennis Center on the Gustavus campus.

The Walz family also promoted TLC camp attendance for all interested youth in Aitkin. They provided scholarship help and promoted the TLC experience vigorously. Every year since Carl's death, large groups of Aitkin players have attended (34 in 2013). In addition, the Walzes have brought their extended family, including a relative from France, to either a family or an adult camp.

Their daughter, Emily, who started playing because of Carl, benefited immensely from the camp exposure. She remembered her camp experiences as follows:

> The camp does so much more than teach tennis skills; it combines tennis mechanics and strategy with games, humor, music, variety shows, sportsmanship, mental training, life lessons and philosophy, promotion of humanitarian service, and most importantly, love. TLC holds a special place in the hearts of the Walzes. Unfortunately, we did not get to return with Carl the next year. However, we have been back each year since because of the love and support we receive from the "family" at TLC and the way Carl's memory and spirit live on there.

Emily was so touched by her TLC experiences that she became a camp instructor when she reached college, thereby realizing one of her brother's dreams. In turn, TLC has influenced her to become a social studies high school teacher and a tennis coach.

After graduating from college, Andy Walz developed an East Africa program for Wilderness Inquiry, a nonprofit that makes the outdoors accessible to everyone, including those with disabilities. He led trips to Kenya and the Kambi Primary School near the base of Mt. Kenya. His family accompanied him on some of the trips. They took supplies, books, recreation equipment, and tennis rackets for the students at Kambi. The Walzes returned from Kenya, wanting to build new classrooms to replace the inadequate horse stable that had served as a school.

The Walz family, with the support of TLC and many others, raised money for eight classrooms. There were no administrative costs, because Andy and the Kenyan project manager donated their time. The money raised covered only materials and local labor. There is a deep pride in the African community regarding their school. The Walz family has gone back to the Kambi School several times, but the most memorable occasion was the dedication of the first two classrooms. They were guests of honor at a festive ceremony that celebrated their cooperative work together.

United States Tennis Association (USTA) Family of the Year

Heidi, Andy, Cindy, Joe, and Emily Walz, 2009 USTA
Family of the Year

The loving, volunteer service that the Walz family has poured into the lives of so many people after the death of Carl is remarkable. Their generosity has touched almost every family in the Aitkin, Minnesota, community. From there, it has spread to TLC in St. Peter, Minnesota, and many other communities in the upper Midwest. Next, it has stretched across the world to Africa and a rural village near the base of Mount Kenya.

In recognition of what they have accomplished, the Northern Tennis Association (NTA) gave them the 2007 NTA Family of the Year Award. Neal Hagberg, Director of TLC, concluded the award presentation saying:

> "Joe and Cindy have given to their children the belief that they can make a difference in this world. They have shown that love is more important than money, fame, trophies, or a USTA ranking. Love is even more powerful than death. The Walzes are the living embodiment of "tennis begins with love."

The Northern Tennis Association submitted their winner for consideration as the national Family of the Year Award. The decision was predictable. On March 22, 2010, at the USTA national meeting in Dallas, Texas, the Walz family received the 2009 USTA Family of the Year Award, given "to the family who in recent years has done the most to promote amateur tennis, primarily on a volunteer basis." The USTA press release ended with the following quote: "Their story is one that inspires many to reconsider what we are doing with our lives and how we can live our lives more meaningfully."

Section IV

TLP APPLIED TO COLLEGE COACHING

*The accomplishments of the Gustavus players and teams
undercut the suspicion that a sportsmanship emphasis
or large squads diminished the chance of winning.*

Some coaches and players have wondered why I emphasized sportsmanship rather than winning in the Gustavus tennis program. There were two important reasons. First, my priority was to teach sportsmanship as a life lesson. When pursued intentionally by an athletic team, lifetime bonds with teammates, coaches, and opponents resulted. Second, we focused on the things over which we had control. We emphasized positive attitude, conditioning, good diets, intensive drills, full effort in matches, intelligent strategies, relaxation techniques, etc. Since winning lay outside our control, we did not emphasize it.

Others have wondered about the exceptionally large teams that Gustavus fielded. Often the squads were near or over 30 players, resulting from the *no-cut* policy that I used. With so many players, how did the top players get the coaching attention they needed to excel? How did the players not making the top group stay motivated? The answers to these questions are revealed in the following chapters.

The accomplishments of the Gustavus players and teams confirmed my conviction that a sportsmanship emphasis or large squads did not diminish our chance for winning. I ended my head-coaching career in 2009 with more wins than any other collegiate tennis coach. Yet, the emphasis was never on winning.

Often, players coming into the Gustavus tennis program had not been exposed to the Tennis and Life Philosophy (TLP) in their high school training. However, when they learned and used our approach, their motivation and competitive accomplishments frequently skyrocketed.

The first 11 chapters in this section focus on events in the history of the Gustavus tennis program that illustrate how TLP worked in the lives of our players. Their actions and testimonies revealed surprising accomplishments, mature insights, and lasting loyalties to teammates that often stretched for lifetimes. Players, alumni, and parents frequently perceived themselves as part of the ongoing Gustavus tennis "family."

1980 NCAA III Championship team: Dan Westlund, Shaun Miller, Paul Holbach, John Mattke, Jim Hearn, and Coach Wilkinson

The final four chapters in this section are different in emphasis. In two of them, I tackle the ethical issue of stacking, which occurs when coaches put or leave their players in incorrect order. At the request of the NCAA III Men's Coaches Committee, I devised a plan that provided an objective, verifiable way for determining lineups. In the next chapter, I address another national issue—the importance of doubles. In a collegiate dual match, should all three doubles be worth 14% of the total points? This occurs when all three doubles together are worth one point. Or should all three doubles be worth 33% of the total points? This occurs when each doubles match is worth one point and when combined, worth three points. The final chapter in this section (Gustavus doubles) is unique in this memoir, intended for readers who are interested in the subtleties of advanced doubles strategies.

21

SIX PILLARS OF THE GUSTAVUS MEN'S TENNIS PROGRAM

Kevin personified the team-oriented approach that I prioritized.
He never complained about playing #3 singles on the team during
his sophomore and junior years, even though it kept him from
competing in the NCAA singles tournament as a sophomore.
Again in his junior year, Kevin was almost denied access to
the tournament because he was a #3 player. After he was
admitted, he went all the way to the national singles final.

In October of 2004, during my 35th anniversary year as the Gustavus head coach, my former players honored me with a sculpture, which now stands in front of the Swanson Tennis Center. Sculptor Nick Legeros created a boy with a smile on his face, jumping over a net, with his left hand holding a racket and his right hand extended to shake his opponent's hand. The boy's energy, upbeat attitude, and sportsmanlike gesture capture the essence of the Gustavus tennis program.

So do the words that are inscribed on the net. Before the sculpture was created, former player Marc Miller ('83) asked me to write down words of wisdom that guided my coaching approach. Next, he arranged my response on the net portion of the sculpture. At the top, forming the net tape, are the Three Crowns. In the middle, arranged in squares that resemble the spaces created by the net strings, are the Serenity Prayer, quotes from Arthur Ashe Jr. and other words of wisdom. The sculpture succinctly captures the mission of the Gustavus men's tennis program, which I led from 1970 until 2009. At the bottom is a quote that touts the fundamental goal of all sporting activity... "Have fun!"

Wilkinson sitting next to the sculpture that
was donated by former players in 2004

Throughout the years, I have depended on six different resources, which I have called the six pillars: (1) parents, (2) players, (3) opponents, (4) alumni, (5) assistant coaches and (6) my wife, Barb. Each had a unique but complementary role in achieving the program's success. Together they helped me create an environment that encouraged sportsmanship, produced many victories, and made coaching fun. Without each pillar, I would have struggled to effectively serve teams that always exceeded 20 players and sometimes reached 40.

Parents, the first pillar

Parents were crucial. When I called recruits, parents often answered the phone. I usually took time to talk with them first. By doing so, I learned important things about the recruit and their aspirations for their son. When campus visits were planned, I encouraged the parents to join him. As a result, they could experience the academic opportunities, student support resources, tennis facilities, and my approach to coaching.

I liked to explain to parents the program's Three Crowns philosophy. These were three things within their son's control. When parents understood that success in the Gustavus program did not depend on winning or playing well, which were outside their son's control, they could decrease the pressure he might feel. I wanted the parents to focus on the Three Crowns, not their son's team position or his win-loss record.

Most importantly, parents were cheerleaders. They needed to emphasize only what their son had done well. He needed to know that his parents were proud of him and his accomplishments. On the other hand, suggestions for improvement should be left to me. I liked integrating them into their son's practice plans in a non-threatening way that would not undermine his confidence.

Parents usually brought their sons to freshmen orientation. In the late afternoon, parents were expected to leave. At that time, Barb and I invited them to our house for dinner. We sought to reassure parents that we were concerned about their son personally, socially, academically, and tennis-wise. We wished to do everything we could to make their son's college experience fulfilling.

To accomplish this goal, I needed the parents' assistance. Often, their son would share problems with them before they talked to me. A "heads-up" on a troublesome issue could help me immensely. After I contacted the student and addressed the problem, I would get back to the parents with ideas as to how they could help.

Parents were frequently invited to participate in team activities. I encouraged them to attend home matches, bring refreshments, and even accompany us on road trips. I made that easy by publicizing our trips early, reserving extra rooms at our hotels, and inviting them to team meals. Parents often helped by driving, hosting meals, or providing housing.

My weekly updates by email put a positive spin on events. They also laid out the schedule for the coming week. I encouraged parents to attend matches and cheer for good shots by their sons as well as their opponents. Of course, they were expected to never show displeasure with opponents' line calls.

A yearly fund raising event called the Tennis GALA involved parents in several important ways. They could play doubles with their sons in flighted tournaments that were adjusted to various skill levels. Parents provided both lunch for all participants and prizes for flight winners. Since alumni also attended, bonds were established between different generations and player eras. Parents of current players soon realized that they were part of an ongoing tennis family that did not end when their son graduated.

Each tennis season culminated with a banquet to which all parents were invited. It followed the conference championship and preceded the NCAA III tournament. Team members were expected to dress sharply in sport jackets and ties. They honored each other with gifts, stories, and compliments. Parents got to know everyone, even when our *no-cut* policy produced teams as large as 40 players.

Most importantly, the banquet allowed me to express appreciation for each player in front of his parents. Regardless of his position on the team, each was praised equally. I mentioned team wins and prospects for the NCAA III tournament, but they were not my focus. Instead, I concentrated on personal attributes that best prepared each son for a meaningful life of service to others.

Players, the second pillar

Current players were my continuing priority. All of the other pillars depended on this one. Molding young men into a true team could be challenging. If they had experienced tennis primarily as an individual, not as a team member, they could have grown dependent on personal recognition and special favors. If their primary goal were to be number one on the team, it would create tension between teammates. One person's success would have been another person's disappointment. I wanted to avoid that.

Instead, I wanted the Three Crowns to guide team behavior. This was a standard that all could achieve every time they stepped on the court, even if they did not win or play well. If players chose negativity, half effort, or poor sportsmanship during practice sessions, there were consequences. I interrupted practice and required additional conditioning for everyone on the team. Players would try harder when they realized that their shortcomings impacted the whole team, not just them.

In team matches, negative behavior from one player could have the effect of pulling the whole team down. Conversely, a positive, full effort performance would be uplifting, regardless of the score. Players sometimes thought that self-directed negativity only involved them. Not true. A doubles partner could easily interpret negative behavior as being directed toward him. The same was true for opponents. Self put-downs indirectly told opponents that their points came from our errors or poor play, not their skill.

During intra-squad matches, I enforced a very strict code. There could be no challenges of opponent's line calls, either verbally or with body language. If there was a problem, players needed to talk to me afterwards in private. Compliments were expected after good shots, followed by "thank you" from the recipient. After matches, each player told the other what he had done well. Winning players were not to brag, but losing players could tell others how well their opponent had played.

Position on the team caused anxiety for some players. Every time they won a practice set against a higher ranked teammate, they thought they should be moved up. When intra-squad tournaments were played, the thoughts were even stronger. Instead, I wanted matches between teammates to be a means for improvement but not a basis for team position comparisons.

With each passing tennis season, it became increasingly apparent that there was a need for an objective system to determine team position that did not depend on intra-squad results. At first, this idea seemed counter-intuitive. However, Shaun Miller ('82) helped me realize that challenge matches and outside competition were different psychologically. He became a five time national champion but seldom won a challenge match.

Before I created a system that prioritized competitive results against outside competition, team position was hard for some to understand. The players knew the values and expectations that I promoted, and so they would say, "Coach, how can you put player X above me after I defeated him twice last week in practice? Why am I behind player Y, who didn't play tournaments last summer and has frequently missed practices?"

Understandably, players were frustrated when someone with natural talent and a poor work ethic was placed higher on the team. Some saw this as coaching hypocrisy. "You say that the Three Crowns are important, but then you reward someone who is not practicing them." In their frustration, they did not realize that the Three Crowns were helping them reach their potential, but they were not the standard that determined lineup order. Instead, it was competitive results against outside competition.

Other expectations improved team unity. Doubles partners needed to do four things between every point (1) smile, (2) have eye contact, (3) make physical contact with their partner, and (4) say something positive. In addition, it was important for teammates to watch the last players finish, even after the team outcome had been determined. When highly ranked varsity players stayed to watch junior varsity players, a positive team dynamic was reinforced.

Also, upbeat team meetings were important. I encouraged players to tell each other the impressive things their teammates had accomplished. Compliments needed to be specific, delivered with eye contact and a smile, and then returned with a "thank you."

Furthermore, our team-oriented approach was enhanced when an upper classman adopted a freshman, helped him adjust to college, and made him feel special. This ran counter to the traditional approach, often found on other teams, where first year students were treated as servants and demeaned during initiation periods.

Finally, I gave equal attention to all of my players, not just the ones at the top of my lineup. That included planning the schedule so that everyone had playing opportunities. I scheduled both difficult and easy opponents and played extra junior varsity matches whenever the opposing team had extras. Sometimes, I used pro sets instead of full matches. My priority was competition for everyone.

Opponents, the third pillar

Positive relationships with opponents made competition fun! My interaction with opposing coaches helped set the tone. Two months before the match, I would reconfirm. For home matches, I recommended restaurants and motels. If visiting teams needed practice courts, I would see that they were reserved. In the week before the match, I called the coach again. If there were changes in my lineup, I wanted him to know. I learned over time that there should be no surprises at match time.

When we entered another playing site or when opponents arrived at our facility, I liked greeting them. By showing a personal interest in the coach and his players, I built an important bridge. I encouraged my players to do the same. When we learned the opponents' names and showed an interest in what they had achieved, it greatly improved on-court relationships.

Establishing trust with the opponents was an important objective. That began with the understanding that our team would not challenge the calls of opposing players, either verbally or with body language. Calling the lines fairly, regardless of the opponent's calls, enhanced trust. If there was any doubt, the shot was good. If we could tell that one of our own shots was out, we called it on ourselves. If opponents had a better view of lines on our side, we allowed them to overrule our "out" calls. We wished to convey a primary interest in correct calls and fairness.

We also complimented opponents' good shots instead of putting ourselves down. We did not show temper, which would have suggested that our opponents' successes came from our poor play. We called the score before each point and made "out" calls immediately and clearly. We refrained from calling foot faults, double bounces, distracting movement, or ball touches on opponents. We did not say "Come on!" when our opponents made an easy error. Instead, our players complimented our opponents when they hit good shots and remained humble when we did well.

This polite approach was extended to officials as well. They were the moral authority on the court. Even if they made mistakes, we did not argue with them or blame defeats on their errors. Instead, we shook their hands after the match and thanked them for their assistance.

After the match, our players complimented the opposing coach and his players for what they had done well. Often, I reinforced this praise with an email or phone call to the coach and the officials.

Carleton coach Stefan Zweifel and Wilkinson enjoy a lighthearted
moment after their 2008 dual match

Alumni, the fourth pillar

The Gustavus tennis program developed a feeling of community, even family, between players, parents, and opponents. I marvel at the continuing, close relationships that connect so many. Gustavus alumni and even some of their parents continue to play in the GALA for more than 35 years after graduation. Teammates from every era since 1970 continue to gather for regular reunions with each other.

The GALA, a flighted round robin tournament for alumni, parents, and current players, began in 1992. It continues as a well-attended event, sometimes drawing participants from both coasts. I will never forget the GALA that celebrated 35 years of my coaching. Marc Miller ('83), Raman Jayapathy ('85), Bruce Jackson ('90), and Tommy Valentini ('02) organized the sculpture project and raised the money to pay for it. They recruited many alumni and then organized a banquet that featured stories from every era of my coaching. Steve Edlund ('73) created a video with pictures of the GALA and greetings from everyone in attendance.

I am thrilled that the Gustavus tennis program has helped foster lifetime friendships between so many former players. This is so different from my own experience at the University of Iowa, where my tennis team first gathered almost 50 years after we graduated. Also, I am pleased that so many

Gustavus graduates continue to play tennis well. That, too, is different from my own experience.

The continuing interaction with alumni has helped current Gustavus players clarify their own values, make business contacts, and plan potential career paths. This happened not only at the GALA, but in other situations as well. For example, the team traveled each year to Milwaukee, where we competed at a beautiful indoor club owned by John Gambucci ('81). By always displaying gracious hospitality and strong loyalty to the Gustavus tennis program, he was a powerful role model for current players. So was Shaun Miller ('82), a five-time national champion while at Gustavus. He and his wife Melanie have hosted the team in their beautiful home each time we journeyed to Fargo to play Concordia.

Alumni and parents have also served as coaches when circumstances made it impossible for me to be with the team. For example, Ryan Haddorff ('95) and his father Bob kept the team undefeated while I traveled to Australia in 1997 to compete for the United States on the 55-and-over Austria Cup team. On another occasion, Tim Butorac ('75) accepted coaching duties for a 2003 winter trip to Hawaii. Barb was undergoing a bone marrow transplant operation for multiple myeloma and I needed to be with her. In other situations, split teams playing in two locations at the same time have benefited from the coaching advice of tennis team graduates.

Weddings of former players often have drawn many teammates. For example, Andy Schmidt ('97) was married in Seattle after completing postgraduate degrees at the University of Iowa and the University of Washington. Still, seven out of the ten men in the wedding party were Gustavus teammates. Also, when Eric Butorac ('03) got married at the age of 30 in Newport, Rhode Island, 20 tennis team members journeyed there to share his big day.

When tennis players came into the Gustavus program, they became part of a tennis family. They formed relationships with teammates, parents, alumni, and coaches. Tennis drew them together, but personal ties, more deep and important than the sport, permanently bonded many of them. Their loyalty to each other and their collegiate tennis experience formed an important pillar for the Gustavus tennis program. Their contacts directed new players to the program; their contributions helped fund it; and their personal interactions with the varsity provided a powerful, mentoring influence.

Assistant coaches, the fifth pillar

I have been blessed with many assistant coaches who were previous varsity players. They included Rich Hughes ('81), Erik Samuelson ('88), Steve Molen ('89), Eric Stacey ('94), Dan Carlson ('94), Ryan Haddorff ('95), Ryan Dussault ('99), Tommy Valentini ('02), Kevin Whipple ('03), and Ben Lundell ('05). Each has played a unique and important role. In every case, my assistant coach was steeped in the traditions and values of the Gustavus tennis program, having experienced it themselves for four years. Their personalities, leadership skills, positive attitudes, and playing skills made them a perfect fit. Often the players felt more comfortable going to them, instead of me, for private lessons or individual counseling.

Having another coach who loved and knew the players was invaluable. When important decisions involving team policy were made, a second viewpoint was extremely helpful. When a problem was brewing between team members, my assistant often got wind of it first. Or when a player needed extra help, my assistant was often available.

Kevin Whipple ('03) has continued as an assistant coach after my retirement in 2009. He has continually raised the bar. His passion runs deep and his creativity seems endless. Besides leading effective practices that stress positive behavior and strategic play, he assumes other important roles as well. He films highlight videos of each player that features their best shots and favorite music. In order to attract prospective high school students, Kevin has produced a video that promotes the Gustavus tennis program. He also has taken both head and action shots of everyone on the team and prepared the pictures for display in the indoor tennis center.

Barb, the sixth pillar

For all 39 of my head coaching years at Gustavus, Barb was a supportive partner. Together we directed Tennis and Life Camps, the source of income that made college coaching possible for me. Barb was the head cook for many team meals, the hostess for the annual Christmas party, the accompanying mother on many team trips, the coordinator for the annual GALA, a site director for numerous regional ITA tournaments, the Swanson Tennis Center cleanup coordinator after the facility was badly damaged by the 1998 tornado, a devoted fan, and a counselor when the guys needed it.

Most importantly, Barb supported me when coaching demands took me away from home. Long hours of practice often ate into the evening hours and removed me from parenting responsibilities. She was always there to cover. As a result, our daughters always had a parent who was present to love them and to give them support with their homework. Many spring trips for the tennis team did not coincide with high school vacations for our girls, so Barb was at home while I was gone for a week. The same thing happened in May, when the team often qualified for one, and sometimes two, national tournaments. Without Barb's continual support, I could never have directed an ambitious collegiate program that was supported by five other important pillars: parents, players, opponents, alumni, and assistant coaches.

Steve and Barb head to the tennis court in 1979

22

BUILDING COLLEGIATE SPORTSMANSHIP IN THE EARLY 1980s

*Arthur Ashe Jr. told me that opponents' line calls should never
be challenged, no matter how obvious the mistake. For me,
this was a paradigm shift. I had believed that challenges were
necessary, though always expressed in a polite, respectful way.*

Age of the "Super Brats"

In 1981, Ian Barnes of the *Daily Express* in London gave John McEnroe the
title "Super Brat" after his embarrassing behavior at Wimbledon. In a second
round match against Tom Gullikson, McEnroe threw a fit after disagreeing
with a line call by umpire Ted James. "You guys are the pits of the world,
you know that," he yelled. When McEnroe was docked a point, and then
another point by referee Fred Hoyles, he wailed, "You cannot be serious!"
The label "Super Brat" and his quotes have lived in infamy. John even chose
the latter quote as the title for his 2002 memoir.

McEnroe went on to win Wimbledon in 1981, but his outrageous behavior
led the tournament committee to deny him membership in the All England
Club, an honor that had been automatically bestowed to all previous
champions. In response, John skipped the dinner that honored the winners
saying, "I don't want to sit around with 70 to 80 year old stiffs who criticize
my behavior." The women's champion Chris Evert tried her best to
apologize for the actions of her fellow American.

The other "Super Brat" was Jimmy Connors. His on-court behavior could be
vulgar… giving the finger to a linesman or strutting around the court with
the tennis racket handle between his legs. Sometimes, he yanked on the
handle in a grotesque, suggestive manner. In 1977, he insulted the
Wimbledon establishment by refusing to participate in the parade of former
champions at the tournament's centenary celebration. The following day he
was loudly booed at the tournament, which did not seem to bother him.

Jimmy was strictly anti-establishment, refusing at first to join the Association of Tennis Professionals (ATP) and playing in only three Davis Cup matches, even though he was ranked #1 in the world for five consecutive years.

The age of the "Super Brats" brought a new dimension to poor sportsmanship… the loss of civility. For McEnroe and Connors, the umpires often became the "scum of the earth." The "Super Brats" directed their profanity-laden tirades and accusations toward officials, ball girls, and opponents…whoever happened to irritate them at the moment. Many sports fans in the United States were drawn to both their talent and inappropriate behavior. However, their popularity produced difficult challenges for coaches who wished to advocate civil relationships to their collegiate players.

Seeking to influence collegiate players toward sportsmanship

To counter the influence of the "Super Brats," I designed the Arthur Ashe Jr. Award, emphasizing his legacy of sportsmanship. One player in each collegiate division would receive it. The award's criteria came straight from the Karen Gibbs Award, designed four years earlier for Tennis and Life Camps at Gustavus. Coaches' committees would pick the winners, based on these criteria: (1) sportsmanship, (2) academic excellence, (3) humanitarian concerns, and (4) playing accomplishments.

Initially, the Arthur Ashe Jr. Award included a free trip to the U.S. Open, courtesy of the Head Racket Company. In 1983, Ashe presented the award to Gustavus All-American Rich Skanse ('84). In 1982, he had won the NCAA III doubles title with Shaun Miller ('82), and been an important member of the NCAA III national championship team. Rich wrote in his award application:

> I have come to realize… that I do not want to judge or be
> judged by what I have attained, but by who I am… I try to
> show my humanitarian concerns through the way I present
> myself, both on the court and off. When I play tennis, I try to
> be considerate, fair, and to respect my opponent. I witness for
> who I am by the way I treat my opponent.

Other Gustavus award winners followed Rich: Per Ekstam in 1984, Ulf Gudjonsson in 1989, Ben Lipari in 1999 and Eric Butorac in 2003. Five national winners in 30 years are impressive. No other Division III school had more than two. At the regional and conference level, other Gustavus award winners were: Mark Kruger in 1986, Paul Gustafson in 1992, Andy Schmidt in 1997, Matt Lundmark in 2000, Tommy Valentini in 2001, Daryn Collins in 2002, Andy Bryan in 2007 and 2008, and Krishan Jethwa in 2010.

Rich Skanse receiving the Arthur Ashe Jr. Award from Arthur at 1983

Five guidelines for non-umpired matches

Winning Arthur Ashe Jr. awards did not happen by accident. Gustavus players were trained to be good sports. They followed strictly enforced guidelines that helped them achieve high sportsmanship ideals. In the 1980s, I formulated five guidelines for non-umpired matches to counter the influence of the "Super Brats." The guidelines focused on what players and coaches could do, without officials, regardless of whom we played or how we were treated. In other words, we focused on things within each person's own control. The following guidelines were printed during the 1980s in an ITA publication with the hope that all college coaches and their players would aspire to the recommended behavior.

1) **Do not challenge opponents' calls, either verbally or with body language.** Also, do not call infractions on our opponents, whether they are *Code* violations, double bounces, or late calls. No one likes to be accused, even if it is phrased in a polite manner.

   Mark Kruger ('86), a three time All-American for Gustavus Adolphus College, went through his college career never questioning an opponent's call. In his essay he wrote:

   > It is not the accomplishments themselves that are important, but the experiences, people, and relationships developed along the way while striving to attain these goals...Winning isn't everything. The relationships developed with teammates, coaches, and opponents are much more special. On the court, I play hard and try to win, but at the same

time, try to play in a way that shows respect for my opponent and myself.

2) **Do not criticize an opposing coach or make recommendations concerning player discipline.** On one occasion, I became bothered by the abusive profanity of two players on the opposing team. We had no officials to enforce *The Code*, so I politely suggested to the opposing coach that he apply the point penalty to his players. He looked at me incredulously. "Who are you to talk?" he asked. No, he was not going to discipline his players at such a critical moment. However, he said he would talk to them later.

That evening I pondered this exchange. I had offended the coach, even though I had tried to be polite. He had rationalized away his players' behavior. Because I was an opposing coach, he distrusted my motive. He saw me trying to gain a competitive advantage. This left me with an uneasy feeling. From that day forward, I resolved to never again advise an opposing coach on his players' conduct.

3) **Call lines fairly and give opponents the benefit of the doubt.** If there is any chance that the ball was good, call it "in." If we did not see the ball, if I disagree with my partner, or if we delay in making our call, then the ball is good. Even when we are certain of an "out" call, invite an over rule from our opponents when they had a superior "down the line" view of where the ball bounced. Finally, if we hit a ball out, call it "out" on ourselves (except on a first serve that our opponent returns successfully).

Coaches can have a decisive impact on their players. Coach Jerry Noyce from the University of Minnesota demonstrated this in a dual match against Gustavus. A Minnesota player became frustrated with his poor play, and increasingly irritated by what he perceived to be bad calls from Bill Sternard ('84). However, neither Jerry nor I saw any mistakes.

The Minnesota player finally reached a frustration limit, and intentionally retaliated, calling a ball out that both Jerry and I could see was good. With no prompting from me, Jerry walked out on the court, confronted his player, and asked him if he had purposely called the ball incorrectly. After moaning about the bad calls he had received, the player said "yes." Jerry told him that such behavior was cheating, and reversed his player's call. That action made quite an impression on me.

4) **Set rules of sportsmanship for our team and follow them.** On a southern spring trip to Louisiana in 1981, we played a good Division I school that did not expect us to challenge them. They came into the match with a cocky attitude and started to panic when they realized that we might win. Four of their players were out of control and should have been penalized. The match score was 4-3 in their favor, with close matches at #1 and #2 doubles still on the court. Jim Hearn ('82) and

Shaun Miller ('82), our #1 team, had won the first set, and were on serve in the second. Then it happened. Jim, probably influenced by the non-penalized behavior of our opponents, let his racket fly in a moment of frustration.

We had a team rule that prescribed automatic default for racket throwing. Miller and Hearn lost their chance to beat a good Division I team. I apologized to the opposing coach and explained our team policy. As we finished the #2 doubles match, I heard two home spectators comment that their team could use a rule like ours. I never defaulted Jim and Shaun again. They went on to win the national doubles championship that year.

5) **Congratulate opponents with a firm handshake, eye contact, and specific praise.** Credit them for at least one thing done well, even if we played terribly or they cheated. Resist the temptation to make excuses, which take away the significance of our opponents' accomplishment.

Final reflections on Ashe, "Super Brats" and sportsmanlike civility

Arthur Ashe Jr. told me that opponents' line calls should never be challenged, no matter how obvious the mistake. For me this was a paradigm shift. I had believed that challenges were necessary, though always expressed in a polite, respectful way. After listening to Ashe and deciding to follow his example, I switched to an approach that encouraged me to focus only on my own calls. From a mental standpoint, this helped me immensely. As a result, opponents would no longer get inside my head and decrease my ability to stay focused.

Until the late 1970s, I used what I had learned from Arthur as a tool for controlling my own mind and emotions. I knew that my players and I would be tougher mentally if we focused only on what we controlled. Players who focused on things outside their control, such as opponents' behavior or winning, often grew angry and self-destructive. There were occasional conflicts over line calls in the 1960s and 1970s, but they were handled in a subdued and civil manner. Players sometimes got upset and showed it, but it was usually self-directed frustration that added to their own detriment.

John McEnroe and Jimmy Connors, the "Super Brats," introduced a level of incivility never seen before or since. Their retirement in 1991 was a welcome change. New champions again raised the bar during the following 20 years. By 2011, world champions Rafael Nadal and Roger Federer had taken sportsmanlike civility and community service to an unprecedented level. Reputation Institute named Roger the second most respected person in the world. Only Nelson Mandela was ranked above him. With Roger and Rafael as tennis role models, the job of influencing collegiate men toward sportsmanlike civility became much easier.

Shaun Miller, NCAA III singles and
doubles champion in 1981 and 1982

23

WINNING and LOSING:
THE FRAGILE DIFFERENCE

Winning or losing often hangs on such a thin, unpredictable thread. Fortunate points for us at the end of our final two matches against Washington allowed us to win. On the other hand, a mistaken action by the tournament director in our final match against Trinity contributed significantly to our loss.

In May of 2000, the Gustavus tennis team came within one point of losing in the NCAA III Midwest Regional final. We escaped with a 4-3 home court victory over Washington University from St. Louis, Missouri. Moving on to the national tournament in Kalamazoo, Michigan, we advanced to the final round. There we faced a heavily favored team—Trinity University from Texas. We even overheard the tournament director predicting that Gustavus would lose decisively. The following stories from these two matches illustrate the fragile difference between winning and losing and how little control we have over either outcome. Nevertheless, these two stories reveal that we do have control over factors more important than winning.

Gustavus vs. Washington University

Gustavus upset favored Kalamazoo College during the 2000 spring season and earned the top seed in the NCAA III Midwestern Regional Tournament. Our opponent in the final was Washington University, a team we had defeated 5-2 in Milwaukee three weeks earlier.

All three Gustavus doubles teams started out slowly, losing their serves and dropping behind. Still, there seemed to be little reason for worry. Gustavus had dominated last time, winning each match with a two or three service break advantage. We remained positive, confident that our fortunes would change, but it never happened. Washington University maintained and even expanded their leads, sweeping all three doubles and taking a 1-0 lead in the dual match.

Gustavus regrouped after the doubles. We were shocked but still confident that we could come back and win at least four of the singles. At first, it appeared we would. Mike Hom at #3 singles and Nick Crossley at #4 singles achieved relatively easy straight set victories, putting Gustavus ahead 2-1.

Then the dual match took another unexpected turn. Kevin Whipple, undefeated for the season against all opponents (even Division I), lost at #5 singles. The next surprise came at #6 singles, where Daryn Collins went down in three sets. Gustavus had not lost to any Division III, #6 player all year. Gustavus was behind 3-2 with the difficult task of pulling out both #2 and #1 singles.

At that point, Jay Bemis at #2 singles had lost the first set and was down 5-2 in the second set tiebreaker. He hung in with a positive attitude, refused to give up, and miraculously pulled out the tiebreaker 10-8. Then he went on to easily win the third set, notching the dual match score at 3-3.

All attention then turned immediately to Matt Lundmark at #1 singles. Three weeks before, he had lost to Washington's Arun Nanjappa. This time they had split the first two sets. Matt was down 3-4 in the third set and 15-40 on his serve, but he played two spectacular points to draw the score back to deuce. Six points later, Matt won the game, drew even at 4-4 and again at 5-5.

Both players were attacking the net. Whoever got there first seemed to win the point. Either player could have won if he had picked up an extra point here or there. Fortunately, Lundmark emerged with the last point and a 7-5 victory in the final set. With this clutch win, Gustavus escaped with a narrow 4-3 team victory and the right to advance to the national quarterfinal round in Kalamazoo.

Gustavus vs. Trinity University

Before facing Trinity in the final, Gustavus beat Redlands University from California 4-0 in the quarterfinal round and favored Williams College from Massachusetts 4-3 in the semifinals. The margin of difference was a third set at #6 singles, won by Daryn Collins with the team score tied at 3-3.

Gustavus entered the championship match as a decided underdog. However, previous assumptions proved false when Gustavus won the doubles point and two of the singles matches. With the final match on the court, the team score was tied at 3-3. Nick Crossley, #4 player for Gustavus, had won the first set. At 2-2 and game point for Nick in the second set, the umpire called a foot fault on Nick's opponent. The call gave the game to Nick and a service break advantage.

Nick's opponent was so upset that he blasted a ball in anger across the net and into the far back fence. This was his second *Code* violation for unsportsmanlike behavior, so the umpire gave Nick's opponent a game penalty, making the score 4-2. In frustration the player yelled, "You can't do this to me! You are taking away the national championship!" He demanded that the match be stopped and the head referee summoned. The referee came onto the court, listened to the umpire and the player, and then upheld the umpire's decision.

The Gustavus team watching the match was excited! A team championship seemed imminent. Nick was up a break and in the driver's seat. His opponent had unraveled. He was bursting with anger and resentment, and on the verge of another outburst, which would have produced an automatic default.

As soon as the head referee upheld the umpire's actions, the tournament director yelled from behind the court, "That is a terrible decision!" The head referee, taken aback that the tournament director should criticize his decision, reversed his call and put the score back to 3-2. Nick's anguished, unsportsmanlike opponent now felt vindicated.

The 15-minute delay containing theatrics and protests had interrupted Nick's concentration and allowed him to cool off. His hopes had been raised by the referee and then dashed by the inappropriate intervention of the tournament director. Now, Nick had to put this aside and regain his focus.

Nick did his best under the circumstances. He did not protest the tournament director's action. Instead, he played hard with a positive and sportsmanlike attitude. However, he was unable to hold on. His vindicated opponent pulled himself together, played well, broke Nick twice, and won the second set. The opponent's momentum continued through the third set, ending the opportunity for Gustavus to win a national championship.

Winning or losing

Winning or losing often hangs on such a thin, unpredictable thread. Fortunate points for us at the end of our final two matches against Washington allowed us to win. On the other hand, an overrule of the tournament referee by the tournament director in our final match against Trinity probably changed the outcome.

However, these things did not define us. If we had become negative when the Washington match spun out of control, we would not have been successful. If we had stopped trying to win, we would not have been successful. If we had become poor sports when our opponent misbehaved or erupted in anger directed at the tournament director, we would not have been successful. However, in both matches we made the decision to be successful at the highest and most important level. We demonstrated positive attitudes, full effort, and good sportsmanship. I was extremely proud of my team. I would have been so, even if Jay Bemis and Matt Lundmark had not staged their miraculous comebacks.

Matt Lundmark in 2000

24

CELEBRATING EXCESSIVELY

*At midseason, Gustavus met Kalamazoo College, ranked #2
in the nation. They had everyone back from their team that
had reached the NCAA III finals the year before. Gustavus
had not defeated Kalamazoo in ten years. Nevertheless, Gustavus
prevailed, claiming an exciting 5-2 victory with polite constraint.*

In 2000, a number of the players on the Gustavus men's tennis team took my college course on sport ethics. We traveled to New Zealand and Australia. One of our tasks was to analyze the attitudes of spectators at the Australian Open toward sportsmanship. We discovered that spectators older than 30 believed in the traditional sportsmanship that I emphasized—humility in victory and graciousness in defeat. On the other hand, spectators under 30 thought that victory celebrations in the presence of defeated opponents were still sportsmanlike. Many tennis team members in the class initially agreed with this viewpoint.

However, their perspective was modified two months later in California on our spring trip. Gustavus had won four matches, including a decisive 6-1 victory over highly ranked Redlands University. The last match on the trip was against the University of California-San Diego, a lower ranked team that had lost to Redlands. Gustavus went up 3-0 in the match, but then saw its advantage slip away in a surprising 4-3 loss. Both teams were shocked. As UCSD erupted into uncontrolled celebration, the Gustavus team felt great discomfort with their actions. This experience would serve them well later in the season.

At midseason, Gustavus met Kalamazoo College, ranked #2 in the nation. They had everyone back from their team that had reached the NCAA III finals the year before. Gustavus had not defeated Kalamazoo in ten years. Nevertheless, Gustavus prevailed, claiming an exciting 5-2 victory with polite constraint.

As the season ended, four closely matched teams met in the semifinals of the 2000 NCAA III Men's National Tennis Championship. Trinity University of San Antonio, Texas, faced the favored University of California-Santa Cruz team, and Gustavus took on Williams College from Williamstown, Massachusetts, the defending national champion. The site was the tennis stadium at Kalamazoo College, Michigan.

The Trinity-Santa Cruz verdict came down to the last match between Jeevan Ramakrishnan of Trinity and Danny Kim of Santa Cruz. Everything was a three—#3 singles, a 3-3 team match score, the 3rd set, and a 3-3 final set score. Both teams eagerly anticipated the outcome. All the players on both sides were glued to each point. The Santa Cruz players seated in the stands joked between themselves, perhaps conveying confidence, possibly masking their nervousness. They were the favored team, number one ranked all season, and now, it was coming down to the last few games.

Trinity had so much nervous energy the players in the stands could hardly sit still. After one particularly exciting point, Mike Slutzky shinnied ten feet up a narrow pole, intended only for supporting awnings. Reaching the top, some 20 feet above the court surface, he let out a yell, and quickly descended before the flimsy structure that supported him could collapse.

When Trinity won the final point, a remarkable scene unfolded. Ramakrishnan jubilantly tossed his racket at least 30 feet in the air. Before it came back down, he took off running toward the opposite end of the stadium, knocking over chairs as he ran, pumping his fist, and yelling, "Bring it on!" His excited teammates jumped up out of their seats and over the guard rail that separated the stands from the courts. Racing to the other end of the stadium, they mobbed Jeevan, rolling on the ground, cheering, unable to contain their celebration.

On the other side of the net, while Ramakrishnan's racket was still in the air, Danny Kim dropped to his knees and crushed his racket on the ground, breaking it in half. Crestfallen, having let his favored team down, he put his forehead on the ground, buried his head under his arms, and remained there, not moving, for several minutes.

After minutes of celebration, the Trinity coach told Jeevan to go back and shake hands with Danny. Neither competitor seemed the least bit concerned that this formality had gone neglected.

The other semifinal match between Gustavus and Williams was equally close, but a different model of competition prevailed. Gustavus scored first, sweeping all three doubles and going up 1-0. Then, Williams won three singles matches for a 3-1 lead. Next, Mike Hom and Nick Crossley won for Gustavus at #3 and #4 singles, drawing the score even at 3-3, leaving the dual to be decided at #6 singles. Miles Hawley from Williams had won the first set, but Daryn Collins from Gustavus notched the second set in a tiebreaker. Everything depended on the final, third set. The air was filled with excitement and anticipation. A hard fought baseline contest determined the outcome, and Collins from Gustavus emerged the winner.

After the match was completed, Collins walked calmly to the net and shook Hawley's hand. Both opponents offered compliments to each other. Following this exchange, teammates of both players congratulated the contestants and then all members of both teams. Williams' players graciously offered the Gustavus team best wishes for success the following day.

The next day, just before Gustavus played its championship match, David Johnson, the Williams coach, came over to the Gustavus team and wished them good luck. "The level of sportsmanship yesterday was simply outstanding," he said. David had been affected by the traditional sportsmanship that both his and my teams had modeled, where winners were modest and losers were gracious.

2000 NCAA III 2nd place team: Asst. Coach Ryan Dussault, Michael Hom, Josh Heiden, Mark Jones, Matt Lundmark, Jay Bemis, Kevin Whipple, Nick Crossley, Tommy Valentini, Daryn Collins, Coach Wilkinson

25

ACHIEVING THE IMPROBABLE

*During the fall of his senior year in Mobile, Alabama,
John won the 2008 ITA National Singles title. In the
semifinals, he eliminated the defending national champion
from Washington University. In the finals, John defeated
an Emory University player who had been a five-star,
high school recruit with a top-30 national junior ranking.*

In 2005, John Kauss was a Minnesota high school tennis player trying to decide which college he should attend. Even after his senior year, he had not advanced beyond the first round of the state high school singles tournament. A rival Minnesota Intercollegiate Athletic Conference coach told John that he should not attend Gustavus, because he was not good enough to make the varsity team. However, Kevin Whipple, then tennis pro at the White Bear Indoor Club, had worked with John and recognized his potential. After talking with Kevin, I encouraged John to enroll at Gustavus.

John's transformation from an average high school player to an outstanding collegiate champion came gradually. By the end of his freshman year, he had not earned a varsity position in either singles or doubles. John broke into the singles lineup in his sophomore year, but his results at #3 singles were inconsistent. His drive for excellence often left him frustrated and angry. When things were not going his way, he could not hide his disappointment.

In John's junior year, he made a conscious change in attitude. Instead of emphasizing winning, he prioritized the Three Crowns. John chose to remain positive, even when things were not going his way. He responded to coaching advice positively and tried different strategies when his preferred one was not proving effective. He began to treat others with more respect. Winning was no longer his priority, yet he was winning much more.

Remarkable results started to occur. At the 2008 ITA National Indoor Tournament, John played brilliantly. He won all of his singles and doubles matches convincingly and helped lead the Gustavus team to its fourth national indoor team championship.

During the fall of his senior year in Mobile, Alabama, John won the 2008 ITA National Singles title. In the semifinals, he eliminated the defending national champion from Washington University. In the finals, John defeated an Emory University player who had been a five-star, high school recruit with a top-30 national junior ranking. These singles victories caught me by surprise. So did his trip to the doubles final with partner Mike Burdakin. I had scheduled an earlier flight home. Rescheduling a flight proved difficult, so I gladly drove John and Mike back to Minnesota on a joyful, cross-country road trip.

John Kauss, 2009 NCAA III #1 seed in
singles and doubles

As John's confidence grew, he achieved more memorable milestones. In the winter, John qualified for one of three male positions on a U.S. collegiate team that competed in France against amateur teams from many other countries. In the spring season, he went undefeated in Division III singles and doubles competition. Consequently, John was seeded #1 in singles and #1 in doubles with partner Mike Burdakin at the 2009 NCAA Division III National Tournament.

After graduation, Kauss became a tennis coach and pro. He discovered that his change in perspective was at the heart of the message he was sharing with his students. He knew that the Three Crowns had caused his own transformation and success. John wrote the following to me a year and a half after graduation.

> At first, I rejected your teachings about tennis and life. I was too prideful to see that focusing only on the things in my control is the right way to go on about tennis. This has helped me in life so much as well. You helped me realize that tennis was not at all about winning and losing, upon which I based my attitude and my disposition. Once I accepted that winning was out of my control, I became a much better player, much more relaxed on court, and relaxed about the curveballs life throws at you.
>
> I now find myself teaching my students the exact same mentality you taught me. I hope my kids can learn the lesson sooner than I did, but nevertheless I am so glad that I did. I know the Three Crowns are very important and true. You have changed the way I now look at life.

2008 MIAC and ITA National Indoor champions: 1st row, Aaron Zenner, Kevin Stickney, Andy Bryan; 2nd row, Asst. Coach Tommy Valentini, Mike Burdakin, Nick Hansen, John Kauss, Charlie Paukert, Ben Tomasek, Coach Wilkinson

26

OVERCOMING ANGER AND
THE NEED TO WIN

*When I first came to the Gustavus tennis team, I needed to win.
I had learned that wanting to win, more than anybody else,
would equal victory in any competitive event. However, only
within the past two years, did I realize that this attitude had
adverse side effects, not only on me, but on my opponents as well.*

Ryan Skanse was a highly ranked Minnesota high school player who spent considerable time at the Nick Bollettieri Tennis Academy during his teenage years. He attended Minnehaha Academy, was runner-up in the state high school tournament, and graduated in 1987. After attending the University of Minnesota for a year, where he was unable to play because of an injury, he transferred to Gustavus in 1988.

Given Ryan's training and competitive experience in high school, I was expecting more noteworthy tennis accomplishments during his first two years at Gustavus. However, he struggled in college competition, losing matches at the #3 position that he was capable of winning. Ryan was his own worst enemy, consumed with anger and frustration when he was not playing well. Usually the anger was directed at himself, but that was not always the case. On one occasion, Ryan and a hothead from an opposing team became very upset with each other during a match. They were ready to interrupt play to have a fistfight. Only my intervention prevented this from happening.

At the beginning of Ryan's junior year, a different personality began to emerge. His outlook on competition, opponents, and winning changed. At the same time, his level of play jumped considerably. Ryan moved into the #1 singles position for Gustavus and reached the semifinals of the 1991 NCAA III Singles Tournament. He and his partner Dave Jussila won the national doubles title. In Ryan's senior year, he played consistently for the whole season with no emotional outbursts. He made it all the way to the NCAA III singles final where he lost in three close sets to the defending national champion.

Ryan Skanse, 1992 NCAA III singles finalist

What produced this dramatic change in personality? What allowed him to utilize the skills that had been there before, but were sabotaged by his anger? What took him from an inconsistent and emotional #3 player one year to one of the top competitors in the nation for the next two years? The answers become clear in an essay that Ryan wrote during his senior year, explaining his philosophy of competition. The essay was part of the award application process for Division III Senior Player of the Year.

> When I first came to the Gustavus tennis team, I needed to win. I had learned that wanting to win, more than anybody else, would equal victory in any competitive event. This was supposed to be the driving factor that would allow me to play to the best of my ability. However, only within the past two years, did I realize that this attitude had adverse side effects, not only on me, but on my opponents as well.
>
> Tennis was really never that fun for me, and there were numerous times when I thought that quitting would be the most logical answer. When things were not going my way, I would

become so enraged on the court that afterwards it scared me to think that my emotions could control me in such a way. What was I doing wrong? After struggling with this for many years, the answer I found has had the most impact, not only on my tennis game, but on my life as well. I found that wanting to win, more than anything, produced the result of needing to win at all costs. My self-worth was based on being a better tennis player than someone else. When I lost, I felt like a failure. But when I won, the sun had never shined so bright.

Finally, I have come to understand that tennis is just a game, meant to be enjoyed, not an activity that means life or death. The lesson I am learning is to put tennis into life's proper perspective. I now realize that respecting my opponent and giving it my best effort, rather than winning or losing, is the true meaning of tennis.

It is important for me to understand that continued perfection is an extreme rarity in a game of such precision. I tell myself before each match that I am going to miss some shots. Doing this takes the pressure and frustration off when I miss in a crucial situation. Ironically, by taking out the need to win and the fear of losing, I am now winning more than I ever have.

This new attitude has been influential on my life. It seems that life is just like a game of tennis. People are competing in all aspects of life. Therefore, the principles of competing on the court can be applied to life's daily challenges...The growth I have experienced in collegiate tennis is to realize the enjoyment of the game. Now, every time I step on the court, it is possible for me to win, regardless of the final score. After four years of collegiate tennis, I can truly say, for the first time in my life, that I love the game of tennis.

How ironic. When winning was no longer the priority, everything changed. Ryan switched his focus to full effort, good sportsmanship, and positive attitude. He could be successful every time, regardless of the final score. When success was always achievable, tennis became fun again. Ryan had internalized the wisdom of the Serenity Prayer.

When this happened, Ryan discovered that he could apply the prayer to all areas of his life. Being appreciated or thanked was outside his control, but appreciating and thanking others was not. Getting an "A" on a difficult, competitive exam was outside his control, but studying hard to master the material was not. Winning a contract or maintaining a job was outside his control, but giving full effort to do the best work possible was not.

At first, it was hard for Ryan to stay focused on the things within his control, and to let go of the things that were not. But when he did, a new world of possibilities was opened to him, both on and off the tennis court.

Coach Wilkinson, Dave Jussila, and Ryan Skanse, 1991
NCAA III doubles champions

27

SACRIFICING A NATIONAL TITLE
FOR A BEST FRIEND

As I played my last college matches, I no longer feared
losing. What should have been the most pressure filled
situation of my tennis life was not. My willingness to
default the NCAA III singles final did not come from
an innate unselfishness that I possessed. Rather, it came
from the important lessons I learned in our program.

An Episcopal priest at the University of the South in Sewanee, Tennessee, told his congregation a story that he had read in the national news. Kevin Whipple from Gustavus defaulted the 2003 NCAA III singles title to his doubles partner Eric Butorac. The pair had reached the doubles final as well. A long singles semifinal by Eric in the morning, a short rest period before the singles final, and a doubles final to follow, prompted the pair to make a special request. Could they play the doubles final first? The tournament referee agreed, but the NCAA committee refused. Not wishing to jeopardize the doubles title, Kevin defaulted to Eric. Then the pair won the doubles championship in straight sets, 6-2, 6-2.

"I like that story," the priest said. "It says something about friendship. As the years go by, I'd like to know more about the enduring respect that will develop between these two friends as they grow old."

The priest went on to tell a story about Damon and Pythias, friends since birth. King Dionysus sentenced Pythias to death for treason. Pythias requested that he be set free for several days to put his family matters in order. The king refused, but then relented, when Damon offered to take the place of his friend Pythias until he returned. The king believed that Pythias would not return, and that Damon would be killed instead. When Pythias returned, the king in astonishment said:

The sentence is revoked. I have never believed that such faith and loyalty existed between two friends. I am wrong. You shall be rewarded with your freedom. But I ask that you in return do me one great service: teach me how to be worthy of a friendship such as yours.

Tying this story to a Biblical reference, the priest quoted Jesus in John 15:12.

This is my commandment, that you love one another as I have loved you… You are my friends if you do what I command you. I do not call you servants any longer… but I have called you friends.

The priest ended his sermon by saying:

The story of Jesus is one of friendship—God's friendship for all humanity, the invitation of friendship towards all of those who surround us… This is the witness of friendship that we hold at the center of our faith—the friend, Jesus who was willing to give his life for all those whom he called friend, the entire human family, you and me included. We take our places, gathered around our friend, the one at the center of our faith, the one who draws us together and inspires our common life.

A story of two friends

Kevin Whipple grew up in St. Cloud, Minnesota, and Eric Butorac in Rochester, Minnesota. Both came from out-state locations and shared a common challenge. Since most of the important tournaments were located in the Twin Cities, Kevin and Eric had to travel in order to play. Most of their top-ranked rivals were locals playing close to home. Another factor connected Kevin and Eric. Neither of their families had the money to send them to national tournaments or academies. While other top players in the state often traveled, Kevin and Eric developed their talents almost exclusively within Minnesota.

Similar backgrounds contributed to a deep personal bond between them. They liked getting together and practicing tennis. Some of the time Eric went to St. Cloud, but more frequently, Kevin came to Rochester. They took advantage of the free tennis instruction and drills offered by Eric's father, Tim, and the pros that worked under him at the Rochester Indoor and Outdoor tennis clubs. They developed into two of the top players in the state, destined to clash for the state high school title in their senior year.

When they played in the high school final, Kevin expected to win, based on previous tournament results. However, Eric pulled an upset. Twelve years later, after 12 ATP professional doubles tournament titles, Eric still referred to the 1999 Minnesota State High School singles title as one of his greatest tennis accomplishments. On the other hand, Kevin was devastated. Later he wrote, "The outcome of that match was all I cared about. I needed it... After losing to Eric, I quit tennis and gained a lot of weight."

Both Kevin and Eric chose Division I tennis programs, even though I had made an all-out effort to recruit them to Gustavus. They assured me that we were their second choices, but Eric went to Ball State University in Indiana and Kevin to New Mexico State. However, Kevin was unhappy there from the first week. He had reported overweight and out of practice, which did not help his chances. By midway through his first semester, Kevin contacted Gustavus and a mid-year transfer was set in motion.

When Kevin arrived, I was shocked at how much weight he had gained. Soon, however, he was back on track. His effort was noticeable as he conditioned hard and quickly dropped the extra weight. He immediately earned a spot at #5 singles. A singles player in high school, Kevin had little experience in doubles. He accepted the challenge to acquire volleying skills and learn doubles strategy. Kevin entered the doubles lineup during the 2000 NCAA III national tournament, just in time to help us finish second.

Kevin's positive experience at Gustavus certainly influenced Eric. They had remained in frequent contact with each other. As time away from classes on road trips and combative, unsportsmanlike behavior between Division I opponents weighed heavily on Eric, the thought of coming to Gustavus became more appealing. It was the place where his father had won a national championship, where his mother and father had met, and where his best friend, Kevin, was going to school. Midway through his sophomore year at Ball State, Eric decided to transfer.

Two great friends were reunited. They roomed together, studied together, hung out together, played doubles together, and worked together in the summer time. Kevin and Eric were inseparable. Their friendship strengthened within a tennis team environment that stressed team unity and putting teammates before oneself. One of the biggest challenges for many tennis players, who grew up playing tennis individually, was putting aside a "me" centered approach. That was not a problem for Kevin and Eric, as their bond to the team grew and their personal friendship with each other deepened.

As a doubles team Kevin and Eric won two ITA Division III national championships, but bids to win the NCAA III crown in their sophomore and junior years came up short. In singles, Eric reached the NCAA III finals in 2001, and Kevin did the same in 2002. With their teammates, they won the ITA Division III National Indoor Tournaments in both 2002 and 2003. In their senior year, Kevin defeated Eric in the ITA Midwest Region final, thereby earning the right to play #1, a position that Eric had held the previous two seasons. At the ITA national tournament, Kevin received the top sportsmanship award. At the awards banquet that preceded the 2003 NCAA III Singles and Doubles Tournaments, Kevin was named Senior Player of the Year, and Eric was given the prestigious Arthur Ashe Jr. Award for sportsmanship, scholarship, humanitarian concerns, and playing excellence.

A tournament dilemma and an NCAA reprimand

As the 2003 NCAA III Singles and Doubles Tournaments unfolded, Eric and Kevin progressed through the draws. Kevin dominated each of his singles opponents, advancing to the final without losing a set. Eric had the tougher route. In the quarterfinals, a change in strategy was necessary to eke out a three set victory. After that, two more doubles matches lay ahead, but Kevin and Eric breezed into the finals with straight set victories.

On the final day, Eric's semifinal match against the top seed was even tougher than the quarterfinal match the day before. After losing the first set and going down a break in the second against an outstanding opponent, Eric wondered what he could do to change the tide. Everything he had tried up to that point had not worked. I told him, "Hang in there, have fun, and hope that his level of play falls off." It did. Eric broke serve, won the second set, and then went on to take the third set.

But victory came at a high price. Eric was feeling the onslaught of cramps. His match had lasted until nearly noon, his singles final was scheduled for an hour later, and the doubles final, which had been scheduled for 1:30 p.m., would need to be pushed back. Given the circumstances, Eric and Kevin asked the tournament referee for an adjustment in the schedule. "Can we play the doubles final at 1:30 p.m. as scheduled and then play our singles final afterwards?" He agreed, but the NCAA III tournament committee did not. They ruled that the order of the singles and doubles finals should not be reversed.

Next, Eric and Kevin asked, "Can we not play the singles final and be considered co-champions?" Again, the answer was no. "If you both refuse to play, the singles title will be vacated. Neither of you will be recognized as an NCAA III singles champion." That was not acceptable to either of them. The only way that they could avoid playing the singles first was for one to default to the other.

That was an agonizing position for both of them. They wanted to play the singles final but not at the expense of a doubles championship. Eric and Kevin had fallen short in their previous two tries. They did not want that to happen again. Kevin knew that a long singles final, like the one they had played the previous fall in the Midwest Regional final, might leave Eric unable to play doubles.

Given the circumstances, Kevin chose to default. The decision made no one happy, especially Eric. He did not want the singles championship by default. Eric was deeply bothered. Kevin empathized with Eric, but he was still determined to default. The doubles championship meant more to Kevin than the singles. However, in order to ease Eric's discomfort, Kevin agreed to tell others that the match had been determined by a coin flip, which he lost.

The NCAA III committee was very upset by Kevin's decision and even more so when Eric and Kevin told national news that the title had been determined by a coin flip. For the committee, it trivialized and degraded a national championship. They believed that not playing the championship singles match first created an unfair advantage for Eric and Kevin in the doubles. From the committee's perspective, the original order of play needed to be honored. Consequently, they sent an official letter of reprimand to Al Molde, Gustavus athletic director. They faulted Kevin, Eric, and me for behavior that was "detrimental to the NCAA Division III Men's Tennis Championships." The committee felt that I should have forced Kevin and Eric to follow the original schedule.

Why Kevin chose to default

Many observers predicted that Kevin would later regret his decision to default. "Who in their right mind would pass on an opportunity to be an NCAA III singles champion?" they asked. However, they were wrong. Many years later, Kevin remains more convinced than ever that he made the right decision.

However, Kevin becomes very uncomfortable if he is portrayed as an unselfish saint who sacrificed for his friend. Recently he wrote to me,

> My decision had more to do with our program than it does with me. If I had played my college tennis for any other program and been in this situation, I would have been unwilling to default. Four years earlier, when I lost to Eric in the state final, I quit tennis and gained a lot of weight. I only cared about the match outcome. I needed it.
>
> As I played my last college matches, I no longer feared losing. What should have been the most pressure filled situation of my tennis life was not. I had so much fun that season and each one before it. I was proud of myself for the work ethic that I showed on a daily basis. Playing in our program already had taught me that this was all that really mattered. My willingness to default that match did not come from an innate unselfishness that I possessed. Rather, it came from the important lessons I learned in our program.
>
> I've been told by a lot of people that what I did was wrong, but I've never heard this opinion from anyone who played for us. The people who came through our program, more than any other, know what's truly important in life. They understand what happened that day, while others often cannot. I hope this

story is remembered as one that makes the Gustavus tennis program and everyone who has been a part of it unique.

Which viewpoint was right?

Was the NCAA III committee right? Were the actions of Kevin, Eric, and me worthy of an official reprimand? Or was Kevin right? He credits the Gustavus tennis program and its adherence to the Three Crowns as the basis for his decision to default. He claims that four years earlier, in the state high school finals, before he enrolled at Gustavus, he never would have considered a default.

Kevin continues to believe that he made the right decision. What about you, the reader? If you had been in Kevin's position, would you have done the same as he? If not, what would have been your course of action? What would you do for a best friend in this situation?

Coach Wilkinson, Kevin Whipple, and Eric Butorac with the 2003
NCAA III doubles championship trophies

28

NO-CUT APPROACH TO COLLEGE TENNIS

*I don't know what his number on the team was, but I do
know, and what I will always remember, is that he was treated
exactly the same as the number one player on your team.*

No-cut tennis, a popular alternative at the high school level

The *no-cut* approach to tennis is firmly endorsed by the United States Tennis Association (USTA) as a key strategy for promoting tennis. On its web site, the USTA encourages high school coaches to register their *no-cut* teams. More than 2,850 coaches have reportedly adopted the approach. They are encouraged by the incentives of a recognition certificate, a press release, free *no-cut* hats, games and drill books, free subscription to a magazine, and consideration for an award presented at the USTA Tennis Teacher's Conference. The USTA writes on its web site:

> *No-cut* School Tennis Teams play a critical role in growing tennis by allowing students of all abilities to join a team representing their school. This opportunity helps create well-rounded student athletes, develops leadership and teaches responsibility.

The benefits of *no-cut* tennis listed on the USTA web site include:

1) A *no-cut* policy sends a message that developing kids is important to the coach and the school.
2) Schools gain more support from parents and the community by offering everyone a chance to participate-regardless of ability.
3) A positive experience on a *no-cut* team will encourage students to continue to participate in this lifetime sport beyond high school.

Why *no-cut* tennis is uncommon at the college level

Unfortunately, at the college or university level, *no-cut* tennis is uncommon. Few coaches carry more than 12 players. For them, splitting practice time and team budgets with more players shortchanges everyone and stands in the way of a winning approach. Most coaches want to give specialized attention to the most talented players on the team. Consequently, high school coaches may support *no-cut* at their level, where widespread participation is a primary goal, but college coaches have not supported it at their level, where winning is more important.

How Gustavus men's tennis used *no-cut* tennis for 39 years

While most college programs had limited rosters, I decided to buck the conventional approach, using a no-cut approach at Gustavus from 1970 through 2009. Our team size often ranged between 20 and 40 players. Anyone who was willing to accept the obligations of a challenging program was welcomed. Rigorous conditioning and intensive drilling were demanded. Surprising to some, our approach both increased participation and produced winning teams.

Some players quit when they realized their skills were not sufficient to merit a top varsity position. In other words, they cut themselves. However, most players took pride in being a team member, no matter what their position.

Quitting or self-cutting was different than being cut. Quitting was a choice that each player could make, regardless of his ability. It was an action completely within his control. By contrast, being cut, often based on the results of tryout matches, lay outside each player's control.

I always put the emphasis on what each person could control. Those factors were positive attitude, full effort, and good sportsmanship. No matter how unskilled a player might be, he could be successful when measured by those priorities. This core philosophy drove me naturally toward a *no-cut* approach. Cutting players for losing or not playing well struck me as being hypocritical. I would be eliminating them from the program for reasons outside their control.

The large teams that were spawned by a *no-cut* policy produced many advantages. Inexperienced players developed within our program and sometimes played on the varsity team by the time they were seniors. The availability of many good practice partners facilitated improvement. The attitudes and work ethics of the junior varsity often spurred the top players to work harder. Also, the presence of many supportive teammates on the sidelines boosted the players who were competing.

I took important steps to make the team experience meaningful for everyone. I ran two, and sometimes three, separate practices, which allowed me to give more individual time to each player. They could pick a practice time that fit their class schedule best. Also, everyone, regardless of their position on the team, received opportunities each week to compete against outside competition. Often, we played four teams on the same day to facilitate this goal. For me, the most touching affirmation of my *no-cut* approach came in a letter from the father of a player ranked below #20 on the team. He wrote, "I don't know what his number was, but I do know, and what I will always remember, is that he was treated exactly the same as the number one player on your team."

Gustavus 1997 team, one of many that included nearly 30 players.

29

TEAM FIRST

*Heading into the NCAA III tournament, I faced a difficult
decision. Gustavus had fashioned an impressive record using
eight players. We were the #1 team in the Midwest Region
with a victory over Kalamazoo College, then the #2 ranked team
in the country. However, NCAA III rules required Gustavus to
restrict its team to seven players for the national tournament.*

Early in the 2000 season, the Gustavus team read and discussed an article by
Davis Cup star Todd Martin that explained his two most important
principles of team play. One was the importance of an outstanding work
ethic. Martin singled out Alex O'Brien for how he modeled this on the U.S.
Davis Cup Squad. No one on our team was surprised with this emphasis. It
was on the top of almost everyone's "team first" list.

On the other hand, Martin's second point was not anticipated by anyone.
He claimed it was important for players to support the coach on lineup issues.
Even though Martin would have liked to play whenever he was on the Davis
Cup team, he knew that this difficult decision needed to be made by the
captain. Whatever he decided, Martin would support the plan
wholeheartedly. This was vital for team cohesion and effectiveness.

In most of my coaching years, someone on the Gustavus team struggled with
my lineup decisions. I always encouraged players to talk to me privately if
they disagreed. Grousing about it with teammates would create dissension
and undesired pressures on everyone. I promised to explain my reasoning.
However, there were times when the evidence did not point clearly to just
one decision. Nevertheless, the player needed to give full support to my plan.

Our discussion at the beginning of the 2000 season proved helpful. Heading
into the NCAA III tournament, I faced a difficult decision. Gustavus had
fashioned an impressive record using eight players to fill our top six singles
and top three doubles positions. We were the #1 team in the Midwest
Region with a victory over Kalamazoo College, then the #2 ranked team in

the country. However, NCAA III rules required Gustavus to restrict its team to seven players for the national tournament.

One of the eight had to be eliminated. Would it be sophomore Josh Heiden, my #7 singles player, or senior Mark Jones, my #8 singles player? Josh and his partner Nick Crossley had gone undefeated for the entire season at #3 doubles. Josh was a stronger singles player than Mark, an important consideration should one of the top six get injured and be unable to compete. On the other hand, Mark and his partner Jay Bemis were our #2 doubles team. They had lost a few matches, but they had a win over the NCAA III doubles finalists from the year before. I gave the nod to Mark.

There were many good reasons why Josh could have been selected to play, but he did not voice any of them when he was not selected. Instead, he said that he understood, and that next year he would get his chance. During the week of practice before nationals, Josh beat our #1 player in a practice match. At #3 doubles, I experimented with different combinations. However, Josh and whomever I put him with beat whichever team I tried.

Many players would have been saying, "Coach, don't you think you should reconsider? I'm beating everyone in both singles and doubles." But he didn't. Instead, Josh took the pressure off his teammates and me by stepping aside supportively.

Josh was there for the team, practicing whenever someone needed a hitting partner, even though he knew his competitive season was over. He was there at the regional finals, cheering for each of his teammates as they struggled through difficult matches. Josh even decided to miss classes at the end of the semester and to pay for his own plane flight to the national tournament at Kalamazoo.

Todd Martin's article on team tennis had a powerful influence on Josh and the entire team during the 2000 season. However, there was another factor that may have affected Josh even more. One year before, his teammate Mark Jones had faced the same dilemma. He gracefully stepped aside when the seven-man team limit had caused Mark to be removed from the tournament squad. The behavior of respected peers can be the biggest influence of all.

30

"WANNABE" VARSITY PLAYERS

The varsity "wannabe" has a self-centered goal.
He wants to create a competitive opportunity for
himself. When the "wannabe" argues for a position
in the top six, it decreases the chance that he will
relax and play confidently when the pressure is on.

"Wannabe" description

A frustrating challenge for many collegiate tennis coaches is the varsity "wannabe," a player who desperately wants to be in the top six. From his perspective, if it were not for poor selection methods and the biased judgment of the coach, he would be there now. Often the "wannabe" is frustratingly close to his goal, but not there.

A varsity "wannabe" is quick to point out his own accomplishments and the limitations of teammates that play above him. However, by bragging, the "wannabe" puts extra pressure on himself to win. When his opportunities come, he often chokes. In non-pressure situations, he relaxes and plays his best tennis, leading him to believe that he belongs higher on the team.

On the other hand, the varsity "will be" does not anguish about his position just outside the top six. He works hard on his game, remains relaxed when he plays, praises his teammates, takes advantage of the opportunities he is given, never brags about himself, and focuses on the things within his control. A varsity "will be" is a coach's dream, ready to step in when needed and completely supportive of his varsity teammates when he watches from the sidelines.

Some coaches are so frustrated by "wannabes" that they cut their team size to a bare minimum in order to avoid complaints. Coaches sometimes have looked at my large teams in disbelief, picturing 20 or more "wannabes" making life miserable for me. Fortunately, most of my players were not "wannabes".

Typical complaints of the varsity "wannabe"

Experience taught me that "wannabe" complaints generally fit into several categories: Following are the complaints and my response to each one.

1) **Challenge matches should determine who will play in the top six.** However, challenges between teammates are psychologically different than competitions against non-team members. The challenger has everything to gain and nothing to lose, providing an advantage over the person being challenged. In other cases, a mental block against a teammate may be the determining factor. Consequently, challenge matches often do not provide an accurate measure of how a player will perform against outside competition.

    Team position should reflect how team-members compete against non-team members. Therefore, I prioritized USTA tournament results, victories in the ITA fall collegiate tournament, and varsity dual match wins in situations where I used junior varsity players.

    In the final analysis, my decision to insert a player in the top six was based on my judgment. It depended on only one thing—*my objective analysis of the player's competitive record against outside competition.* Whom has he defeated? To whom has he lost? As a coach, I was interested in fielding the lineup that would put the team in the most likely position to win.

    On the other hand, the varsity "wannabe" had a different, more self-centered goal. He wanted to create a competitive opportunity for himself. When the "wannabe" argued for a position in the top six, it decreased the chance that he would relax and play confidently when the pressure was on. Ironically, the more that a "wannabe" pleaded his own case and put down the accomplishments of players in the top six, the more I doubted that he would be successful when the team needed his help the most.

2) **I beat teammates during practice games.** I believe practice should be a place for each player to work on his game and improve. It includes focusing on strokes and strategies that could take the player beyond his present comfort zone. If practice results were to become the basis for team position, players would be pressured to work only on what they already did well. In the process, their games would not have expanded and developed as quickly.

3) **I worked harder in practice, did additional weight lifting, worked on my game during the off-season, obeyed training rules, etc.** All of these accomplishments are admirable. They put each player in the best

possible position to improve. They are in keeping with the priorities of our program and serve as an excellent model to teammates.

However, they are not the basis for determining who will play in the top six or what position a player will occupy. Team position depends only on one's record in official matches against players from other teams.

The story of a varsity "will be."

Conversely, whenever a varsity "will be" would argue on behalf of his teammates, it made a significant impact on me. One such situation occurred before the 2007 National Indoor Tournament. My assistant coaches and I were trying to decide who should play #3 doubles. Playing in one of the top positions was a very big deal for team members, especially because the tournament was played at home in front of the largest crowd of the season. We were trying to decide between John Kauss, Ben Tomasek, and Nick Hansen, and there was no obvious right choice, given their records.

In the midst of this quandary, John wrote the following email to me:

Ben, Nick and I met tonight to talk about this weekend and the doubles situation. Based on how well Ben and Nick have played together in the past, and how Ben has been playing lately, I believe the best team for the third spot is Ben and Nick.

I think that they will have a better chance holding Nick's serve with Ben, who has great, solid volleys and moves very well at the net. Ben's serve will also be complimented by Nick's great closing and put-away shots. Ben's returns have been very reliable, and with the holding of serve, I think breaks will come easier to these two.

I am not saying that I am not confident in my doubles play, but I believe that for this very important weekend, these two are the best. I have a strong desire to be a good doubles player. I am confident to play this weekend, but I want to see the team with the best chance of winning be played. I need to work on many areas of my doubles game, and with time, I think I could be a great doubles player.

I know you are giving this topic a lot of thought, and I thought I would give you my input. However, I know that your decision is final, and whatever team you decide to pick is probably best. If you decide on a different team, I will respect your decision and play my best, no matter what. John Kauss

We accepted John's advice. Ben and Nick played well at the National Indoor and then had a successful season together at #3 doubles. John did not break into the top three doubles during his entire sophomore year. Remember, John's doubles story did not end there. In his junior year, he had a successful season at #2 doubles. Then, in his senior year at #1 doubles, Mike Burdakin and he reached the finals of the ITA National Tournament, went undefeated against Division III competition in the spring season, and were seeded #1 at the NCAA III Tournament.

John was a "will be" player, who did not load extra pressure on his teammates or himself. John's confidence in his teammates helped them to be confident, thereby enhancing their performance. Later, when John got his opportunity, he had nothing to prove. This freed him to establish one of the most impressive records in the history of Gustavus tennis.

Nick Hansen

31

HYPOCRISY?

*There is nothing inherently hypocritical about
the way competitive athletic teams are selected.
However, hypocrisy does exist when coaches who are
committed to sportsmanship abandon it in order to win.*

Can a coach select a team based on their ability to win and also prioritize sportsmanship?

Many coaches build tennis programs on the core values of positive attitude, full effort, and good sportsmanship. These values build competitors into better people—both on and off the court. Furthermore, they are achievable goals for all team members, regardless of their skill level, natural athletic talent, or position on the team.

However, what happens when good sportsmanship comes into conflict with winning? Consider players choosing to call "out" a ball that might be touching the line or choosing to play the ball because there is a slight chance that it might be good. *The Code* requires the latter choice. It is good sportsmanship and the right thing to do, even if a match or championship is lost because of that decision. Many coaches are crystal clear with their players—be honest and follow *The Code*, even if it means losing.

Some players that have internalized this message are puzzled when their coaches pick their varsity lineup based on winning. Are they being hypocritical? Should coaches base their decisions on values that are more important than winning? Should they put superior players in the varsity lineup if they berate themselves, give half efforts in practice, or act confrontationally toward teammates and opponents? If there are junior varsity players that are clearly superior at demonstrating team values, should they replace the varsity players who do not?

Are coaches being hypocritical if they admit that they pick players for the varsity based on their ability to win rather than their demonstration of team values? When I posed this question to the 2013 Gustavus men's tennis team, half of them said "yes" and half said "no." Who was right?

Half of the team said "no."

Gustavus team members who said "no" realized that the core value of sportsmanship and an empirical method for determining the lineup are separate and distinct issues. Each has been presented clearly in the coach's description of his program. Hypocrisy is saying one thing and doing another. The coach would have been hypocritical if he had affirmed one method of determining team position and then used another.

A related analogy illustrates the same point. Gustavus has advertised its commitment to five core values: faith, community, justice, service, and excellence. Teachers, administrators, and posters have reminded students of these values and how they could help "make their lives count." At the same time, the College has awarded honors status at graduation based on one objective rating system—grade point average.

Has the College been hypocritical when it awarded honors status to students with high grade point averages, even though they might rank low in service, community, faith, and justice? Again, the answer is "no." Indeed, the College would have been hypocritical if it had advertised that honors status would be determined by the grade point average and then added other factors into the honors calculation.

Half of the team said "yes."

The Gustavus team members responding "yes" were focused on another issue—not the one presented in the question to which they responded. They recognized the conflict between good sportsmanship and the desire to win. If a coach should claim that sportsmanship is more important than winning and then ignore his players' unsportsmanlike behavior, that is hypocrisy. Similarly, if a college should advertise justice and excellence as core values and then ignore the plagiarism of students, that is also hypocrisy. There need to be consequences for players and students who fall short of core values.

The pressure on a coach to win can lead to inaction on a sportsmanship issue. A self-imposed penalty on one of his own players could cause his team to lose. If the opponent had not been penalized for similar infractions, the coach's tendency to avoid action is increased. A coach may also wish to avoid an embarrassing confrontation with his own player. By "sweeping infractions under the rug," the coach may hope that future violations will not occur as the player matures. This too is hypocrisy.

How a coach can avoid being perceived as hypocritical

Even coaches who act with integrity, consistency, and fairness can be misunderstood. They can stress good sportsmanship over winning and still be called a hypocrite. For example, a player being disciplined may respond, "Coach, you must have seen Joe throw his racket, but you only punish me!" Junior varsity players, particularly varsity "wannabes", may perceive a lax standard being applied to varsity players and a stricter standard to themselves.

A principled coach who emphasizes good sportsmanship over winning can benefit from the following ten recommendations. All reduce the possibility of being perceived as hypocritical.

1) **Explain early in each season the core values of the tennis program.** Show how they have the power to enrich both tennis performances and lives.

2) **Emphasize how important everyone on the team is, regardless of position or ability.**

3) **Communicate clearly why the program's core values and the method for determining the varsity lineup are different.** Emphasize why a change in lineup position is not the correct punishment for inappropriate behavior. However, removal from the lineup or the team may sometimes be necessary.

4) **Lay out specific rules and the consequences for not following those rules.** Secure team and parental buy-in for all rules. A coach needs their support. Implement additional rules as new challenges evolve.

5) **Do not impose a penalty unless the offender knows in advance the consequence for the action, except in extreme, unexpected situations.**

6) **Give praise in public and constructive criticism in private.** Public shaming is never appropriate. Even when administering a point penalty for unsportsmanlike behavior, do it in a low and non-emotional voice.

7) **Request assistance in holding team members accountable to the highest standard of sportsmanship.** A coach, particularly on a large team, cannot observe every infraction. For the sake of the team, players should report unacceptable behavior by others on the team. Everything shared with the coach is kept in confidence.

8) **Invite private, constructive criticisms of your program.** Express appreciation for the feedback and modify behavior as needed. However, request loyalty and respect in public.

9) **Never respond to anyone with anger, profanity, resentment, or sarcasm, no matter how grievous the insult or accusation.** Ill spoken words cannot be retrieved and their effects can linger.

10) **Teach the team that effective behavior modification requires love, caring and personal support, as well as penalties.** Both coaches and players need to reach out privately to any teammate with

unsportsmanlike tendencies. Players enter the program with different backgrounds. A correction that is easy for one may be difficult for the next, depending on his confidence and prior social conditioning.

Trust is the key for dispelling the suspicion of hypocrisy

Tennis coaches select their teams based on the players' proven ability to win. Coaches have differing ways of measuring that ability, but their goal is the same—to pick the best players based on winning. The core value of sportsmanship does not factor into their selections. However, every player is subject to sportsmanship sanctions, which may include removal from the lineup or suspension from the team, depending on the severity of the infraction.

Similarly, all of the teams at the 2012 Olympics selected participants based on their ability to help their team win. The fastest, the strongest, and the most skilled were sorted out in qualifying events that measured competitive excellence. The Olympic core values of friendship and respect played no role in selecting the participants. However, they played an important role in disqualifying athletes that disrespected Olympic ideals by cheating, taking illegal drugs, etc.

There is nothing inherently hypocritical about the way competitive, athletic teams are selected. However, hypocrisy does exist when coaches that are committed to sportsmanship abandon it in order to win.

Trust between coaches and players is the glue that cements relationships and diminishes the unwarranted suspicion of hypocrisy. A good tennis coach builds an atmosphere of trust with his players through communication, respect, and acceptance.

32

STACKING: THE DIRTY LITTLE SECRET

*Ann Koger's characterization of stacking hit the nail
on the head. It has become "the dirty little secret" of
college tennis. By discussing the issue frankly, as we have
done here, stacking becomes less secretive. The next step
is to eliminate stacking by adopting a transparent and
widely accepted standard for measuring lineup strength.*

DEFINITION: Stacking occurs when a coach puts players out of order in a team lineup. College tennis rules require players to be in order of competitive strength. The best singles player on the team should play #1 and the least skilled should play #6. If instead, a coach were to put the #6 player at #1, and then slide all other players down one position, where they each would face easier competition, this *could* change a 0-6 disadvantage into a 5-1 advantage. This move would sacrifice the #1 position in order to pick up the other five. Most stacking is not that blatant. By switching a #1 and a #2 player, a coach could change a 0-2 disadvantage to a 1-1 tie, enough to convert a 4-5 team loss into a 5-4 win.

Veteran coach Ann Koger from Haverford College refers to stacking as "the dirty little secret" in college tennis. She writes from 29 years of experience. Her devotion to tennis has earned her spots in the USTA Middle States and the Black Tennis Halls of Fame.

> I agree that stacking has become the "dirty little secret" in college tennis. I run into it regularly…

> I keep good records on my team. I have moved players up or down according to their winning percentage, usually one position either way. I have never, to the best of my knowledge, been accused of stacking.

> However, the players on my teams, over the last six to seven years, have pointed out and complained about opposing teams' line-ups. They say, "Something seems wrong with their line-up." Then they ask me, "What

do I think?" I give my opinion. Then they ask, "What can we do about it?"

Education among coaches and rules that deter stacking are definitely needed. However, the education concerning stacking should extend to the conference offices. Many of those conference offices have not a clue about tennis. They make rulings that make no sense.

It is sad that college tennis has come to this. I guess *The Code* and sportsmanship have gone the way of win at any cost. What kind of example are we showing our student-athletes and others?

Accusations and resentments

Another successful season was drawing to a close. Gustavus had won the conference championship and qualified for the NCAA III Regional Playoffs at DePauw University in Greencastle, Indiana. For the second straight year, advancement to the NCAA III final eight came down to a team dual match with the same university. Again, the result was the same as the previous year. Gustavus emerged with a close, hard fought victory.

What happened next was both surprising and disconcerting. The opposing coach rushed toward me, not to offer congratulations, but to loudly denounce my cheating. He focused on my choice of player at #2 singles. For the second straight year, my #2 player had lost decisively to a good opponent, whose outstanding return of serve had neutralized my player's serve-and-volley game. From the other coach's perspective, they would have won if my #2 man had played where he belonged, lower in the lineup.

Upset and venting his frustration, the coach confronted me on the court where the last match had finished. I was speechless. I said nothing as he criticized me in front of our players and parents. Finally, the mother of another player on my team had more than she could stomach. She stepped forward and went jaw to jaw with the coach. Meanwhile, I slipped away to congratulate our players for a job well done. We had advanced to the final eight!

Fourteen years later, this coach still continued to regard me as a cheater who had unfairly deprived his team of the opportunity to reach the final eight. Such feelings exist between many coaches, although most do not complain publicly. For example, I felt victimized in 2003 when Gustavus hosted the NCAA III Championship. Our team was particularly strong at the top, where Kevin Whipple and Eric Butorac played #1 and #2. Eric had reached the NCAA III singles final in 2001, while Kevin had done the same in 2002. Everyone knew that we had a virtual lock on #1 and #2 singles as well as #1 doubles. We were not as strong at the lower positions, even though we had won the 2003 Indoor National title earlier that year.

Our semifinal opponent had good depth, but no outstanding players that could compete with Butorac or Whipple. Consequently, they took an inconsistent player with a big game, who should have been playing #6, and put him at #1. They gave away the #1 position, which they would have lost no matter who on their team played there. This pushed their more consistent players down, where they matched up well against our bottom four.

A quick glance at our opponent's records confirmed this strategy. At #1 the top singles player was 5-11, at #2 the record was 8-12, at #3 it was 14-5, at #4 the record was 16-4, at #5 it was 17-4, and at #6 the record was 15-4. The following year, when the team added another strong player to their lineup, the #1 player from 2003 dropped out of the lineup, while all the other players remained in it. This added confirmation to the conclusion I had reached the year before. Our opponent, by stacking their lineup, cost us a spot in the 2003 NCAA III Championship final.

Longing for an accepted lineup system that ends stacking

Upon further reflection, I later realized that I too had a player out of order. My stacking was not intentional, but it was clearly stacking. My #3 player had a 10-13 record, and the rest of my team had records of 21-6, 22-4, 19-5, 16-8, and 18-5. Why did I not move him down? When we won the ITA National Indoor Tournament early in the season, he had played very well at #3. As the season progressed, he seemed to lose his confidence, losing to players who were inferior in ability. Not wishing to further diminish his confidence, I left him at #3, hoping he would regain his early season level of play. However, it never happened. By the end of the season, #6 may have been his appropriate position.

I have always been opposed to illegal lineups. So are most coaches. Yet, I persuaded myself that my out-of-order lineup was OK. So do many other coaches who also consider themselves ethical. This realization left me wondering. *Could a widely accepted system be created that would automatically put players in the proper order?* If so, a continuing source of frustration and resentment between coaches would be eliminated.

Most coaches are ethical. They would like to create a competitive environment that eliminates stacking and distrust. Most stacked lineups are unintentional. I would not have played a stacked lineup in 2003 if there had been a transparent and universal standard for measuring lineup strength. I would have moved my #3 player down.

Most coaches do not protest stacked lineups because it produces tension and accomplishes nothing. We resent stacking. We think it's unfair. We tend to talk negatively about the coaches who do it, but very seldom to their faces. We regret the frustration that it produces in our players and their parents, but we accept it as inevitable. We don't talk publicly about it, because it would sound like excuse making or "sour grapes."

Ann Koger's characterization of stacking hit the nail on the head. It has been "the dirty little secret" of college tennis. By discussing the issue frankly, stacking becomes less secretive. The next step is to eliminate stacking by adopting a transparent and widely accepted standard for measuring lineup strength.

Andy Bryan, 2008 NCAA III doubles 2nd and 2007
ITA national singles 2nd

33

ANTI-STACKING PLAN

The Intercollegiate Tennis Association recommended the Anti-Stacking Plan as a guide to all coaches in setting their lineups. Some conferences have put it into their conference regulations. As the principles of the Anti-Stacking plan become better understood and the potential benefits are realized, more coaches will adopt it.

NCAA III takes action to stop stacking

In 2008, at the NCAA III men's coaches meeting, the stacking issue was raised. Many reports of unethical lineups and inappropriate victories led the NCAA committee chairman to put the issue front and center. A spirited discussion revealed many problems and a lack of solutions. The main issue was the lack of consensus on how to determine *order of strength*. Each coach had his own method for determining strength and setting the lineup order. There was no objective way to address the problem, yet a majority of coaches agreed that huge problems in certain coaches' lineups did exist.

At the request of the NCAA chairman, I agreed to tackle the problem. After consulting with other coaches at the NCAA III championship, I drafted a proposal that established *winning percentage* as the only legitimate, fair measure of competitive strength. On the one hand, it seemed logical. Pro tennis rankings and league standings in all sports are based on wins against all opponents.

On the other hand, the plan struck some coaches as radical. They asked:

- How can you compare a win-loss record at #1 singles with any other position?

- How do you distinguish between wins against quality opponents and wins against lesser ones?

- Should a close win be treated the same as a blow out?

- How do you put a player with an outstanding record ahead of a player with a poor record, if he does not win in challenge matches?

- Should matches played indoors or in bad weather situations be given less value?

- How do you move a freshman with an outstanding record above a senior captain?

Coaches like to take many of these issues into consideration and then make lineup judgments that defy objective verification. This can be a problem when inscrutable calculations get mixed with a competitive desire to win.

Some coaches see player matchups as a legitimate part of competitive strategy, even though collegiate tennis rules specifically outlaw it. They reason that basketball, football, and most team sports permit matchups. In fact, good coaching in these sports is determined by matchups that exploit the opponents' weaknesses. Why should tennis be any different?

In short, it is different because the rules are different. Tennis requires that players be arranged in *order of strength*, not according to how they match up.

Anti-Stacking plan cuts through ambiguities

In 2013, Gustavus men's tennis ended its fifth season using the recommended plan. The results were impressive. The win-loss records of everyone on the team were similar. If a #1 player struggled in comparison to the #2 player, he moved down. If a #6 player excelled in comparison to the #5 player, he moved up. Everyone understood why and when the moves were made.

The Anti-Stacking plan at Gustavus cut through all the ambiguities. It offered a definitive way of determining lineups that was completely transparent and subject to public scrutiny. Opposing coaches could see it being used consistently in a fair manner. Players on the team could understand why they were moved up or down. Parents of the players, who are often anxious about the position their son plays, could understand. Lineup positions were determined by *winning percentage*, not coaching prejudice, favoritism, or an illegal matchup strategy.

In stark contrast, an analysis of all teams participating in the 2010 NCAA III men and women's tournaments revealed that 50% of the teams had singles lineups out of order. There seemed to be three important reasons.

1) Coaches were unaware of many ITA lineup rules, even though they were reprinted in the match scorebook that they all possessed.
2) Coaches defined *order of strength* in many different ways. If opposing coaches protested, ethics committees were reluctant to act in the absence of clearly defined principles for determining *order of strength*.

3) The biggest problem was "parking." Coaches decided early in the season that a particular lineup was correct. Then they left the players at those positions, regardless of their records.

Anti-Stacking plan for singles

The Anti-Stacking plan for determining *order of strength* in singles lineups contains six requirements:

1) To start the season, a coach may rely on competitive results, challenge matches, and intuition to set the lineup.

2) During the first 10 dual matches a coach may adjust the lineup after every match, but *winning percentage* is the only basis for changing lineup order. A coach can move a singles player up only if his *winning percentage* is better than the player he is replacing. The player at #1 should have a record that is equal to or better than the player at #2. The player at #2 should be equal to or better than the player at #3, etc.

3) Coaches are responsible for NOT leaving players in the same position too long. A one to five percentage difference can trigger a change. If the difference reaches 10%, the coach should definitely act. By keeping the percentages of adjoining players in the lineup somewhat equal, the coach is continually in a position to make appropriate changes based on the most recent results. If the coach waits until the spread becomes 20% and then makes the mandatory change, he or she locks into a more permanent change that does not prioritize the most recent results.

4) After players have completed 10 matches, changes in the singles lineup may occur only at half-month intervals on March 1, March 15, April 1, April 15, and May 1. Only a one-position move up or down is permitted at each date. If the tenth match should occur on April 3, the next position move would be on April 15. Only spring season matches are included in the 10-match total.

5) After 10 matches, a coach is required to move a singles player up one position if the winning percentage is 20% greater than the player above. In the case of a #1 player who has won 70% of his matches and a #2 player who has won 89% of his matches, a switch is possible but not required. However, it is best that coaches make switches before a 10% threshold is reached. A player is exempted from mandatory changes until he or she has played 10 matches.

6) Mandatory switches start at the top and move down the lineup. For example, if #1 has a 50% winning percentage, #2 has a 70% *winning percentage*, and #3 has a 90% *winning percentage*, #1 and #2 switch positions. The #3 player remains at the same position because the former #1 can only drop one position on a given date.

7) When a player returns to the lineup after an absence of less than three weeks, the coach places this individual in the lineup at the same position

he or she held before the absence. If the absence is more than three weeks, the player may be inserted at a lower position, depending on the situation and the judgment of the coach. New additions to the team, possessing established competitive results, may enter the lineup anywhere at the coach's discretion. Junior varsity players entering the lineup start at #6, regardless of their previous *winning percentage* in varsity matches.

8) Coaches are encouraged to inform their next opponents of any lineup order changes two days in advance. However, last minute deletions from the lineup because of sickness, injury, or conflicts are always possible.

Anti-Stacking plan compared to current ITA rules

The Anti-Stacking plan for determining *order of strength* is consistent with present ITA rules, except for two points, both of which facilitate illegal matchups.

1) Present ITA rules permit two players of equal strength to switch, regardless of their records.

2) Present ITA rules permit switches every match. The proposed guidelines do as well during the first 10 matches of the season. After that, switches are restricted to half-month intervals.

The Anti-Stacking plan for determining *order of strength* in singles lineups contains three new provisions.

1) The *winning percentage* of all matches in the spring season is the sole criterion for determining *order of strength*.

2) Any switch where the person being moved up has a lower *winning percentage* than the person being replaced would be against the rules. Also, any switches after the individual has played 10 matches must be made at half-month intervals.

3) Adjacent players in the lineup must be switched when the *winning percentage* of the lower player is 20% better. However, it is best that switches be made before a 10% threshold is reached.

Benefits of Anti-Stacking plan in singles

1) The Anti-Stacking plan makes *winning percentage* the basis for lineup order changes. If mistakes occur, coaches will prompt each other to make corrections. The objective standard of *winning percentage* removes ambiguity and creates ethical transparency. Coaches will know when they need to make switches. Distrust of other coaches will be minimized. Suspicions of stacking will be greatly reduced or alleviated.

2) The Anti-Stacking plan eliminates distinctions between quality matches and easy matches, indoor and outdoor matches, close matches and blowouts, or matches played in good and bad weather conditions. These subjective considerations would complicate the issue and make the system less objective. On the other hand, *winning percentages* are based

on players' records that can be found on their respective college web sites.

3) The Anti-Stacking plan has a correcting mechanism. Everyone knows that a win at #6 is different than a win at #1. A #1 does not need to be moved to #2 until #1's *winning percentage* is 20% worse than #2's. This would allow the coach some discretion, yet not too much. A player can only drop one position every half month, so the *winning percentage* at #6 has no bearing on him. Any movement down gives the player a half-month to establish a better record against presumably easier competition and thereby move back up. However, it is always the total record, not just the record at the new position, which determines the winning percentage.

4) The 20% difference that triggers a mandated change on certain dates is an arbitrary but well-chosen percentage. This also allows the coach some discretion, but not too much. If the trigger is below 20%, the coach's ability to factor in other knowledge is decreased. For example, the coach may anticipate that a given player's winning percentage will soon be better than the person below without a position switch. However, if the difference between adjacent players in the lineup moves to 20% or more, and no change in position is mandated, too little emphasis is being placed on *winning percentage* comparisons.

5) The Anti-Stacking plan makes it easier for players and parents to understand and support lineup adjustments. Coaches are sometimes reluctant to make lineup switches because it communicates a lack of confidence in the player. Now it will be clear that some switches are mandated, not optional.

Anti-Stacking plan recommended but not required by the ITA

In the summer of 2010, the Intercollegiate Tennis Association (ITA) considered the Anti-Stacking plan. Much opposition still existed. If the Anti-Stacking plan became a required rule, coaches would be forced to give up an area of responsibility that historically has fallen within their domain. Many thought only an insightful coach could divine the complex issue of team position. For those who crafted their lineups strategically (and perhaps illegally), it meant they would have to forfeit one of their winning tools.

The ITA stopped short of requiring coaches to follow the Anti-Stacking plan. However, they did recommend it as a guide to all coaches in setting their lineups. Some conferences have put the Anti-Stacking plan into their conference regulations. As the principles of the Anti-Stacking plan become better understood and the potential benefits are realized, more coaches will adopt it.

1995 MIAC Championship team: Ryan Haddorff, Brad Olson, Rob Castille, Paul Jeffries, Todd Bowlby, Jon Koenigs, Andy Schmidt, Adam Beduhn, Noel Stout, Coach Wilkinson

1980 Gustavus men and women's tennis teams at Millsaps College in Jackson, Mississippi. The teams traveled together by van and cheered each other on.

34

DOUBLES SCORING CONTROVERSY

Doubles should equal singles in importance.

The evolution of doubles scoring

Doubles scoring, the doubles format, and the importance of doubles have changed over the past four decades. In 1970, each doubles match was two-out-of-three sets and counted one point for the winning team. The total points for every dual match was nine, so the winner needed five victories. It remained that way until 1995. During these 25 years, tiebreakers were added in 1973 and have remained. No-ad scoring, which was introduced in the early 1980s, came and went within a decade.

In 1995, two fundamental changes in both the men and women's tennis format occurred, which far eclipsed the other relatively minor changes. The first was to switch doubles from two-out-of-three sets to an eight-game pro set (with a tiebreaker if the score reached 8-8). This addressed the troublesome length of team dual matches, which could stretch for more than six hours. The second was to place the doubles first, before the singles. When singles came first, the dual match outcome could already be settled before the doubles began. This happened whenever one team won either five or six of the singles matches. By putting the doubles first, coaches guaranteed that the doubles would be meaningful. Under the former plan, some coaches were not even playing the doubles if one team achieved five or six victories in singles.

In 1995, the Division III men adopted a third fundamental change, but the women did not. The men decided to make the three doubles worth one point. In other words, once a school won two out of the three doubles matches, it was awarded the doubles point. If a third doubles match was still in progress when the doubles point was decided, it was often suspended. Next, the six singles were played, with each worth a point. The total points for a dual match became seven instead of nine, and the relative importance of doubles in scoring decreased from 33% to 14%. The change was defended on the ground that the shortened doubles format made the matches worth less. Proponents claimed that three eight-game pro sets were the equivalent of one three-set singles match. However, the women's coaches did not buy that argument. The parting of ways between Division III men and women's coaches in 1995 set the stage for a conflict that emerged a decade later.

In 2006, the NCAA III men's committee reconsidered the scoring change, pushed along by the NCAA, who wanted consistency between the men and women. When it became apparent that the women's coaches were unwilling to change, the matter was put before the men's coaches at the 2006 NCAA III national tournament. Virtually every coach in attendance agreed that Division III men should continue allocating only one point to the doubles. When a straw vote was taken, the vote was 32 to 2 against change.

However, the Division III NCAA Committee wanted to put the men and women on the same match-scoring page. They probably suspected that the majority of the men's coaches in the nation would support the three-points plan, even if the coaches in attendance did not. Consequently, the committee asked me to write a position paper supporting the three-points plan and the coach from Middlebury College to craft a defense of the one-point plan. The following summer, both positions were presented to all Division III men's coaches, and the vote tally was recorded. The outcome of the survey would determine policy for Division III men.

Why doubles should count one or three points

Following are the primary reasons why Division III men's coaches were encouraged in 2006 to support either the one-point or the three-point position.

The "one-point" position

1) **The shortened eight-game format for doubles automatically reduces its importance.** The typical hour for an eight-game pro set is one-third the possible length of a long, three-set singles match. Therefore a doubles match should be worth one-third of a singles match.
2) **An eight-game pro set is a "crap shoot."** Anything can happen. A good team can get off to a poor start, go down a service break, and have no chance to recover. Giving three points to a "crap shoot" rewards the lucky and penalizes the more skilled teams. One can anticipate many undeserving teams pulling upsets.
3) **Going down 0-3 after the doubles creates too big of a hole for the trailing team.** It has to win five out of the six singles. That is not fair. It is too big of a hurdle.
4) **Our role model should be what the best collegiate men do, not the plan of Division III women.** Division I men count only one point for all three doubles.
5) **The one-point plan for all three doubles has served us well for over a decade.** What is the reason for changing? Virtually all of the nation's top Division III coaches favor the current scoring position.

The "three-points" position

1) **Doubles should be equally important as singles, yet doubles is allotted only 14% of the total points under the one-point plan.** Under the proposed three-points position, doubles matches count for only 33% of the total points. However, this is a step in the right direction. The current imbalance under the one-point position is unsettling, given the fact that more than 80% of all adult tennis played is doubles.

2) **An increased emphasis on doubles facilitates the role of Division III tennis coaches as educators.** Their players do not receive athletic scholarships. They are primarily students and secondarily tennis players. Most incoming freshmen on college teams have spent most of their earlier years playing singles. However, most of their tennis after college will be doubles. Coaches have the opportunity to share doubles knowledge and develop skills that will benefit their players for a lifetime. Making doubles worth just 14% of the total points decreases the incentive for coaches to spend time on doubles and undermines their role as educators.

3) **The inconsistency between Division III men, which allots one point for doubles, and Division III women, which allots three points for doubles, produces confusion.** So does the inconsistency between Division III men and all other non-Division I teams—men and women in Division II, NAIA, and Junior Colleges. The confusion is compounded by the difficulty to understand why each singles match should count one point and all three doubles matches together should be worth one point.

4) **The argument that an eight-game pro set for doubles is worth one-third of a two-out-of-three-sets singles match because of their relative length is not valid.** By analogy, one would argue in track that the half-mile run should be worth half of the mile race, and that the 100-yard-dash should be worth only a small fraction of either event. The length of time to complete doubles has nothing to do with its importance. In track, events do not vary in importance because of their length. The same should be true for tennis.

5) **The assertion that an eight-game pro set produces a "crap shoot" is not supported by the facts.** If it were true, then the best teams would have spotty records, caused by the unpredictability of eight-game pro sets. Instead, all of the Gustavus doubles teams from 2000 to 2003 produced outstanding records. For example, in 2001 and 2002, Michael Hom and Daryn Collins even went undefeated at #2 doubles for two consecutive regular seasons. This would not have happened if doubles' results were unpredictable. By analogy, in swimming or track, shorter distances would produce less predictable winners. Again, this is not the case.

Decision on doubles reached and ideas for the future

The ballots went out to all of the Division III men's coaches in 2006 with instructions to read both position papers before they voted. The ballots were cast and a verdict was reached. More than 80% of the coaches voted for the three-point plan. Beginning in 2007, scoring again included three points for doubles.

Why was there such a discrepancy between the position of the coaches attending the national tournament, who favored the one-point plan by over 90%, and the position of coaches nationwide, who favored the three-points plan by over 80%? For me, the answer was clear. For coaches who had built their success by recruiting top singles players, the one-point plan seemed fair. However, for the majority of coaches, the thought that singles should account for 86% of the point total seemed unfair.

Now, it is time to push the envelope further. Doubles should equal singles in importance. Therefore, doubles should be worth two points and singles one point. If one team should sweep the doubles and lose all the singles, or win two doubles and two singles, the match would be a tie. In such cases, a tiebreaker between two corresponding singles players or two doubles teams (based on a coin flip) would settle the dual match outcome.

Is it necessary for doubles to be increased to full two-out-of-three sets to be considered equal to singles? Definitely not. The 8-game format for doubles is a keeper. The better teams win. The intensity is high, and dual matches finish in a shorter time frame.

35

GUSTAVUS DOUBLES

*No team better illustrated the depth of Gustavus doubles than
Raman Jayapathy and Riley Horan, our #3 team in 1984.
When the NCAA III committee disqualified a team for poor
sportsmanship in the team competition, Raman and Riley got the
vacated spot, setting the stage for an amazing string of victories.*

Four decades of doubles excellence

For the four decades (1970-2009) that I coached men's tennis at Gustavus,
the team was widely respected for its doubles accomplishments. The

capstone on that reputation
is the unprecedented
professional doubles career
of Eric Butorac. No other
Division III tennis player
has succeeded so well in
doubles against the world's
best players. He has
defeated Rafael Nadal,
Mike and Bob Bryan, and
many others in Association
of Tennis Professionals
(ATP) doubles
competition. Eric has
competed in the finals of
the Australian Open, won
15 ATP titles, and been
ranked #9 as a team with
his partner.

Paul Holbach 1980 NCAA III doubles champion
with John Mattke

Eric's father, Tim Butorac, and Dave Petersen, an unseeded team, surprised the 1973 NAIA tournament field by winning the national doubles title. In 1974, they proved that their title was not a fluke by reaching the finals again. These accomplishments established Gustavus as a national tennis power and earned for the school the first national championship in any sport.

Next, John Mattke and Paul Holbach reinforced the Gustavus doubles reputation by earning All-American doubles recognition for four consecutive years between 1977 and 1980. In 1977, they reached the NAIA semifinals, and in 1978, they advanced to the finals. The following year, Gustavus joined the NCAA III. Mattke/Holbach made their mark there by finishing second in 1979 and winning a national championship in 1980. Mattke went on to an outstanding ATP professional career in both singles and doubles, ranking near the world's top 100 during the middle 1980s.

Then came Shaun Miller, who won a 1981 NCAA III doubles title with Jim Hearn and a 1982 title with Rich Skanse. Shaun won a singles title in 1982 and participated in NCAA III team titles in both 1980 and 1982, giving him five NCAA III national championships, more than anyone else in Gustavus men's tennis history. The team title in 1980 was the first national NCAA III team championship for Gustavus in any sport.

Jim Hearn 1981 NCAA III doubles champion with Shawn Miller

During the rest of the 1980s, Gustavus was blessed with an abundance of outstanding doubles teams. They included Duke Paluch/Mark Kruger, who reached the NAIA semifinals in 1983; Bill Sternard/Rich Skanse, who advanced to the quarterfinals three times during 1983 and 1984 in NAIA and NCAA III tournaments; and Jim Allen, who reached the NCAA III quarterfinals with Mark Kruger in 1986 and with Ulf Gudjonsson in 1987.

However, no team better illustrated the depth of Gustavus doubles than Raman Jayapathy and Riley Horan, our #3 team in 1984. When the NCAA III committee disqualified a team for poor sportsmanship in the team competition, Raman and Riley got the vacated spot, setting the stage for an amazing string of victories. They advanced all the way to the NCAA III doubles final.

During the 1990s, the string of doubles accomplishments continued. In 1991, Rich Skanse's younger brother Ryan teamed with Dave Jussila to win another NCAA III doubles title for Gustavus. Other Gustavus teams reaching the NCAA III quarterfinals were Gordon Reid/Joel Lobland in 1991, Reid/Skanse in 1992, and Paul Jeffries/Ryan Howe in 1994. Todd Bowlby/Paul Jeffries was ranked #3 in the nation in 1996. In 1998, Todd Bowlby/ Ryan Dussault finished second in the national ITA tournament and were seeded #2 at the NCAA III tournament. The next year, Ryan and Matt Lundmark reached the NCAA III semifinals.

The next ten years were remarkable. In 2000, Matt Lundmark and Michael

Charlie Paukert 2008 NCAA III doubles finalist with Andy Bryan

Hom reached the NCAA III doubles final and led a team that lost 4-3 in the national team finals. Eric Butorac shared three national titles with his partner Kevin Whipple in 2002 and 2003. In 2001 and 2002, they played together with four other doubles All-Americans—Michael Hom/Daryn Collins (undefeated in dual match play), and Josh Heiden/Nick Crossley (ITA Midwest Regional champions). Gustavus did not capture any NCAA III team titles during this time period, but it did earn two ITA National Indoor titles in 2002 and 2003.

Other Gustavus doubles players excelled in the following years. Adam Morgan and Brett Morse-Karzen were three time doubles All-Americans between 2004 and 2006. Andy Bryan reached the NCAA III quarterfinals with Jesse Brauer in 2007 and the finals with Charlie Paukert in 2008. In 2009, John Kauss and Mike Burdakin put the final exclamation point on my collegiate doubles coaching career by finishing second in the national ITA tournament, going undefeated against Division III competition during the regular season, and earning the #1 doubles seed at the NCAA III tournament.

After my retirement, Gustavus doubles continues to excel under Coach Tommy Valentini. Amrik Donkena and Mya Smith-Dennis reached match point in the 2012 NCAA III doubles championship final. For two consecutive years, they have earned All-American honors. What explains the continued success experienced by Gustavus players?

Gustavus doubles explained

Gustavus excels in doubles because we concentrate on doubles skills and strategies. Strong first and second serves, hit to the correct targets, are critical. So are consistent service returns that dip low in the front part of the opponents' court, both cross-court and down the lines. Even though topspin returns are most common, our players are expected to be equally confident with underspin. A soft chip against a big serve or an underspin lob on the right occasion is crucial. Also, topspin lobs off easy bouncing balls later in the points can cripple opponents who play too close to the net.

Volley skills are vital. Many players come into our program afraid to stand close to the net when balls are being blasted at them. They need to overcome that fear. Next, they need to feel confident angling those balls away for winners– or hitting soft drop volleys. Also, many incoming players have not concentrated on approach volleys. Instead, they stop and play the ball after it bounces. Good doubles players need to move through the low volleys, keep their racket head above the ball so they can impart underspin, and hit the volleys to the most strategic targets.

Most players coming into our program have not been trained in positioning and movement. When serving, they are accustomed to assuming one standard position, instead of mixing up the standard position with the "I" and "Australian" formations. Constant changes permit our players to take away favorite targets from returners. It forces them to pick less desirable return targets, ones at which they might be less effective. Next, we teach "poaching" and "switching," which most of our new players have never used before. "Poaching" is an opportunist movement at the net that is made at the last second. On the other hand, "switching" is a preplanned movement, made earlier than "poaching," which requires both serving partners to move to the opposite side of the court and to be set.

When returning serve, we emphasize an offensive position for the returner's partner. We use it when the returner is hitting well and keeping the return down, away from the server's partner. The returner's partner needs to play half way up in the service box, and then move forward in anticipation of a good return. "Poaching" and "switching" play an important role for teams that assume this offensive position. There are many offensive opportunities to "poach" when the returner's partner is close to the net. Also, "switches" can be called in advance, where the returning team agrees to move before the serve is struck.

With so much "poaching" and "'switching," the fake is another important part of doubles strategy. If the opposing team knows that movement always signifies a "poach" or a "switch," this gives them an advantage. Therefore fakes, made at the right time, add to the confusion of the opponents and their temptation to look away from the ball when striking it.

However, most players coming into our program find the offensive position uncomfortable. They feel safer when they stay at the service line, thereby giving them more time to respond to a "poach" by the server's partner. In the process, they sacrifice offensive opportunities at the net in favor of a defensive strategy. However, the service line area is called "no man's land," not an effective place to be when trying to play defensively.

The better defensive strategy for the returning team is "two back." It is used when the returner is unable to get the return down and away from the server's partner. Picking the right position at the right time is a strategic decision based on what is happening. It can change continually during a match and may switch according to which opponent is serving.

These are the highlights of the doubles strategy that we teach. Often, it takes endless doubles drills and more than a year for our players to play our system effectively. When they do, they play doubles at a level that far exceeds the untrained approach that most of them had when they entered our program. It is no accident that Gustavus has fashioned an enviable record in doubles over four decades and that Eric Butorac headed into his pro career prepared to excel in doubles.

Section V

"BUILD IT, AND THEY WILL COME"

Beginning in 1992, the two-million-dollar Swanson
Indoor Tennis Center was built in stages. Interior
improvements came in 1995, and again in 1998,
when it was rebuilt after being destroyed by a tornado.

Outstanding tennis facilities that now serve Gustavus and Tennis and Life
Camps (TLC) stand on land where a cornfield existed in 1990. It took
dreams and perseverance for the indoor and outdoor courts to become a
reality. The development of continually improving facilities went hand in
hand with the TLC mission.

Aspects of the movie classic *Field of Dreams* have interesting parallels to the
development of tennis facilities on the Gustavus campus. In the movie, an
Iowa farmer who loves baseball decides that he will convert some of his
cornfields into a beautiful baseball diamond. The film's classic lines, "Build
it, and they will come," and "Is this heaven? No, it's Iowa," are easily
recognized almost 25 years after the film was released. The idealistic, perhaps
deluded, farmer hopes that the spirits of past baseball greats will somehow
come to play when his classic baseball field is completed.

His persistence and dreams are rewarded. Spirits from the past file out of the
surrounding cornfields at dusk to play again the game they loved. They
included Shoeless Joe Jackson and seven of his Chicago White Sox teammates
(later called the Chicago Black Sox), who were accused of conspiring with
gamblers to throw the 1919 World Series to the Cincinnati Red Sox. They
were permanently banned from baseball, amid much controversy. In that
series, Shoeless racked up twelve hits and no errors, a record that stood until
1964. If he had been trying to throw the series, many wonder why he
performed so well.

Another of the players was Archibald Wright "Moonlight" Graham, who
played in just one major league game for the New York Giants on June 29,
1905. Instead of continuing to play baseball, he became a doctor and
selflessly served the people of Chisholm, Minnesota for 50 years. For
"Moonlight" to be included among the baseball greats is significant for the
movie's theme. A selfless servant of others is a true baseball hero, one who
deserves to be included in any gathering of baseball greats. This deference for
higher values adds to the appeal of a movie that celebrates magic, baseball,
and a romantic longing for the past.

I was amused when our daughter Deb and Dave Aasen, instructors at TLC in 1991, wrote and performed a skit that was a parody of *Field of Dreams*. Dave was the farmer in southern Minnesota, a few miles from Iowa, pretending to be me, an Iowa native, who created a tennis Mecca out of cornfields. Deb was my wife Barb, speaking with a strong German accent, cautioning her idealistic husband to be realistic. But Dave persisted, listening to the voice that said, "Build it and they will come." Other TLC instructors, pretending to be greats from the past, did appear magically, and of course one of them asked, "Is this heaven? No, it's TLC."

The Swanson Tennis Center (STC) and the Brown Outdoor Courts now stand on land that was formerly a cornfield. When Gustavus chose not to build an indoor tennis center on campus, Barb and I hired a real estate agent, purchased 14.5 acres of adjoining farm land, and donated it to the College. It included the property beginning at the college ring road and stretching north beyond the now existing STC and college physical plant buildings.

Beginning in 1992, the two-million-dollar STC was built in stages. Interior improvements came in 1995, and again in 1998, when it was rebuilt after being destroyed by a tornado. Little of the construction and maintenance could have occurred without financial support from a variety of sources, including TLC, the Greater Gustavus Fund, Gustavus alumni and parents, friends of Karen Gibbs, and insurance payouts.

"Build it and they will come" is precisely what happened. We built it, and they have come—more than 50,000 TLC campers over a 37-year period. So have varsity men and women tennis players and many other Gustavus students with tennis interests.

36

GYM FLOORS AND ELASTIC LINES

The most ingenious tennis space created by Dr. Klotz
was the main basketball floor, the same place where
Don Nelson established Big Ten record performances.
Within two minutes, we could convert the basketball floor
into a tennis court. On a couple of occasions, we played
at half time during televised Big Ten basketball games,
in front of a Field House audience of some 10,000 fans.

Being taught to improvise

The University of Iowa had no indoor tennis courts in the early 1960s when I played varsity tennis. Nevertheless, I could practice during the winter months, thanks to the ingenuity of my coach, Dr. Don Klotz. He created tennis practice areas in unlikely places within the Iowa Field House, a large barnlike structure that served varsity basketball, indoor track, baseball, wrestling, and gymnastics.

When gymnasts and intramural sports were not using the wooden floor in the north gym, it became a tennis court after a tennis net was stretched between volleyball poles. We could play matches there, even though multiple lines on the floor for tennis, basketball, volleyball, and badminton made line calls challenging. The wood floor, made faster by the chalk dust from the gymnasts, created difficulties for a baseliner.

Another practice site was the large dirt area at the west end of the Field House, where baseball practiced, the Reserve Officers Training Corps marched, and track and field athletes ran and jumped. The unpredictable surface rarely yielded a true bounce. The best strategy was to not let the ball bounce, except on service return.

More frequently, we used the wrestling practice area, up near the rafters on the south side of the Field House. The ceiling was approximately 18 feet high, and the distance between the building support pillars was less than the width of a regular tennis court. When the wrestlers were not using the space, we stretched a net between the pillars. We outlawed angle shots, given the close sidewalls, and lobs were virtually impossible.

However, the most ingenious tennis space created by Dr. Klotz was the main basketball floor, the same place where Don Nelson established Big Ten record performances. Within two minutes, we could convert the basketball floor into a tennis court. On a couple of occasions, we played at half time during televised Big Ten basketball games, in front of a Field House audience of some 10,000 fans.

The quick conversion to a tennis court was ingenious. The tennis lines were black elastic tapes, which we hooked onto small nails that had been tapped into the sides of the raised basketball floor. We achieved proper net height and cable tension by attaching chains to both ends of the net cable, and then securing the chains on hooks that had been installed under the bleachers on both sides of the basketball court. Next, we put sawhorses under the net cable where the net posts belonged. Finally, by adding a block and tackle with a rope cinch to one end of the net cable, we could achieve the right net height with a couple of tugs on the rope cinch.

Building a collegiate tennis program at Gustavus

From 1963 to 1970, I served as the University of Iowa assistant varsity coach as I completed my MBA and Ph.D. course work. After accepting a faculty position at Gustavus in 1970, I agreed to coach tennis on a volunteer basis. My biggest challenge was finding a place to practice indoors. The Twin Cities, which were 65 miles away, had a couple of indoor tennis clubs, but they were too far away and beyond our budget.

There were two gymnasiums on the Gustavus campus—one in the Myrum Field House and the other in Alumni Hall. Myrum housed a wooden basketball floor, raised one foot above a dirt floor and surrounded by wooden bleachers. In earlier years, Myrum had been used for ice hockey, but now it was limited to basketball, physical education classes, and an occasional John Denver concert. Denver sang there three times and met a Gustavus student named Annie Martell, who later became his wife.

Few would have guessed that this facility could house a tennis court. There were no nets, backdrops, tennis lines, or tennis surface, and permanent basketball backboards hung ten feet above the floor. However, this was the same challenge that Dr. Klotz had solved when he converted the University of Iowa basketball floor into a tennis court. I followed his example, and our primary indoor practice facility for the next ten years materialized.

The other gymnasium on the Gustavus campus was Alumni Hall, used for gymnastics, volleyball, dance, and some intramural basketball. A 22-foot ceiling and a 90-foot length did not discourage me from considering this space for tennis. Just below it was a lounge, which had been converted into emergency office space for Gustavus administrators after the administration building burned in the spring of 1970. Athletic activity in Alumni Hall shook the ceiling of the administrators below, causing a ban on athletics until after business hours.

Converting Alumni Hall to tennis was less challenging than Myrum Field House. The net and its cable were attached to a block and tackle with a rope cinch, and then hooked to eyebolts on both sides of the gym. The school added permanent, white, tennis lines to the floor, complimenting an array of volleyball and basketball lines that were already there. Stray balls were easy to retrieve, except when they dropped into stairwells at two corners of the gym and ended up in the locker rooms two stories below.

While the tennis court conversion was easier, learning to play there was not. The low ceiling eliminated defensive lobs, but well placed offensive lobs that stayed just below the roof were very effective. With only six feet behind the baseline, backcourt play was difficult.

Our practice and playing conditions were primitive. Nevertheless, we became a tennis power and won a national team title. No other school from the northern half of the United States was among the top finishers. Warm climate schools wondered how we improved so much during our long, Minnesota winters. When we told them about Myrum and Alumni, they found the story hard to believe.

1972 MIAC Championship team: 1st row, Pat Carey, Mike Helgeson, Rick Schowalter, Craig Senn, Bruce Meese; 2nd row, Dave Kubes, Steve Edlund, Tim Butorac, Brad McMinn, Coach Wilkinson

37

GUSTAVUS OUTDOOR TENNIS COURTS

Before 1979, we played many intercollegiate matches
at the South Courts. A special memory was our 1974
match against the University of Iowa. We won 7-2, led by
All-Americans Tim Butorac, Dave Petersen, and Kevin Ylinen.

The Gustavus outdoor courts are full every fall, when 225 players from 30 colleges and universities gather for the Intercollegiate Tennis Association (ITA) Midwest Regional Championship. All 36 courts in St. Peter—5 at the high school, 4 in the city park, 21 campus outdoor courts, and 6 indoor courts in the Swanson Tennis Center (STC)—have matches with other players waiting. The College hosts this tournament every year, as no other college in the upper Midwest has the required number of courts.

Coaches, relatives, friends and players marvel. Sitting on the hillside that overlooks the nine Gibbs Courts, they gaze at the Minnesota River Valley, clothed in striking red, orange, yellow, and green colors. The blue sky and warm sunshine enhance the magical view, more breathtaking than any other spot on campus. "How fortunate you are," one parent remarked, "I can't imagine a prettier spot from which to view tennis."

"How did your outdoor campus courts come to be?" people have asked. The question refers to the nine Gibbs Courts, perched dramatically on a hillside; the three South Courts, nestled next to soft pine trees; and the twelve Brown Courts, overlooked by a spectator tower. Responding to this inquiry, I share the following story of fund raising, court construction, campus politics, and related events.

Gibbs Courts

When I started coaching in the fall of 1970, there were four courts on the northern side of campus—two (side by side) on the hillside beneath North Dormitory and two more (end on end) under Sorenson Dormitory. We used these courts for men's varsity practice, but a wide grassy area between them made coaching difficult. However, this space below Link Dormitory was appreciated for a non-tennis activity when snow was on the ground. Gustavus students used it for "traying," a daredevil activity that required food trays from the cafeteria. Sitting on them at the top of the hill, enthusiasts pushed off and plummeted downward across the open space toward 7th Street below.

We did not want to ruin their fun, but we longed for six courts in one location, a number that would accommodate practice space for larger teams and permit all six singles matches in a varsity meet to be played simultaneously. However, the College lacked the funds and the commitment to address our needs. I soon realized that we needed to raise the money ourselves.

Our inspirational force for fundraising was Karen Gibbs, the Gustavus player who had died from bone cancer in August of 1977. We sought to honor her memory by creating the Gibbs Tennis Center. It would include six courts and support facilities that would fill an open breezeway beneath Link Dormitory. Included in the project were a kitchen, a large study/computer room, an entrance lobby, storage rooms and a large lounge overlooking the tennis courts.

Karen Gibbs Lounge in 1982

Friends of Karen and mine met frequently; and we mapped out an ambitious fund raising drive. Our primary fundraisers were doubles events at several tennis clubs in the Twin Cities area. Skilled tennis players who could afford generous contributions paired with Gustavus varsity and alumni players for exciting evenings of competition and socializing.

By late 1978, we had raised $180,000. Gustavus Physical Plant Director Dale Haack drew up the plans, secured the approval of Financial Vice President Ross Bloomquist, and provided the engineering and construction expertise. With help from a Twin City tennis court-building company, we created the Karen Gibbs Tennis Center.

In October 1982, a memorable dedication ceremony celebrated Karen's life and the facilities built in her honor. Pictures of Karen, quotations from her, and tributes from Professor Bob Esbjornson and sculptor Paul Granlund adorned the walls. In front of the lounge, overlooking the courts, stood "Venus Nautilus," a sculpture by Paul Granlund honoring Karen. It showed a woman, emerging with arms outstretched from the spiral of a nautilus shell, symbolizing Karen's struggle against cancer and her indomitable drive to succeed.

Venus Nautilus," 1982 sculpture by Paul Granlund
honoring Karen Gibbs

Over the following year, fundraising and planning continued. The two oldest courts were destroyed, and five new tennis courts were constructed. By the summer of 1983, we had nine courts, retaining walls, terraces, bleachers, hillside seats, and walkways. The total project, led by the engineering skill of Dale Haack, transformed the area into a beautiful tennis complex. All of these costs were covered by contributions from tennis enthusiasts, the Greater Gustavus Fund, and Tennis and Life Camps (TLC).

From 1984 through 1997, the Gibbs Tennis Center was the outdoor center of collegiate tennis during the school year and TLC during the summer. This role was interrupted on March 29, 1998, when a tornado demolished much of the campus and left the Gibbs Courts unplayable. Tennis fences were bent, their foundations were lifted out of the ground, and gaping holes were left in the playing surface. For the rest of the collegiate spring season, the teams used high school courts in Mankato for their practices.

Nine Gibbs Courts overlooking the Minnesota River Valley

Also, TLC was severely challenged. We depended on twelve outdoor courts, four indoor courts, a dormitory, a dining service, and classrooms. Immediately after the tornado, we expressed optimism to the 900 people already registered. Two weeks later, however, we knew that Gustavus would be closed for repairs all summer. How were we going to salvage our business? How could we avoid refunding thousands of dollars and endangering the future of TLC? We could not picture another nearby place with the resources to accommodate our needs.

Then, out of the blue, came the telephone call that I will never forget. Paul Brosnahan, a former TLC camper and a lawyer from Winona, proposed that we come there for the summer. At first, I was incredulous. How could it be that his community had everything that we needed…and that it would still be available in the middle of April? "Come and see," he encouraged me. That is precisely what we did.

The city of Winona and the campus of St. Teresa welcomed us with open arms. Several years before, the College of St. Teresa had closed, and its property was purchased by a nonprofit foundation that prioritized Winona community development. The foundation added several buildings to the campus, including a six-court indoor tennis facility. They also built 12 outdoor courts. Unbelievable! These were precisely the tennis facilities that we needed. What about a dormitory, dining service, classrooms, and staff apartments? They owned those too. By some stroke of luck, everything we needed was still available.

We had to pinch ourselves. Was this really happening, or was it just a dream? We returned from Winona absolutely giddy. TLC would continue on an attractive campus, bounded by the Mississippi River and gorgeous bluffs. Registrations continued to pour in. On June 1, we loaded everything we needed, including nine ball machines, into a moving van and made a three-hour journey to our new summer home.

In 1999, TLC was back using the Gibbs Tennis Center. However, the indoor tennis arrangements were changed. Previously, we had used four indoor courts in Lund Arena, which was a short walking distance from the Gibbs Courts. Instead, the College now asked us to depend on the Swanson Indoor Tennis Center (STC), located on the far northwestern corner of campus. How would we get students back and forth in a timely manner between outdoor and indoor sessions that alternated every 50 minutes? By renting a school bus.

For seven summers, while the Gibbs Courts were still used by TLC campers, I was the driver of what was affectionately called "The Magic Bus." Every 50 minutes, all summer, I picked up campers and dropped them off at their required destinations. Friendly greetings, music, and get acquainted activities made the trips magical for many, but I longed for the day when so much transporting would not be necessary.

In July 2005, that day finally came. The construction of new courts near the Swanson Indoor Tennis Center (STC) made transporting unnecessary. TLC no longer depended on the Gibbs Courts. It was a time for both celebration and remorse. TLC could now operate more efficiently, but campers would no longer experience the beautiful Gibbs Courts, the breathtaking valley below, the Gibbs Lounge, or the "Venus Nautilus" sculpture. Furthermore, they would not observe the 2002 renaming of Link Dormitory. Thanks to the recommendation of President Dennis Johnson, Link Dormitory became Gibbs Dormitory, marking the first time in school history that a campus building would be named after a Gustavus student

South Courts

When I first arrived on campus back in the fall of 1970, there were three courts (side by side) on the southeastern corner of the campus. Built in 1961, they were newer, in better shape, and more conducive to coaching than the four courts at the Gibbs site. Some days I assigned men to play practice matches there, but on other days the women's tennis club used the courts. In 1974, women's tennis became an official varsity sport, and our opportunities to practice there became less frequent.

Before 1979, we played many intercollegiate matches at the South Courts. A special memory was our 1974 match against the University of Iowa. We won 7-2, led by All-Americans Tim Butorac, Dave Petersen, and Kevin Ylinen. In 1979, two new Gibbs Courts ended the period when the South Courts was the preferred venue.

After the tornado of 1998, the South Courts again played a crucial role. While all other courts on campus were destroyed, the southeastern corner of campus escaped the storm's greatest fury. Our last conference home match that season—against St. Olaf—was played on those three courts.

There was a simple beauty to the South Courts, nestled next to pine trees and just below the dormitories at the south end of campus. Students appreciated the presence of courts generally not committed to the tennis teams or any other organized activity. Also, their location on the edge of campus, next to many private homes in St. Peter, provided nearby residents easy access to tennis courts. Even though they have served Gustavus and the community well, the College decided in 2013 to eliminate them.

Brown Courts

In 2001, a generous gift from Wayne and Sandra Brown, parents of former varsity player Greg Brown ('87), led to eight new outdoor courts in front of STC. Other donations helped create a spectator tower in 2003, just in time for the NCAA III men's national championship. In 2004, Nick Legeros crafted a beautiful sculpture and rock garden in front of STC. Former players Marc Miller ('84), Bruce Jackson ('89), and Raman Jayapathy ('85) raised money from alumni to pay for this project.

TLC instructor Dave Lachman teaching campers on the
four newest Brown Courts in 2010

Spectators watch a 2011 match on court #1 from the Brown viewing tower

However, an important goal still eluded us. We sought four more courts on the eastern portion of the physical plant grounds, a sparsely used area just to the north of existing courts. It had a pine tree perimeter on two sides. By adding spruce trees to a third side, we could create a protected, natural site.

Gustavus and TLC needed twelve outdoor courts near STC, not just eight. With twelve courts, the men and women's teams could practice at the same time. Two dual matches (each requiring six courts) could be played simultaneously.

In 2004, my push to achieve this goal proved difficult, even though we had raised the money ourselves to build the four courts. Who was going to pay for the maintenance of these and all the other courts on campus? After this and other questions were resolved, Gustavus President Jim Peterson gave his approval, and construction of the final four Brown Courts began. By July 2005, all twelve Brown Courts were ready. A new era of TLC efficiency began, and my seven summers of transporting students by bus between the Gibbs Courts and STC were over.

Court maintenance and commitment to lifetime activity

Maintenance of asphalt courts in an alternating cold and hot weather climate is a continuing challenge. Temperature changes create contraction and expansion, producing frequent cracks in the playing surfaces. If not patched regularly, outdoor courts deteriorate quickly. TLC revenues now cover most of the repair costs.

A winding route over a 40-year period has put Gustavus in an enviable outdoor tennis facilities position. For the future, Gustavus has a plan that benefits TLC, varsity tennis programs, physical education classes, the tennis club, intramurals, and recreational players. Concurrently, it reinforces the College's commitment to wellness, lifetime sports, physical fitness, and family relationships.

View from the observation tower looking toward the entrance of the Swanson Indoor Tennis Center

38

SWANSON INDOOR TENNIS CENTER

*Sixteen people were playing tennis in Swanson
Indoor Tennis Center (STC) when the tornado struck.
When they heard the freight train sound that accompanies
tornadoes, they rushed to the cement block classroom,
got down on the floor, and covered their heads.*

First-time visitors to STC on the Gustavus campus are often amazed. The natural lighting during the day and the direct lighting at night; the 65-foot ceiling at the center; the six beautiful blue and green courts with generous spaces between each one; the spectator areas above and behind each court; the lobby, classroom, and viewing lounge, all featuring pictures, trophies, and awards representing the history of tennis at Gustavus; and the large electronic scoreboards—all create an unparalleled ambiance.

STC is a magnet for players and their fans. By 2013, three NCAA III national tournaments, eleven Intercollegiate Tennis Association (ITA) national indoor championships, and many Midwest regional championships had been hosted at STC. The Minnesota Intercollegiate Athletic Conference (MIAC) uses STC for all season-ending playoff tournaments. The Minnesota State High School Association and the Northern Tennis Association schedule many regional tournaments at STC. Furthermore, STC is the headquarters for TLC.

Quest for an indoor tennis center

For 20 years, indoor tennis courts on the Gustavus campus proved to be an elusive goal. Detractors believed that tennis was an outdoor sport only, that the College should not invest in a "frivolous" sport venue, and that a tennis center detracted from campus beauty.

After two years of using makeshift tennis courts for practice, we wanted real indoor tennis courts. In 1972, I proposed that an air structure be placed over two existing outdoor courts beneath North Hall. The cost was less than $100,000. I had the support of President Frank Barth. He saw the value that such a facility would bring to the campus. However, important faculty leaders disagreed. Barth did not think it was prudent to continue his support, and so my first dream for an indoor tennis facility vanished.

The next opportunity for indoor courts came in 1975, when the indoor Lund Hockey Arena was completed. The first plan showed permanent bleachers down to rink side, but Athletic Director Lloyd Hollingsworth insisted that Lund Arena should be multi-purpose—more specifically, large enough to accommodate four tennis courts when hockey season was over. We purchased a tennis carpet to cover the cement floor, added curtains behind the courts and divider nets between them, and built tennis net standards that could rest on the carpet without being anchored. The facility helped us in the spring season, when rain and snow often forced us indoors. Also, it was crucial for TLC, which began in 1977. However, Lund Arena did not provide indoor courts for most of the school year. From October until the middle of March, we still depended on the cramped, lightening-fast, basketball floors in Myrum Fieldhouse and Alumni Hall.

In 1980, an indoor tennis club on the south side of Mankato offered practice opportunities before mid-March. It was an 18-mile drive, usually late at night. Practice started at 10 p.m. and ended around midnight. On one occasion, our van slid off a slippery road. Fortunately, no one was injured. Getting back to dormitory rooms at 1 a.m. was not ideal, but it was a price that dedicated varsity players paid to excel at their sport.

In 1983, new hope for indoor tennis arrived when Gustavus decided to build a new athletic center that would expand Lund Arena. All coaches were encouraged to offer their recommendations. I suggested that we build a four-court tennis facility on the south side of the hockey arena. After hockey season ended, we would have eight courts. By that time, the men's tennis team had won two NCAA III team championships and many individual national titles. It seemed as if we were in a position to have our plans prioritized.

However, tennis needs were passed over. State of the art basketball, indoor track, swimming, volleyball, gymnastics, and racquetball facilities were added, but nothing was done for tennis. I was crushed. How could the College prioritize even racquetball over tennis? It was not even a varsity sport.

Next, my attention turned to the abandoned Myrum Fieldhouse, which could house three tennis courts if the basketball floor were eliminated and the dirt floor were paved. However, the administration wanted to tear the building down and create a green area in front of the Sorenson, Link, and North Dormitories.

By 1984, my challenge was clear. President John Kendall thought that the College had done enough for indoor athletic facilities. Their future projects would be academic buildings.

Critical help from Lloyd "Bud" Swanson

Support needed to come from elsewhere. I turned to Lloyd "Bud" Swanson, CEO of First Federal Savings and Loan in Minneapolis. Bud had a special interest in tennis, nourished by several successful years on Gustavus tennis teams. After graduating in 1935, he continued to play tennis for most of his life. Bud knew personally how important indoor courts were to tennis enthusiasts in Minnesota. He marveled at what our program had accomplished and wanted to help.

Bud was in a unique position to assist. First, he was a member of the Gustavus Board of Trustees, the governing body of Gustavus. Even the president of the College answered to the Board. Bud was an esteemed Board veteran who could sway other Board members with his quiet but reasoned approach to issues. Second, he was treasurer of the Greater Gustavus Fund, an independent foundation that supported Gustavus causes. Bud's opinion on how the foundation's funds should be spent at the College made a difference.

However, the opposition was formidable. A big breakthrough came when Bud convinced fellow Board member Tom Dahlstrand to donate $100,000 to a future indoor tennis center. Also, he pledged $150,000 more in the future. His gift forced the Board's hand. If they refused the gift, they risked offending Tom and endangering future gifts.

The Board prudently accepted the gift in 1985 and authorized the indoor tennis center project with the understanding that no College funds would be allocated to the project. The responsibility for fundraising fell primarily on me. I invited two more $100,000 donations—one from Suzanne Jackson and the other from Doug and Carole Skanse. Bud and other smaller donors connected with the tennis program also lent their support. The Greater Gustavus Fund, thanks to Bud, contributed frequently. Finally, profits from TLC brought us to our $750,000 goal.

I was ecstatic. By 1988, we had accomplished our goal. The plans for a four-court, indoor facility had been drawn up with the support of Physical Plant Director Dale Haack, Vice President for Advancement Bob Peterson, and Development Officer Paul Tillquist. Herb Baldwin, campus landscape planner, had identified an ideal location for the proposed tennis center. He had placed it just west of the football stadium, in keeping with the existing campus plan. We anticipated Board approval.

When I heard about the post Board meeting report, I could not believe my ears. A new campus plan by an outside landscape architectural firm, unbeknownst to Baldwin, Peterson, or Tillquist, had been presented and approved. It included a new mall extending westward from Christ's Chapel. Proposed buildings lined both sides of the mall, and the aging football stadium was scheduled for elimination. So was the proposal for the tennis center, which would have been located in the middle of the newly approved mall.

Going off campus to build a tennis center

Again, I was crushed, but not willing to give up. Earlier potential sites—south side of Lund Arena, west side of the football stadium, and the Myrum Fieldhouse space—were all on campus. Obviously, any new proposed site needed to be off campus. The Board agreed. They instructed President Kendall to purchase a 13-acre section of farmland on the northern side of campus, and he agreed to do so.

With the new site in mind, I changed my thinking from a four-court, brick and mortar building to a six-court, air structure. Two more courts would provide an optimum number for collegiate dual matches and more practice space for our large varsity teams. Going with an air structure would help us to stay within budget.

For the next two years, I raised and contributed more money. Concurrently, I spoke with air structure engineers and Twin City contractors, who would build the courts, locker rooms, and mechanical room. Board member Roger Carlson met frequently with me at this time and maintained support with other Board members. Without Roger's assistance, I could not have pursued an aggressive construction strategy.

The process would have moved more quickly if President Kendall had purchased the land immediately. Each time I checked, he assured me that he was working on it. After a year and a half, I heard rumors that the farmer who owned the land was refusing to sell to the College. I knew I had to take the initiative. In 1990, I hired local real estate agent Barbara Haack to buy the land. In short time, she successfully negotiated a purchase of 14.5 acres for $110,000. As soon as the papers were signed, Barb and I donated the land to the College, with the provision that it be used for tennis. President Kendall initially refused our gift, but reluctantly accepted it in 1991 under pressure from the Board.

Still, the proposed, million-dollar tennis center was no guarantee. Therefore, Barb and I agreed to shift the tennis center further north, more out of sight from the rest of campus. The donated property closest to campus was designated for proposed athletic fields. Next, we wrote a letter guaranteeing that the College would assume no costs for construction. Also, projected revenues and expenses showed a minimal burden on the College. Finally, the Board gave its approval in late June.

In July 1991, we were set to build. Inflation of the air structure was set for the end of October. On Halloween, one of the great, early blizzards of the century struck. Several air structures in our area collapsed under the pressure of heavy, wet snow and driving winds. Thank goodness, we were not ready a week earlier. Our air structure might have gone down immediately after it went up. Snow remained on the ground for the rest of the winter, so inflation of the air structure was postponed to the summer of 1992. After 20 years of opposition and postponements, we finally had an indoor tennis facility. We named it the Lloyd O. Swanson Indoor Tennis Center in honor of Bud.

Swanson Indoor Tennis Center, located next to the 12 Brown Outdoor Tennis Courts

Still, there was more to accomplish. My complete vision for STC included a classroom, viewing lounge, elevator, and spectator viewing area above and behind the courts. These features were omitted from the original construction in order to meet budget. So my fundraising and contributions from TLC continued until more construction could be authorized in 1995. Warren Wunderlich, Physical Plant Director, I & S Engineering, and I worked together to produce an optimum design that benefited both players and spectators.

Tornado destruction

On March 29, 1998, a F3 tornado more than a mile wide hit the campus squarely, destroying buildings and breaking 80% of the windows on campus. STC came to an abrupt end. The air structure was torn to pieces and spread across the countryside, as far as 120 miles away. One white piece of fabric was lodged high in a tree in front of our home, a continuing reminder of the tornado's force. Sixteen people were playing tennis in STC when the tornado struck. When they heard the freight train sound that accompanies tornadoes, they rushed to the cement block classroom, got down on the floor, and covered their heads.

A trophy case above the classroom was lifted into the air and ripped apart. A two-foot splinter pierced the tire of a car still sitting in the parking lot. Trophies were smashed and scattered about. The steel in the structure was twisted. Glass was broken and pictures were ruined. The air structure that used to cover and protect the interior was gone, exposing everything to the snow and rain that followed.

Swanson Indoor Tennis Center after the March 29, 1998, tornado

When the tornado struck, Gustavus students were on spring break. I was in Phoenix with the men's tennis team when we saw the reports on national television. The picture that struck me the hardest was one of Carole Langsjoen, standing in the remains of her living room. The walls and second story of her beautiful home were gone. I had been there many times in the early 1970s, bringing wooden rackets that needed to be restrung to her husband Arne, a chemistry professor at the College.

My first call was to Barb, who had gone to Sioux City, Iowa, to visit my mother. She was safe, but the same could not be said for our home. It suffered $50,000 worth of damage, but was still standing. Three other homes on our short street next to the College were completely destroyed. Barb returned to St. Peter the next day and spent the following week coordinating cleanup efforts for both our home and the Swanson Tennis Center. She was extremely grateful for the outpouring of help from family and friends that worked with her for over a week.

The team and I returned a week later. The College was shut down, so I sent our players home. One dormitory was completely destroyed. Gustavus suffered over 50 million dollars of damage. It appeared that no classes could resume that spring, but miraculously they did. In late April, students returned and completed their school year.

Improvement opportunities created by the tornado

Even while in Arizona on the spring trip, I put our contractors on notice. We wanted STC replaced, improved, and ready by August. The new air structure needed heat sealed seams instead of stitched ones. The first structure had begun to leak water through the stitch holes when it was raining. Another issue had been the noise created by loud blowers on the side of the air structure. By putting them 15 feet away from the air structure and connecting them to underground tunnels that entered through the floor, we created a quieter environment. This also solved another problem. Ice sliding off the top of the air structure had sliced the fabric where it was attached to the previous blowers, creating gaping holes in the side of the air structure and the need for emergency action.

Another change was desirable. The first air structure had a cap that trapped snow, forcing workers to climb up 65 feet to shovel away the heavy drifts. The smoother top on the new air structure minimized drifts. While no climbers have gone up the new air structure to shovel, there was one occasion when they should have. Accumulating snow from two successive storms caused the south end of the structure to sink quickly to the floor under the weight, and then explode upwards after the snow slid off. This caused a split in the side of the air structure, which we temporarily covered with big pieces of ply board. This near disaster could have been avoided if we had manually cleared the snow after the first storm.

Two additional improvements made the new air structure even better. The first was the construction of a three-foot-high foundation wall around the perimeter. The old ground-level foundation made snowplowing challenging. It was difficult to avoid cutting the fabric while removing deep snow from the sides of the air structure. The second improvement was changing the lights. The original ground-based lights were directed up to the 65-foot ceiling. There the light was reflected back to the tennis surface. This left the light too dim for players tracking hard-hit tennis balls. The lighting improved greatly when we hung the lights from the ceiling.

Many other things were done to meet the August 1998 completion goal. The twisted steel and broken glass, water-soaked and glass-embedded furniture and carpets, destroyed pictures and trophies, ruined tennis courts and back curtains—all had to be replaced. Sometimes, I wondered if everything could be ready for that fall semester, but we prevailed. Warren Wunderlich, the physical plant director, supervised numerous contractors and pushed them to complete the work. A brand new facility awaited the students when they returned.

STC's vital role for Gustavus

Through challenges and changes, STC has become a home for the Gustavus tennis family. Pictures and awards on its walls go back to 1892, when tennis at Gustavus began. STC is a special place on campus, where players are remembered and celebrated. They can share with friends, parents, children, and even grandchildren their memories of bygone days.

**TLC Instructor Nikolai Johansen playing on court #1 in the
Swanson Indoor Center**

Also, STC is the home of TLC. The office headquarters on the second floor
helps us serve more than 1,500 campers each summer. Pictures of former
campers are preserved in scrapbooks that line the office walls. Campers'
tennis games and lives are changed by what they experience on the courts and
in the classrooms of STC. Pictures of staff from every year, Aasen Award
recipients for outstanding teaching, and Walz Award winners for remarkable
service to local communities—all reinforce positive values.

Finally, STC welcomes all Gustavus students—physical education class
participants taking tennis, intramural players, tennis club members, and any

student wanting to enjoy indoor tennis for no charge. Faculty members and players from St. Peter and the surrounding region take advantage of court time, leagues, tournaments, and lessons—all under the direction of Heidi Carlson, STC manager.

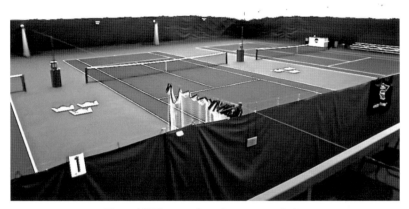

View of STC courts from the spectator balcony

Now, STC is widely viewed as an important asset to the College. Many potential students and their parents are first introduced to the College in STC. Players regularly use indoor courts seven out of nine months during the school year. In the summer, TLC depends on this air conditioned, indoor facility. Although the pathway to its existence was arduous, in retrospect, the final facility far exceeds what an easier route would have produced.

Section VI

TLP APPLIED TO MY TENNIS PLAYING

The thought "don't make a mistake" increases
dramatically the chance that I will make an error.

I have divided my tennis playing experiences into two segments—those before coming to Gustavus in 1970 and those afterwards, as my Tennis and Life Philosophy (TLP) crystallized. My new approach to tennis opponents kept competition fun for me and contributed importantly to the longevity of my playing career. I never challenged an opponent's line call—either verbally or with body language. I did not put myself down or show temper, thereby implying that my opponent's success was caused by my poor play. My trusting approach influenced opponents, even those with reputations for poor sportsmanship, to respond congenially to me.

Tennis became more fun, the longer in my life that I competed. I anticipated playing tennis tournaments all the way into my 90s. The higher national rankings that I achieved as I grew older can be attributed in part to my internalization of the Tennis and Life Philosophy (TLP). I became better at letting go of everything that was outside my control—especially winning and playing well. As I learned to focus on a positive attitude, full effort, and good sportsmanship, I found myself relaxed in high-pressure situations, unafraid of failure. I defined success by the things I controlled. Ironically, the less I focused on winning, the better my competitive results became.

My emphasis on positive attitude kept me from dwelling on mistakes or keeping track of negative statistics. I loved playing points that determined games, because I knew I played my best then. I could not have maintained that attitude if I had dwelled on past game-point mistakes. That only would have increased the likelihood for the mistake to surface again in a similar, future situation. The thought "don't make a mistake" increases dramatically the chance that I will make an error. My strategy was to remove the memory of past mistakes by putting them out of my mind immediately. Accordingly, my mind on game-points was filled with images of ones that I had won.

Taking this approach a step further, I tried to avoid blaming losses on my mistakes or poor play. Instead, it was better for me to remember the good play of my opponent and to give him full credit for the win. Did this approach stop me from giving attention to weaknesses in practice? Definitely not! But it did stop me from giving them an undue emphasis.

Another important strategy for my tournament competition was keeping it in balance with other priorities. My playing was always sandwiched between family, teaching, coaching, and other professional responsibilities. Tournaments never took me away from home for more than a few weeks in any calendar year. Often, Barb accompanied me to the more interesting destinations. The following tennis stories describe some of the competitive experiences that I enjoyed between my 30th and 61st birthdays.

Wilkinson competing in 1972 at the age of 31

39

CHARMED BY CAROL CHANNING

She was dressed strikingly, but it was the platinum
blond, bouffant hairdo, the huge, dark sunglasses, the
large diamond rings, the huge smile, and the gushing,
affected way of speaking that showcased her persona.
Even though I was supposed to be receiving the trophy,
the whole presentation seemed to be more about her.

In 1971, I advanced to the singles final of the Missouri Valley Sectional Championship in Kansas City with an upset win over top seeded Cliff Bucholtz, who was previously ranked #18 in U.S. singles and #4 in doubles. I was playing very well and feeling confident that I would win the title for the third time. Dale Miller, my opponent in the final, lacked a record that matched Cliff's.

Just before the final, we learned that Carol Channing, a nationally known singer, actress, and comedienne, would be presenting the trophies. She was in Kansas City for much of the summer, doing her own show at the stately, open-air Starlight Theatre, a famous city landmark since the 1950s. Because of her busy schedule and tight timelines, the trophy presentation had to be made before the final. This was a curious way of doing it, but it offered both my opponent and me the chance to have our picture taken together with a national star.

Channing was a flamboyant beauty who radiated stardom. Cameras flashed everywhere as spectators tried to get their own pictures. She was dressed strikingly, but it was the platinum blond, bouffant hairdo, the huge, dark sunglasses, the large diamond rings, the huge smile, and the gushing, affected way of speaking that showcased her persona. Even though I was supposed to be receiving the trophy, the whole presentation seemed to be more about her.

In 1971, at 50 years of age, Carol was old enough to be my mother. However, she did not look or act her age. Already in the 1940s, she was a Broadway star in the musical comedy, "Gentlemen Prefer Blondes." Its hit song, "Diamonds are a Girl's Best Friend," continued to define her. In 2012,

Carol was still performing the song, having outlasted four husbands and looking surprisingly young.

After the trophy presentation, I lost in the final. How ironical that my cherished record of this Missouri Valley Championship is a picture of Carol Channing presenting me a trophy that I did not win.

Carol Channing presenting the Missouri Valley
championship trophy to Wilkinson in 1971

40

PLAYING IN MINNESOTA'S PREMIER TOURNEY

The good players came because the tournament and the social events surrounding it were so much fun. Also, home stays in the wealthiest mansions on Lake Minnetonka and the chance to fraternize with the Twin Cities social elite were enticing extras. Tennis legend Andre Agassi won his first professional tournament at Minikahda in 1987.

From the late 1950s through the 1980s, the Minikahda Invitational was the premier professional tournament in the upper Midwest. It was held in mid-August at the Minikahda Club, overlooking the western shore of Lake Calhoun in Minneapolis. The manicured clay courts, the smell of the freshly cut grass on the adjoining golf course, the temporary bleachers filled with fans, and the stately clubhouse all added to the allure of this prestigious, end-of-the-summer event.

Former Minikahda tennis pro Bill Kuross was the promoter who persuaded top international stars to come. Bill had played at the U.S. national singles and doubles championships during the 1950s, so he had good connections. However, that was not enough. The good players came because the tournament and the social events surrounding it were so much fun. Also, home stays in the wealthiest mansions on Lake Minnetonka and the chance to fraternize with the Twin Cities social elite were enticing extras. Tennis legend Andre Agassi won his first professional tournament at Minikahda in 1987.

I played Minikahda many times during the 1970s. My favorite tournament was the one in 1971. In the quarterfinals, I was pitted against Haroon Rahim, the top player from Pakistan and all of Asia. That year he was the top singles and doubles player on a UCLA team that had won the NCAA team championship.

I won the first set against Rahim and lost the second. Everything came down to the third set. At 3-3, I broke serve to go up 4-3. I said to myself, "If I can hold serve two more times, the match is mine." That thought undermined my performance. Mentally, I did not stay in the present, taking one point at a time. I lost the deciding set 7-5.

In the doubles, partner Jim Ebbitt, the Big Ten #1 singles champion, and I faced two legends in the semifinals. One was Alex Olmedo, the best amateur player in the world in 1959. For two years, he was undefeated in Davis Cup play for the United States in both singles and doubles. His partner was Allen Fox, 1961 NCAA singles champion and top-10 ranked U.S. player five times. This time, I did not need to lament afterwards how we came close but lost. Both Jim and I served big and returned serve well. We dominated 6-3, 6-3 in a match that lasted only an hour.

Ebbitt/Wilkinson defeating Olmedo/Fox at the 1971 Minikahda tournament

41

DRAFTED BY THE MINNESOTA BUCKSKINS

In late February of 1974, the Minnesota Buckskins
drafted me in the 13ᵗʰ round. I reported for tryouts
at the Oakdale Racquet Club in Minnetonka
together with my doubles partner Jim Ebbitt.

World Team Tennis began in 1974, just as the national tennis boom was moving into full throttle. The Minnesota Buckskins was one of 16 teams, situated in leading metropolitan markets across the United States. Larry King, the husband of Billie Jean King, was the league's co-founder.

George MacCall, former U.S. Davis Cup captain, was the first commissioner of the league. Burt McGlynn, chairman of McGlynn Bakeries, became the owner of the Minnesota franchise. At the time, McGlynn's bakery departments were situated in over 35 Target stores. The Met Center, the home of Minnesota North Stars of the National Hockey League, was also the home of the Minnesota Buckskins. The steep sides of the Met Center put the fans close to the action and the air conditioning provided maximum comfort during the summer months when the 44-match league schedule was played.

World Team Tennis was driven by the vision, energy, and popularity of Billie Jean King. In September 1973, she had become a national symbol for women's liberation, thanks primarily to her "Battle of the Sexes" match with Bobby Riggs, a 55-year-old former Wimbledon champion. The match was billed as a $100,000 "winner-take-all" event, but actually both contestants were guaranteed an additional $150,000, making it the most lucrative tennis match ever played.

Earlier in the year, Riggs had set the stage by beating Margaret Court, the #1 woman player in the world. The score was 6-2, 6-1. Riggs bragged that he was an elderly, out-of-shape man who came out of retirement to play, and still he could beat the top woman player. Riggs cast himself as a "male chauvinist pig," using the victory as a put-down of all women players. It was more than Billie Jean could stomach. With the honor of all women at stake, she accepted the challenge that she had refused earlier in the year.

The stage was set. Riggs, the consummate promoter, made appearances on "The Tonight Show" with Johnny Carson, "60 Minutes," and the "Today Show." On each show he presented an anti-women message. Suddenly, people with no previous interest in tennis were captivated by the drama that was to play out at the Astrodome in Houston. Four muscular men dressed as Egyptian slaves carried King to the court in Cleopatra style. By contrast, Riggs entered in a rickshaw, drawn by a group of beautiful models dressed skimpily in revealing outfits. Riggs gave King a large lollipop, which was in keeping with his "Sugar Daddy" persona, and she presented him with a piglet, which symbolized his "chauvinist pig" image.

Thirty thousand watched in person while 90 million worldwide viewed the spectacle on television. King had watched Margaret Court get humiliated in the previous match with Riggs. She was determined to not let it happen again. Instead of playing her normal aggressive game, King played near the baseline and ran Riggs from side to side, forcing him to cover the entire court and tiring him in the process. King was in control from start to finish, winning 6-4, 6-3, 6-3. In the process, she drove a stake into the heart of male chauvinism and established herself as an adored, feminist liberator.

Celebrity status put King in position to be the driving force pushing World Team Tennis and gender equity forward. For the first time ever, men and women were playing on the same professional teams with equal salaries. Mixed doubles was the final featured match in each team competition, thereby putting mixed gender competition front and center. Traditional tennis etiquette, which emphasized quiet fan behavior and polite applause for winners, was replaced by partisan cheering. World Team Tennis wished to create an exciting brand of tennis that appealed to broad audiences. Star players in the first year included Bjorn Borg, Jimmy Connors, Chris Evert, Evonne Goolagong, Illie Nastase, Martina Navratilova, and John Newcombe.

Billie Jean King was the player/coach for the Philadelphia Freedoms. Owen Davidson had the same position for the Minnesota Buckskins. He came to Minneapolis with impressive credentials and a close connection to King. Together they had won eight Grand Slam titles in mixed doubles. Just before taking the Buckskins position, he had won the 1973 U.S. Open men's doubles title with John Newcombe, defeating Rod Laver and Ken Rosewall in the finals.

In late February of 1974, the Minnesota Buckskins drafted me in the 13th round. I reported for tryouts at the Oakdale Racquet Club in Minnetonka together with my doubles partner Jim Ebbitt, a 1972 University of Minnesota graduate and Big 10 champion at #1 singles. One year before, we had won the U.S. Professional Tennis Association Indoor doubles title together.

The Buckskins intended to carry four men and four women on their roster. After signing three international male stars, they announced that the fourth man on the team would be either Ebbitt or I. After a week of tryouts, which included playing doubles with and against Davidson, Ebbitt got the final position.

After the 1974 season, the Buckskins and seven other teams disbanded. Other cities added, but the league struggled and suspended operations after the 1978 season. It resumed play in 1981. Billie Jean King became the league commissioner and its primary owner in 1984, when she retired from competitive play. The league still thrives in 2014, even after King's retirement as commissioner in 2001.

Wilkinson competing in 1972 at the Minikahda tournament

42

MY RIVALRY WITH JERRY NOYCE

Our rivalry remains a source of great pride for both of us.
We always played each other with trust, respect, friendship,
and good sportsmanship. Thirty-five years after our signature
match, Jerry was the master of ceremonies at my retirement
celebration. Rivalries do not get any better than ours.

When I moved to Minnesota in the fall of 1970, Jerry Noyce was the reigning sectional champion. He had played #1 for the University of Minnesota in the 1964, 1965, and 1966 seasons. Jerry had settled in Minneapolis after graduation and had continued to play at a very high level. Our rivalry for the top ranking stretched over much of the 1970s.

No match better epitomized the intensity and closeness of our battles than the singles final of the 1975 National Public Parks Tournament. Neither of us was projected to advance that far. However, on my way to the finals, I eliminated Elmataz Songol, a 1973 Egyptian Davis Cup team member, who had been assigned to the Egyptian Embassy in Washington. Meanwhile, Jerry beat Bill Babcock, who had just returned from playing ATP pro tournaments in Europe. Sports writer Joe Soucheray wrote in the *Star Tribune*:

> Jerry Noyce and Steve Wilkinson will play at noon today at the Nicollet Tennis Center to decide which one will become the first National Public Parks men's singles champion from Minnesota since Dick Hairline of Minneapolis won the title in 1946.
>
> In recent years, Noyce, the tennis coach at the University of Minnesota, has come closest to a singles title. He went to the finals of the tournament in Detroit in 1971 and was at break point in the second set of that match when he tore a muscle in his calf. This year's tournament is Wilkinson's first national public parks tournament.

Perhaps the most decisive moment determining the outcome came before the match began. Given the threat of rain, match officials asked us to consider shortening the match from three out of five sets to two out of three. Jerry had no preference, but I wanted the longer match. Consequently, the match format remained unchanged. If it had been shortened, the match outcome would have been reversed.

For the first three sets, Jerry's high-powered serve was almost untouchable. In the newspaper summary, I was quoted as saying, "I couldn't even see the ball at first. I had to move eight feet behind the baseline to get my racket on the ball." Jerry won the first and third sets with a service break in each. If he had won one more point in the second set, I would have lost in three straight sets. On the deciding 4-4 point in the 9-point tiebreaker, I hit a tough service return at Jerry's feet as he followed his serve to the net. Fortunately for me, his half volley hit the net tape.

At the beginning of the fourth set, I still faced an uphill battle. To make matters worse, I lost my serve and went down a break early in the set. Fortunately, I was able to break back late in the set, sending the match into a tiebreaker, which I won 5-2. Rain delayed the fifth set, giving both of us a chance to catch a breather. When play resumed, I held my serve five more times and got one service break. Four hours and 42 minutes after the match had begun, I emerged with a 4-6, 7-6, 3-6, 7-6, 6-4 victory. Jerry was quoted afterwards:

> I had all the chances. I was always ahead. I had it in three straight, then in four sets, and I let it get away. I wasn't so tired physically at the end as I was burned that I hadn't put away the match earlier.

Less than an hour after the singles ended, Jerry and I stepped back onto the court, this time as doubles partners. Again, we were stretched to the limit. Two and one half hours later, we won the doubles championship. After almost eight hours of play within a nine-hour period, both Jerry and I were exhausted.

Our rivalry remains a source of great pride. We always played each other with trust, respect, and good sportsmanship. The same was true for the matches between the teams we coached—Jerry, at the University of Minnesota, and I, at Gustavus. Thirty-five years after our signature match, Jerry was the master of ceremonies at my retirement celebration. Rivalries do not get any better than ours.

Also, Jerry's "serve" off the court has exceeded his outstanding serve on the court. While coach at the University of Minnesota, he created the Baseline Tennis Club, a nationally recognized tennis booster club. At the same time, he was vice president of the Northwest Racquet, Swim and Health Clubs and Chairman of the USTA National Collegiate Tennis Committee. Next, he moved on to become the founder and CEO of a national health organization, which led President George W. Bush to pick him in 2007 to serve on the President's Council of Sports and Fitness.

Wilkinson and Noyce after their last tournament match
against each other in 2000

43

PLAYING IN THE NATIONAL 35-AND-OVER TOURNAMENTS

"In building his championship ascent,
Bob Carmichael was lucky to beat professional
Steve Wilkinson 7-6 (5-4), 6-4 in the semis."

In 1978, two national tournaments in Houston provided my fondest memories of 35-and-over tennis. At the USTA Clay Court Championship, I was seeded 12th, but wins over sixth seeded Adrian Bay in the round of 16 and fourth seeded Peter Van Lingen in the quarterfinals put me into the semifinals against top seeded Bob Carmichael from Australia. Carmichael was still active on the ATP circuit, where he had won one singles title and twelve doubles titles. In 1978, he had reached the finals of four ATP tournaments and had won one of them.

I focused on dictating play by mainly attacking the net behind hard and deep shots hit down the middle of the court. Occasionally, I mixed in low underspin shots that stayed short. Both shots took away Carmichael's angles, which existed when the approach shots were close to the sidelines. My strategy put considerable pressure on his passing shots. I was reaching them and winning the points with effective angle volleys.

Long, consistent rallies from the baseline were the norm by most clay court players. My aggressive tactics proved frustrating to Carmichael, whose frequent outbursts should have gotten him defaulted. An *Inside Tennis* reporter wrote:

> In building his championship ascent, Carmichael was lucky to beat professional Steve Wilkinson 7-6 (5-4), 6-4 in the semis. On set point in the tiebreaker, 4-4, Carmichael notched a fault and Steve moved in almost up to the service line. Bob's serve with two thirds pace hit about six inches in from the line and big Steve hauled off with his forehand, hitting out at about 150 miles an hour, out about two feet beyond the baseline.

Carmichael went on to win the tournament, but in the process he never seemed happy. The *Inside Tennis* reporter wrote:

> Compared to his opponents in the tournament, the very determined personality of Carmichael appeared to dominate the play. He hit the ball hard on groundstrokes and serves with enough accuracy, especially on big points, to win. When he'd miss, the intense Aussie, who says "tennis does not come easy to him," would contort his face and go into his now famous soliloquies of inner remorse. But these spasms of anguish did not appear to impair his play on the next point.

Carmichael reached the finals of three more ATP doubles tournaments in 1979. His retirement after that year did not surprise me. He just did not seem to have much fun when he played.

My other Houston tournament in 1978 was the USPTA 35-and-over National Indoor. In the semifinals I played top-seeded Ron Holmberg, who had played in the U.S. Open from 1953 to 1972. He was ranked among the top ten U.S. players nine times during the 1950s and 1960s. *The USTA Official Encyclopedia of Tennis* describes him as one of "the leading players of his day." *World Tennis* magazine wrote, "Holmberg can do more with a tennis ball than any other player of his era. There is no shot that is beyond his aptitude… His touch, power and stroke making are beautiful to watch."

In 1978, Holmberg was not the player that he had been during the '60s. He still had all the shots, but he did not move to the ball as well. Consequently, I won against someone whose resume far exceeded mine.

Wilkinson competing in the National Public Parks tournament in 1976

$$44$$

CHASING NATIONAL TITLES IN PHILADELPHIA

*My nostalgic memories of Germantown include the smell of
freshly cut grass; players clothed in white, moving gracefully to
low skidding balls that seldom bounced over the 6-foot high,
portable back fences that separated each bank of courts.*

Beginning in 1986, the first year that I was eligible for 45-and-over
tournaments, I began a late summer tradition that lasted for 14 years. The
U.S. national grass court tournaments for men in the 45, 50, and 55-and-
over age categories were held together in Philadelphia.

The tournament headquarters was at the Germantown Cricket Club,
founded in 1854 and currently designated as a U.S. National Historic
Landmark. From 1921 to 1923, the club hosted the United States National
Tennis Championship, a predecessor to the U.S. Open. Also, the club was
the site of several Davis Cup finals from 1924 through 1927.

Today, the Germantown Cricket Club is a primarily white, upper class
fortress in the midst of a black, poverty-challenged, residential area. Stone
walls surrounding the grounds and a guarded gate serve as a constant
reminder of the stark contrast between the social realities inside and outside
the walls. However, just east of the club are homes that still reflect an earlier
day when the area belonged to the white, upper class of Philadelphia.

In one of those houses, just a half block from the club, lived Bill Tilden,
picked by a 1950 Associated Press poll as the greatest tennis player of the half-
century. "Peggy," an elderly club member, shared with me her fond
memories of riding in the rumble seat of Tilden's roadster when she was a
young girl. The Germantown Cricket Club was Tilden's club—the place
where some of his best victories were achieved. For seven years, he
completely dominated international tennis, winning six straight U.S. national
singles titles from 1920 through 1925.

My nostalgic memories of Germantown include the smell of freshly cut grass;
players clothed in white, moving gracefully to low skidding balls that seldom
bounced over the 6-foot high, portable back fences that separated each bank

218

of courts; and the sound of balls hitting the strings, but no noise coming from the feet or bouncing balls.

My trips to Philadelphia inspired me to reach high. For the first time in my life, achieving a top U.S. tennis ranking in my age group and playing on international cup teams representing my country seemed achievable.

Steve and Barb Wilkinson at the Germantown Cricket Club in 1997

45

WORLD CHAMPIONSHIPS IN SOUTH AMERICA

*Playing internationally in Uruguay involved more
than tennis competition. We were sport ambassadors
for the United States. What a rare opportunity!
Representatives from 32 countries socialized with each
other, drawn together by our common love for tennis.*

Playing for a world team championship in Uruguay

In 1989, a dream came true. I was selected for the U.S. Dubler Cup team, a
Davis Cup equivalent for players 45-and-over. We were scheduled to
compete against 31 other countries in Montevideo, Uruguay. Joining me
were Jim Parker from Houston, Texas; Keith Diepraam from Midlands,
Texas; and Len Saputo from Walnut Creek, California. Our coach was John
Powless from Madison, Wisconsin. Also, Barb and Len's wife, Vicki,
accompanied us.

Playing internationally involved more than tennis competition. We were
sport ambassadors for the United States. Representatives from 32 countries
socialized with each other, drawn together by our common love for tennis. A
giant barbeque party—touted as the largest that anyone at the Carrasco Club
had seen—was a featured social event. So was the day trip excursion to Punta
del Este, which included a trip to the harbor to see the Whitbread Round-
the-World yachts. They were in port before their next leg of the journey to
Freemantle in Western Australia. Many of our participants found their own
country's boat and had their pictures taken together with the crews.

On other evenings, when our American entourage dined together at local
restaurants, we were struck by how late everyone ate—even families with
small children. Supper began at 9 p.m. and peak time seemed to be between
10 and 11 p.m. Meat dominated most of the main entrees. The size and
thickness of the steaks exceeded anything I had experienced in the United
States. If one ordered chicken, they served whole, medium sized birds. We

enjoyed long leisurely meals together, combined with savory South American wines.

Easy victories over Uruguay in the round of 16 and Great Britain in the quarterfinals set the stage for difficult challenges in the semifinal against Italy and the final against Germany. The deciding doubles match between Keith Diepraam/Jim Parker and Bodo Nitsche/Gunter Krauss could not have been closer. The score was 5-7, 7-5, 7-6(3). With joy and relief we celebrated our world title. Our reflections in the large, silver Dubler Cup were a welcome culmination to an eventful week.

Len Saputo, Steve Wilkinson, Keith Diepramm, Captain John Powless, and Jim Parker with Dubler Cup trophy in Montevideo, Uruguay after winning the world 45-and-over championship in 1989

Playing for a Pan American team championship in Argentina

The next team competition on our South American trip was in Rosario, the second largest city in Argentina. This was the site of the Steven's Cup, an international team competition under the direction of the Pan American Games. A half-year before the competition, we had wondered if Rosario would be able to host the event. Uncontrolled inflation (about 700% per month) had left shop owners unwilling to open their doors. Hungry people had broken into the shops to take food, which then led to looting for more expensive items. The police, discredited because of suppressive activities under the previous government, were ineffective in controlling the situation. However, the crisis quickly passed and Rosario remained the site of the Steven's Cup.

An unexpected experience was our relationship with the youngsters of Rosario. Each afternoon, the courts were flooded with ball boys and ball girls, many of them sons and daughters of club members. The children were very skilled at tennis themselves. We would hit with them. I was surprised how well they had mastered both topspin and underspin. They were eager for autographs, hats, and wristbands—basically anything we would leave with them. Their infatuation with us made us feel like celebrities.

Friendships with Argentine families blossomed as they opened their homes and their hearts to us. We invited one of our competitors and his family to share Christmas with us two months later, and they accepted. We had a wonderful time together as they experienced snow and a white Christmas for the first time.

For the Steven's Cup I played #1 singles, Len Saputo played #2, and we shared the doubles responsibility. After victories over Venezuela, Puerto Rico, and the #2 team from the United States, we faced host Argentina in the finals. The championship came down to the final doubles match. We won the first set 6-2 and came close to clinching the title in the second set, but they hit some brilliant shots and pushed the match to a third set.

I could feel the excitement in the air. The news cameras and the crowd added to the drama. On one point, I drove the ball hard at our opponents' feet four times. My fifth shot went wide and the crowd erupted. Time after time, they made difficult saves. When they broke our serve at 5-5 on a great volley, the crowd began to chant and sing, "Vamos, vamos Argentina! Vamos, vamos a gagnar". Our opponents then held serve to win 7-5.

The place went wild with joy. The Argentinian fans cried and hugged each other. Given the troubles that Argentina had experienced during the preceding year, this victory meant so much to them.

At first, I was very disappointed that we had let the match slip away. Then, I looked up and began to take it all in. Soon, I realized I had never before made so many people so ecstatically happy and probably never would again. The feelings were so strong that Argentina invited Len and me back to Rosario the following year. We accepted, and our international bonds of friendship deepened even more.

46

LEADING AN AMERICAN TEAM IN GERMANY

I went into the match determined to take world
singles champion Peter Pokorny out of his
comfort zone by pressuring his backhand.

An emotional return to Berlin

Len Saputo from Walnut Creek, California, Rob Cadwallader from
Memphis, Allan Carter from New York City, and I were selected to represent
the United States in the 1992 Fred Perry Cup competition in Berlin,
Germany. This was a team competition featuring the world's best in the 50-
and-over division.

The Perry Cup was named after Fred Perry, winner of eight Grand Slam titles
that included three successive Wimbledon Championships in 1934, 1935,
and 1936. From 1933 through 1936, he led the British team to four
consecutive Davis Cup victories. In 1937, he turned pro and moved to the
United States, where he pursued his professional tennis career and started the
famous, laurel wreath clothing line that bears his name.

In 1992, at the age of 83, Perry agreed to be the honored guest in Berlin. We
were thrilled to have a legend in our midst. We talked with him, had our
pictures taken together, and received our awards directly from him.

Berlin was a special location for me, one that evoked positive emotions and
memories. Being back in Berlin evoked memories of 1966, when Barb and I
traveled there together. We decided to visit Communist held East Berlin.
We entered with no delay through Checkpoint Charlie, the border entrance
that connected free and Communist Berlin. However, on the way back out,
Soviet soldiers detained me in a small room for three hours. Barb, who had
passed quickly through a separate entrance for German citizens, was left
worrying about what had happened to me.

In 1992, I was returning to Berlin for the second time, just three years after
the Wall had fallen. East and West Germany were re-united. We could
move wherever we wanted to go, without the presence of tanks, armed

soldiers, barbed wire, and the forbidding wall. The changes brought tears to my eyes.

High on my list to visit in East Berlin was the 100,000-seat track and field stadium, which was built at the order of Adolph Hitler to host the 1936 Summer Olympics. Wishing to promote his belief in racial superiority, Hitler tried to prohibit Jews and blacks from participating, but a threatened boycott caused him to relent. This set the stage for the remarkable, four gold medals achieved by Jesse Owens, a black athlete from the U.S. His success infuriated Hitler, but inspired the rest of the world. As I stood in the stadium, I pictured myself being there. Again, emotions overtook me.

The quest for an international team title for the United States

The United States team was seeded sixth. After a first round bye, we played a tough Netherlands team. The #2 singles players for each team competed first. After a hard fought battle on the red clay, Rob Cadwallader lost. That thrust me into a challenging situation. I needed to win at #1 singles and again in the doubles, or the United States would be making a quick exit from the competition. Fortunately, I won my singles match in straight sets and did the same in doubles with my partner Len Saputo.

Next, we faced Great Britain, the #4 seeded team, which had defeated the United States 3-0 the year before. This time we turned the tables and reversed the score, winning both singles and the doubles. All of the matches were straight sets. Our confidence was growing as we became more accustomed to the strategies that worked best on the slow, red clay.

Our opponent in the semifinals was #2 seeded Austria, led by defending, world, singles champion Peter Pokorny. Most observers figured that we had little chance of beating Austria and virtually no chance of a singles victory over Pokorny. However, our team got a big boost when Rob won the opening match at #2 singles. That took some of the pressure off me. If I could not beat Pokorny, we still had another chance with the doubles.

I went into the match determined to take the world champion out of his comfort zone by pressuring his backhand. On my serve, I combined a high percentage of well placed, first serves with a good mixture of serve-and-volley points. On his serve, I stood inside the baseline, took the ball on the rise, and drove hard shots to the backhand side. When I knew that I had hit an exceptionally good return, I would slip in and try to end the point with a volley. The strategy kept me close for the first set, which I lost in a tie-breaker. Nevertheless, I was confident that my game plan was correct. I was right. I took the next two sets 6-2 and 6-3.

In the finals, we faced the top seeded German team, which had waltzed to the final with easy 3-0 victories over Brazil, Canada, and Switzerland. Harald Elschenbroich, their top singles player, was smooth, consistent, and quick.

He could go for 50-ball rallies and never miss. I tried to pressure him and it worked for a while. We were tied at 3-3 in the first set, but then he won 9 out of the next 12 games.

Our chance for a world title ended with my singles loss. However, in defeat there was still reason for satisfaction. We were a sixth seeded team that finished second. We had dodged the bullet with a tough Netherlands team that had taken a 1-0 lead. Also, we had upset Austria.

Most importantly, the camaraderie between the teams was inspiring. I was touched by the efforts of the Portuguese team, which raised money from all participants to help the Commonwealth of Independent States (formerly the Soviet Union) team. Their car had broken down in Berlin, and they did not have the money to get it fixed.

My own trip home was an occasion for celebration. The Tennis and Life Camps staff eagerly welcomed me back. They had followed my adventures and then shared them with interested campers. Barb was drawn to my stories of Germany after the fall of the Communist wall. What a contrast with the Berlin that we had experienced together in 1966, the year that we were married.

U.S. Perry Cup team members, Len Saputo, Steve Wilkinson, Captain Ned Mansfield, Allan Carter, and Rob Cadwallader with Fred Perry after finishing 2nd in the 50-and-over world championship

$$47$$

DISAPPOINTMENT IN AUSTRALIA

Just one day before our opening match
against the Netherlands, calamity struck.

Competing for a world team championship in Australia

The American 1997 Austria Cup team for 55-and-over players included Joe Bachman from Westerville, Ohio, Allan Carter from New York City, Hill Griffin from Atlanta, and me. Our destination was Canberra, the capital of Australia (not to be confused with the cup's name).

After arriving in Canberra, we received a royal welcome at the United States Embassy. The newly arrived Ambassador Genta Hawkins Holmes invited us to practice tennis on the court in front of her mansion. She and her assistants joined us at courtside for pictures and conversation.

The court surface for the Austria Cup competition was sand-filled, artificial grass, a green carpet covered with sand. In the second half of the 20th century, more and more public facilities and private clubs in Australia switched from natural grass to this new surface. It preserved many of the playing characteristics of grass without the high cost of maintenance. The bounce was low, fast, and irregular. Underspin groundstrokes and slice serves worked effectively on the surface.

However, sand made the surface continually slippery. There was so much sand mixed into the courts at the host site that they looked white instead of green. I had the feeling that I was playing on the beach. Changing directions or just a quick acceleration in one direction usually caused my feet to slip.

Nevertheless, the surface did offer me an advantage over red clay specialists, which made up the majority of senior tennis players in this world competition. I liked grass courts, which were well suited for my attacking game. To play on grass, albeit artificial and exceedingly slippery, could work out well. I practiced with that attitude in preparation for the competition, while my teammates and many other competitors struggled to stay positive.

I knew that our first match was going to be tough. We were pitted against the Netherlands, the same team that we faced first in Berlin five years before. I remembered how we had lost the first match at #2 singles and stared elimination in the face. After the Netherlands, we could have faced Great Britain, just as we had done five years before. It was uncanny how similar the draw was.

However, this time Austria was seeded #1, led by Peter Pokorny, the world champion whom I had upset five years before. The Germans, who had defeated us in the finals in 1992, were seeded #2. The Australians, the only team that was accustomed to the unique slippery surface, were seeded #3. Finally, the United States was given the #4 seed, based in part on our second place finish in Berlin.

Calamity strikes

Just one day before our opening match against the Netherlands, calamity struck. I was at the net and moving wide for a forehand volley. My foot slipped abruptly as I pushed off to reach the shot. I had slipped many times before as we practiced, but this time it was different. A shot of pain went through my left knee, and I fell to the ground. With great difficulty I got back up, limped to the sideline, and sat down. My practicing for the day was ended.

I frantically sought help and advice. The team was counting on me. I tried everything that the physicians and trainers recommended—ice, heat, compression, ultrasound, etc. Nothing worked. There was no way that I could play against the Netherlands. I was frustrated and disappointed.

The United States lost 3-0. All I could do was cheer from the sidelines. Our team did go on to claim ninth place, beating Mexico, New Zealand, and Canada. Meanwhile, Austria won the world championship, depending on the undefeated record of Peter Pokorny.

When nothing improved, I made the hard decision to return home early. In Minnesota, I consulted an orthopedic surgeon. An MRI revealed a broken piece of cartilage in my knee. Surgery was necessary, and my tennis was finished for most of the year.

48

UNDER THE SHADOW OF 9-11

*A guest at our table was the son of a competitor. He
had left his job at the Trade Towers in New York
City to come and watch his father play tennis.*

2001 was my first year in the 60-and-over division. My goal was to earn the
top national ranking in both singles and doubles and to qualify for the 2002
U.S. international team that would compete for the world championship in
Austria. The 60-and-over Von Cramm Cup was named in honor of Baron
Gottfried Von Cramm, a three-time Wimbledon finalist during the mid-
1930s.

To be ranked #1 for 2001, I needed victories in at least two of the four
national tournaments. I arranged my schedule so that I could play three of
the four—the Hard Court in Palm Springs in April, the Indoor in Seattle in
August, and the Grass Court near New York City in September. My doubles
partner for all three tournaments was John Powless from Madison,
Wisconsin.

Playing the 2001 USTA 60 Hard Court Championship

The Hard Court Championship had a special component that I had never
experienced before. The 90-and-over tournament was held in conjunction
with the 60-and-over one. For the first time, I got a close-up look at one of
my lifetime goals. I wanted to compete someday in national 90-and-over
tournaments. This would be the culmination of a well-lived life where years
of a healthy lifestyle would still permit my aging body to perform well.

The enthusiasm for my 90-and-over goal was tempered a little by what I
observed. Nobody was actually running. A slow shuffle better described the
movement that I saw. Players stood in "no man's land" between the service
line and the baseline, hitting balls before they bounced with swinging volleys.
Also, this position prevented the opponent from using the drop shot, a most
effective stroke against someone who moves slowly and plays behind the
baseline.

There was another difference between the 60 and 90-and-over age divisions that puzzled me. "Why do all the 90-and-over matches have umpires, but the 60-and-over matches do not?" I asked the head referee. "There are two reasons," he said. "First, the 90-year-olds cannot see the lines very well, so they need help with their calls. Second, they have a difficult time remembering the score." I thought to myself, if this should be the place where they take their final breath, what a way to go, hitting a service ace or a forehand winner.

Staying for an extra week in California after the Gustavus varsity returned to St. Peter from their spring trip proved beneficial. I won the singles and teamed with John Powless for the doubles title.

Playing the 2001 USTA 60 Indoor Championship

My next stop on the national tournament trail was the 60-and-over Indoor Championship at the Seattle Tennis Club. The location brought back memories from 35 years before. Here my fiancée, Barb, had watched me compete for the first time—an exhibition match against Arthur Ashe Jr. Back then, there were no indoor courts. When it rained, we could wait for hours until play resumed.

In 2001, there were no rain delays, because all tournament matches were played indoors. However, we practiced outdoors, where views of Lake Washington and snow-capped Mount Rainier added to the ambiance.

Again, the singles tournament went as hoped. I won, thereby putting myself in excellent position for the #1 ranking. John Powless and I stumbled in the doubles, losing in the semifinals. We still had a shot at the top ranking, but we needed to win our final tournament of the season—the 60-and-over Grass Court Championship in September.

Playing the 60 Grass Court Championship

I flew into New York City's LaGuardia Airport late in the evening on Sunday, September 9, 2001. John Powless picked me up in his car and whisked us away to Long Island's Rockaway Hunting Club, the oldest country club in the United States and the site of the National 60-and-over Grass Court Championship. The club's original fame came from polo, fox hunting, and steeplechase racing. John and I were fortunate to have bedrooms on the second floor of the clubhouse, thereby eliminating the need for commuting. Although the hunting club name did not suggest a tennis connection, a quick view of the grounds on the following morning revealed 18 grass courts.

Tennis etiquette rules at Rockaway required all-white clothing. Color trim was permitted, but it had to be "minimal and tasteful." I suspect the clothing restriction matched the race restriction for a good share of Rockaway's long history. The formality on the courts was matched by similar restrictions in the clubhouse. The house rules read:

> After 7:00 p.m. men must wear jackets in the clubhouse plus a tie when dining—except for Friday night (or other nights) deemed casual dining. Women should follow a similar code. Jackets are not required on the back terrace during the evenings—but members should not still be in their tennis and golf attire after dark. Blue jeans, leather or rubber flip-flops, sleeveless shirts (for men) are never permitted in the clubhouse or on the back porch.

On Monday, those of us with first round byes practiced. Most of us played on grass only once a year—at the national championship. Those coming from eastern grass court clubs were at a distinct advantage, given how different the surface was from either clay or hard courts. We practiced under a brilliant blue sky in a secluded and privileged environment that seemed so protected and isolated from the world.

On Tuesday morning, John and I headed downstairs for breakfast, eagerly anticipating our first matches of the tournament later that day. The television was on at the side of the dining room broadcasting the news of the day, but we were not paying much attention to it. Instead, our focus was on friends, guests, and the competition that would start at 10 a.m. A guest at our table was the son of a competitor. He had left his job at the Trade Towers in New York City to come and watch his father play tennis.

Experiencing 9-11 up close

Then it happened. As a surreal event unfolded on the television set, we sat in stunned disbelief. A plane had crashed into one of the Trade Towers, setting it on fire. The guest at our table pulled out his cell phone and hit an automatic dial number. He was calling his best friend, who had gone to work that morning in the Trade Towers. His call did not go through. Later in the week I saw the young man again. I asked if his friend had survived. He had not.

At first we thought the plane flying into the Trade Tower was an accident, but soon it became clear that was not the case. After the second Trade Tower fell, I went outside and looked toward New York City, where I could see smoke on the horizon. Next, I went back inside and continued to follow on TV the chain of unfolding events.

While the nation was caught up in post-attack hysteria, the tournament committee had to make a quick decision. Should the tournament continue, or would this be irreverent? Some of the commuting entrants could not reach the tournament site that day. However, if the tournament were cancelled, anyone depending on a flight out of New York airports would be stranded. There were no flights available for the rest of the week.

The tournament committee decided that the tournament would continue. Matches scheduled that day were played, with allowances for commuters who could not reach the site. The time that we spent playing matches was a welcome diversion from the unrelenting attention given to the tragedy.

I finished second in both singles and doubles. My record was sufficient to guarantee me a #1 ranking in singles. In doubles, John Powless and I ended the year with only one national championship. With different doubles champions in each of the four national tournaments, the top ranking was yet to be determined.

All week long, we wondered if planes would be flying again by Sunday. John Powless had a rental car, so we were prepared to drive to Madison, Wisconsin together. However, that plan proved unnecessary. On Saturday, September 15th we received notice that my Northwest flight back to Minneapolis on Sunday morning would occur. This was the first day of flights since 9-11. We were advised to come three hours early, so at 3:30 a.m. John drove me to LaGuardia and dropped me off.

The check-in and flight home were highly unusual. The lines were long because Northwest employees did not arrive until 5 a.m. Everyone who had come three hours early stood in line for an hour and a half with nothing happening. Finally the lines started to move. I was checked in and then moved through a security process that contrasted greatly with what I had experienced less than a week before. When I climbed on the plane, I was shocked. I was one of only three passengers. The other two continued to the West Coast, while I deplaned in Minneapolis.

I had an eerie feeling when I left baggage claim and stepped out into the passenger pick-up area. It was deserted. My plane was one of the first to land since 9-11. No parking was permitted in areas close to the terminal for fear of car bombs. The whole country was in a state of high alert. It would be weeks before the airports would return to any state of normalcy.

End of my tournament career

The beginning of 2002 unfolded as anticipated. I was asked to play #1 singles on the United States 60-and-over Von Cramm Cup team. My team uniform and plane ticket to Austria arrived in the mail. However, just a few weeks before the competition began, we learned that Barb had multiple myeloma, an incurable cancer of the immune system and the blood stream. Her oncologist recommended a bone marrow transplant, but it contained life-threatening risks. I could not leave her.

I called my captain, told him the situation, announced my decision, and offered my apologies. Unbeknownst to me at the time, my tournament-playing career had come to a permanent end.

Steve Wilkinson receives Lifetime Achievement Award in
2012 at University of Iowa

Section VII

GIFTS, GRACE, AND GRATITUDE

Marcus Cicero claimed, "Gratitude is not only the greatest of virtues, but the parent of all others."

Reflecting back upon my life, I realize how many extraordinary, undeserved gifts I have been given by grace. Loving parents, a native country with countless opportunities, a wonderful wife, and safe deliverance from three life-threatening car accidents are several of those gifts. They came my way by chance, not by merit. In other words, I have been blessed by grace. Knowing this, my response is gratitude. Gifts, grace, and gratitude are what I call the three Gs, an important concept that I have stressed in my coaching and teaching.

Gratitude is the same as positive attitude, one of the Three Crowns. Both result from choices that we make every day. No matter what happens to us, we can choose to be grateful and positive.

Gratitude is expressed by smiling, touching, and saying thanks—both verbally and in writing. Tennis and Life Camps has instituted many specific actions, described in previous chapters, which promote the practice of gratitude. I have done the same for my sport ethics classes. For example, I required all students to write letters to their parents and an inspirational coach or teacher. The writing needed to express their appreciation for specific actions that had impacted them.

However, choosing gratitude can be difficult when the people around us have more than we do, or when we have lost what we used to have. These comparisons can put us into a thought process that produces resentment and negativity. Yet, no matter what the situation, gratitude and positivity are possible responses.

Gratitude is an appreciative response to gifts or actions from others. However, sometimes we receive unwanted gifts, which leave us feeling indebted but not grateful. Indebtedness can produce resentment and bitterness, negative emotions that are never associated with gratitude.

Behind any genuine, well-intentioned gift, wanted or unwanted, tasteful or tasteless, is a giver, who wishes to please us. It is the giver that we honor with gratitude—even someone that we may not like. We have the choice to be grateful. We can be sensitive to the feelings of the giver, even if the situation demands that we return the gift.

The life of gratitude is a fulfilling and rewarding one. The following chapters highlight some of the people for whom I am deeply grateful.

Steve and Barb enjoy a hike together on the Olympic Peninsula in April 1966

49

MOUNTAINTOP LOVE STORY

Barb and her family arrived safely in the port city of Danzig,
where her grandparents, aunts, uncles, and cousins lived.
For the next two months, they crowded into a bunker,
hoping to avoid the frequent air attacks. The menacing
behavior of the advancing Russian army, already near
Danzig, instilled even more fear. By March, the threat of
death had become too great. Barb's mother decided they would
try to escape by boat, even though that also posed a big risk.

January 15, 1966, is a day that we will never forget. Nearly 50 years later, Barb and I continue to celebrate that day each year. It marks a most unlikely, mountaintop encounter. The setting was the Mount Baker Ski Area, a piece of heaven in the northern Cascade Mountains, a few miles from the Washington-British Columbia international border.

How unlikely it was that I should meet Barb

Why unlikely for me? One year before, I was a graduate student in an MBA program at the University of Iowa. I had never been to the state of Washington or known that Mount Baker existed.

I ended up in Washington because Dr. Harvey Bunke offered me a job at Western Washington State in Bellingham, Washington. He was leaving the University of Iowa to become president there.

But what got me to the ski slope? I had never gone skiing, did not own any skiing attire, and had no chains for my car—a prerequisite for the final miles of a treacherous, snow covered, mountain road that wound its way up to the ski area. Two friends convinced me to go. Any reservations I had melted away with their encouragement. Skis and chains for the car could be rented. Ski outfits were not necessary. I knew from hikes in the fall how beautiful the mountains were. "But it was nothing," my friends assured me, "compared to the breathtaking scenery in the winter." I was hooked and eager to give it a try.

How unlikely it was that Barb would be on Mt. Baker

Why unlikely for Barb? As a child she narrowly escaped death by Russian soldiers, advancing through West Prussia at the end of the Second World War. The pillaging, raping, and murdering of all civilians (women, children and old people included) was horrific. In January of 1945, Barb, her mother, and two brothers crowded onto one of the last trains leaving her home in Marienburg. Three days later, a bomb destroyed their home and everything they owned, except for what they had carried with them in small suitcases.

Barb and her family arrived safely in the port city of Danzig, where her grandparents, aunts, uncles, and cousins lived. For the next two months, they crowded into a bunker, hoping to avoid the frequent air attacks. The menacing behavior of the advancing Russian army, already near Danzig, instilled even more fear. By March, the threat of death had become too great. Barb's mother decided they would try to escape by boat, even though that also posed a big risk. Only two months before, a Russian submarine had sunk the *Wilhelm Gustloff* refugee ship, sending 9,000 people, half of them children, to a watery grave.

Thousands of refugees gathered at the port on March 25th, hoping to escape to Denmark on the *Mars-Bremen* refugee ship. Five thousand people were allowed on board. Barb, her mother, and two brothers were among the last to make it, but her grandmother, aunt, and cousin, standing next to them in line, did not.

Between January and May, many refugee boats were sunk with thousands of people aboard each one. Barb's mother did not think they would survive. She stood watching over her children throughout the night, hoping that the overhead flares would not reveal their location to the Russians. They sailed undetected to Copenhagen, where Barb, her mother, and two brothers were placed in a detention center behind barbed wire. For two years after the Second World War ended, they lived crowded together in a barrack with many other people, severely malnourished and threatened by disease.

However, Barb and her family survived. In 1947, they were reunited with Barb's father, a German soldier who had been hospitalized with war injuries. They all started a new life together in West Germany. A 1964 visit to Germany by a Bellingham dentist prompted an offer to Barb for employment in his office. In January of 1965, Barb arrived in Washington. One year later, on January 15, 1966, she decided to go skiing at the Mount Baker Ski Area with her roommate.

How an unlikely encounter led to marriage

For most of the day, Barb and I remained unaware of each other. After I arrived, my two friends helped me find appropriate skis to rent and then gave me some pointers on how to ski. However, hanging around with me on the beginner slopes got boring for them. Soon, they went off together on the steep, black diamond runs, leaving me alone for the rest of the day.

That was fine with me. I was not going to risk my life on more difficult slopes. I did not mind being alone as I practiced new skills. The scenery was breathtaking. The sun shone brightly, the sky was a brilliant blue, and sparkling snow adorned the branches of the pine trees—a true winter wonderland.

Near the end of the skiing day, about 4 p.m. it happened. I saw this striking, young woman with beautiful red cheeks. She was alone, practicing elementary skiing techniques. Perhaps it was the magic of the setting or the fact that I had been alone most of the day, but I mustered up the courage to approach her and start a conversation. She responded, and we immediately connected. I learned she was from Germany but working as a dental assistant in Bellingham. What a coincidence, since the ski area drew skiers from Canada and the whole surrounding region.

Twenty minutes after we met, the ski lifts were closing for the day. My friends returned, and it was time to go home. Barb gave me her phone number. I suggested we might get together again, sometime in the next few weeks. However, I could not wait. I called her the next day, and we met that evening. I remained as infatuated as I was the day before.

Our romance developed quickly, in part, because we realized we did not have much time. Barb had planned to return to Germany in May, and I was going back to the University of Iowa in September to begin work on my Ph.D. program. I knew that I would not have time for a long distance relationship. It was then or never.

We were engaged by April and married in Hamburg, Germany. Actually, we were married twice—once in a civil ceremony on August 19th and again in a church service on August 20th. In Germany the civil ceremony is the official one, and the church service is optional. However, we have always regarded August 20th as our wedding day. Barb looked radiant in the gorgeous wedding dress that she wore for the church service. It was a special day, celebrated with many of her relatives and friends. I wish that my family could have been there, but they lacked money, flying experience, and confidence with the language. As for me, I memorized my lines and made a lifetime commitment, even though I understood very little of the German that was spoken in the service.

After the wedding, we took a short walk along narrow, cobblestone streets, leading up to a restaurant in a castle-like building that overlooked the Elbe

Steve and Barb celebrate their wedding day
on August 20, 1966

River. At the festive dinner that followed, Barb's parents toasted us and made me feel welcome, a young man they had met only 10 days before and someone who was spiriting away their only daughter to a distant land, forever.

After a honeymoon that took us through Austria, Switzerland, and Italy, we flew back to Bellingham. We said goodbye to our Washington friends, loaded all of our possessions into a small Volkswagen bug, and headed across the country to Sioux City, Iowa, for a post wedding reception with my parents. The next day, we traveled on to Iowa City for my Ph.D. program and Barb's undergraduate education.

Trying to understand what caused our good fortunes

What a coincidence. What timing. What luck. A young man from Iowa and a young woman from Germany happened to cross paths on January 15, 1966, at the Mount Baker Ski Area. This mountain top experience altered the course of our lives, setting the stage for 47 years of marriage (and still counting), two wonderful daughters, their caring husbands, and four precious grandchildren.

To what do we attribute our good fortunes? Why did Barb survive the Second World War when so many others from West Prussia did not? Why did a conversation with my economics professor lead to a job offer? Why did I decide to go skiing that particular day, something I had never done before, rather than do something else? What if I had not noticed Barb or had lacked the confidence to initiate a conversation? The smallest, apparently insignificant decisions by others or me could have drastically affected the course of our lives. Chance, luck, and accident played undeniable roles.

How Fromm's views on love prepared us for marriage

While fortune affects our lives, there are many things over which we do have control. Figuring this out in the context of potential marriage relationships is always a challenge for young people. That was certainly true for me. I went through four years of college, two years of graduate school, and a half-year of full time teaching without a romantic relationship where I spoke those magic words, "I love you."

Nevertheless, I was learning much about love—what it was and what it was not, what I could control and what I could not. *The Art of Loving* by Erich Fromm, a book that I encountered in my undergraduate years, offered wonderful counsel. I learned that mature love affirms the self-sufficient identity of both lovers as individuals. They do not need each other in order to make either of their lives complete. A person in a mature relationship would not say, "I can't live without you," or "I need you to make my life complete." These quotes suggest addiction. Instead, mature lovers give to each other freely without the need for repayment. It is the commitment to love and serve each other for a lifetime that makes marriage special.

Fromm's view of love reassured me. Every aspect of mature love centered on things within my control. The decisions to love, sacrifice, serve and make a commitment were my choices. If I did not meet a woman to whom I wanted to be committed, that was fine. I did not need a wife. On the other hand, if I did meet someone with whom I wished to share my life, but she was not interested in doing the same with me, that was fine as well.

In any potential marriage relationship, the first important step is establishing intimacy. This means getting to know each other in a close and familiar way. The process begins with conversations—exchanging thoughts, ideas, opinions, and experiences. Next, it entails doing things together—sharing common experiences that both find fulfilling. Out of conversations and shared experiences grow the willingness to share emotions—to become vulnerable and to experience the other person's capacity for compassion.

None of these steps require sexual intimacy. In fact, sex can get in the way of true intimacy, preventing a couple from truly getting to know each other. Sex can be an addiction, as derailing as alcohol and drug abuse. The rush of pleasure that sex produces can cloud the mind to true intimacy, as powerfully as drunkenness. If half of a couple desperately needs the other, this is addiction, not true intimacy or mature love.

When some hear the story of how Barb and I met and how quickly we got married, they think "love at first sight." There is no such thing. Yes, there is attraction at first sight, but that is not love. Mature love requires intimacy, which begins with conversations, shared experiences, and emotional vulnerability.

Our courtship did progress quickly. Our personal stories intrigued each other. We knew ourselves—our beliefs and priorities. Also, my experience in discussing values and teaching ethics helped us cut through more superficial topics and get to issues that really mattered for each of us. We saw each other most evenings, and much of the time we read and studied together. I was trying to stay one day ahead of my honors discussion groups in a humanities course that was integrating 10 different academic disciplines. Talking with Barb, someone who knew music and literature, both helped me and deepened our relationship. Three months after we met, we were engaged.

Why we still celebrate a mountaintop love story

Barb and I are grateful for so many blessings. How fortunate that Barb survived her war torn childhood, that I received a teaching position at Western Washington State, that we both decided to go skiing on January 15, 1966, and that I happened to notice her near the end of the day. That was all luck.

However, the loving relationship that developed between the two of us after we met, the decision to marry after having known each other for only three months, the wedding only seven months after we met, and 47 years of a fulfilling marriage in which we have remained committed to each other—cannot be attributed to luck. We each knew that we had found someone to whom we wished to make a life commitment. We did not anticipate perpetual bliss. We knew that we were committing "for better, for worse, for richer, for poorer, in sickness and in health, until death do us part."

I realize divorce can sometimes be the right decision. No person controls the changing actions and commitments of one's spouse. However, with Barb I made an informed choice based on her willingness to commit, her character, and her history of making and keeping commitments. Although I was initially attracted to her beauty, her personal story, her intellect, her talents, and our mutual interests, these were not the reasons I decided to marry her. I married Barb because I trusted her capacity to make and keep the marriage vows. That is one of the important reasons that we can look back to January 15, 1966, and still celebrate a mountain top love story.

50

A TALE OF TWO DAUGHTERS

Watching our daughters using their professional skills to
advance the nonprofit TLC mission is a dream come true.

"I think I can, I think I can." This mantra is repeated frequently in the
classic children's book *The Little Engine That Could*. Written in 1930 by
Watty Piper, the illustrated story describes a frustrating situation. An engine
pulling a train filled with toys and good food for boys and girls on the other
side of the mountain had broken down. Several other engines were
approached for assistance, but each one refused. When all hope seemed lost,
a little blue engine came upon the crippled train. Would she help? The little
blue engine cautiously agreed, but would she be able to pull the heavy load up
the mountain? When the going was tough, she kept repeating, "I think I can,
I think I can." Sure enough, the little blue engine succeeded, much to the joy
of all the children.

As a small child, I asked my mother to read that story to me, over and over
again. It brought shivers to my spine and laid the groundwork for my
philosophy of life, one based on optimism and hard work. When our
daughters, Stephanie and Deb, asked for stories at bedtime, *The Little Engine
That Could* was frequently chosen. Another generation in our family was
raised with a surprisingly simple and straightforward message—with a
positive attitude and full effort directed toward serving others, all is possible.

Stephanie and Deb heard a similar story when they started attending Tennis
and Life Camps (TLC) three or four times each summer. The camp
philosophy emphasized the Three Crowns (positive attitude, full effort, and
good sportsmanship), which was encapsulated in the life of Karen Gibbs.
Both the little engine and Karen faced great challenges with optimism, hard
work, and a strong sense of commitment to others.

Deb even became so familiar with my motivational talks and yoga meditation
sessions that she could mimic them (with humorous changes added), much to
the amusement of camper friends. Camp songs, created and led by Neal
Hagberg, were embedded in the psyches of both daughters, ready to burst

forth from their lips at almost any moment. Their reputations as TLC "groupies" were well deserved.

They formed lasting friendships with other campers—so strong that Deb wanted to leave small-town St. Peter, live with a friend, and attend Breck School in Minneapolis. Also, both Stephanie and Deb admired the instructors as role models. Continued contact with them all summer, and even year-around with some of the instructors on the Gustavus tennis teams, proved to be motivational. They were like older brothers or sisters.

Daughters Stephanie and Deb after a hitting session with Dad in 1982

As expected, TLC was their best source of tennis knowledge. I was grateful I could be their tennis opponent or partner more than their instructor. Letting others do the teaching is the safe approach for parents, whose primary responsibility is being cheerleaders. When I played with our daughters, our goal was usually a simple one. How many times could we keep the ball going without a miss? My ability to put the ball back to them in a comfortable spot, no matter where they might hit the ball, made our games a fun challenge for both of us.

Our girls played only a few summer tournaments and never became regionally ranked, but they played well enough to have important roles on the St. Peter High School team and to even qualify for the state tournament. Sometimes they felt conflicted, when the techniques and strategies of their high school coach did not match what they had learned at TLC. When they came to me with their concerns, I encouraged them to listen respectfully and to NOT say, "But I learned something different at TLC." However, when they competed, I encouraged them to use what worked best for them.

Daughters Deb and Stephanie after a high school competition in 1986

Perhaps, more important than what they gained attending TLC was what they learned from working at camp. During June, July, and the first half of August, Barb and I were fully engaged. By necessity, Stephanie and Deb were as well, even when they were quite young. We were all part of a family business. This did not seem strange to Barb, who had grown up in a small, post-war German bakery business run by her parents. She and her brothers needed to help if their business were to succeed. Out of such environments come many uniquely qualified and successful youth, grounded in positive values and a work ethic that prepares them for success in an adult world.

This was certainly true for Barb. At TLC she often worked past midnight, carrying out her responsibilities as business and office manager, supervisor of overnight counseling, camp nurse, pro shop and retailing director, dining service and custodial liaison, and parental advisor/comforter. She modeled a work ethic that had a powerful effect on our daughters.

More importantly, Barb encouraged Stephanie and Deb to help. She found jobs that they could do and enjoy, even before they were 10 years old. How empowering it was for them to know that they were contributing to the success of a family business. Our daughters helped fold clothing, check campers in, prepare the night refreshments, run the cash register, sell merchandise, put up signs, stuff and stamp envelopes, and a variety of other tasks. They discovered first hand that work was fun, and that they were skilled and competent.

Reaching their high school years, Stephanie and Deb became tennis teachers in the local National Junior Tennis League program, which served over 200 youth in the St. Peter community. Deb even served as a TLC dorm counselor in her junior and senior years, a responsibility normally restricted to college students.

During their college summers, both Stephanie and Deb were tennis instructors at TLC. They previously had taught youth and a few adult lessons, but TLC gave them the opportunity to teach adults frequently. Being in this position helped their confidence immensely. After graduation, Stephanie became an athletic club desk supervisor and Deb an elementary school teacher.

Deb, Stephanie, Steve, and Barb Wilkinson in 2012

These positions led to future jobs and more demanding responsibilities. Stephanie became an event planner at Carlson Companies; next, at the Minneapolis Chamber of Commerce; and later, at Dain Rauscher Wessels, an equity capital markets firm. When the Royal Bank of Canada (RBC) acquired Dain Rauscher Wessels, other members of Stephanie's department were transferred to New York, London, and Toronto. Stephanie was the only one left in Minneapolis. Her ability to work with executives, organizational skills, attention to detail, and a formidable work ethic are attributes that she credits to growing up in a TLC work environment. Now, she travels around the world coordinating conferences and special events.

Deb, on the other hand, moved from elementary teaching to United Health Group. First, she developed wellness products to service corporate customers. Then she moved into operations, hiring and managing health coaches who helped people lose weight, quit smoking, and reduce stress. This led to new responsibilities. Starting in 2011, she became the Chief of Operations officer in a research and innovations department that collaborates with leading universities. The outcome is scalable and evidence based health services, which can be delivered nationwide with improved health outcomes at more affordable costs.

Deb credits TLC for showing her how to take best practices and turn them into repeatable lessons that anyone with base skills and a love for teaching can implement. She marvels at the TLC staff-training program, which facilitates relatively inexperienced teachers to deliver polished lessons. Also, she cites TLC as an example of operational discipline, effective business practices, and positive leadership—important characteristics for the company in which she now leads.

2010 TLC family campers sing "Happy Birthday" to Jane Arnoldt, our granddaughters' cousin

Both Stephanie and Deb have embraced our decision to make TLC a nonprofit. They now serve on the TLC Board of Advisors, which includes representatives from every tennis nonprofit group in the upper Midwest. The potential of this alliance for growing tennis and creating opportunities for youth and adults is impressive. Watching our daughters use their professional skills to advance the nonprofit TLC mission is a dream come true.

Our grandson, Stephen, eagerly anticipates time with 2013 TLC instructor Amrik Donkena

Most importantly, Stephanie and Deb have grown into adulthood with a continued love for TLC and an eagerness to share it with their children. We admire the activities of our grandchildren—Caroline, Eloise, Stephen, and Audrey—but even more, the positive attitudes that they bring to their schooling, athletic competition, and life. They have attended TLC, and each summer they eagerly anticipate returning—not so much because they are dedicated tennis players, but more because they are attracted to the vibrant instructors, encouraging teaching, and life lessons. As our grandchildren compete in other sports at home, we approve their good sportsmanship and pursuit of excellence while they remain indifferent to winning or losing.

51

ARTHUR ASHE JR.'S BRAVERY

I invited Arthur to be our featured speaker at the 1993 Tennis and Life Clinic. Arthur delayed accepting my offer because of his declining health. When "Sports Illustrated" named him Sportsman of the Year in early December, I figured there was no way that he would come. Nevertheless, Arthur called me on December 15 and said he would accept my invitation.

Arthur Ashe Jr. put my playing career in perspective. In 1965, he taught me that challenging opponents on their line calls was not the right approach. Instead, my goal was to create mutual trust and respect. Arthur's perspective kept playing fun and helped me focus on the things within my control.

In 1992, Arthur's example again proved influential. He knew at that time that his days were numbered. Arthur had contracted AIDS from a tainted blood transfusion. Even as his physical stamina decreased, he continued to reach out and serve.

I invited Arthur to be our featured speaker at the 1993 Tennis and Life Clinic. We had designated racial minority participation in tennis and AIDS relief as our charitable priorities. Arthur delayed accepting my offer because of his declining health. When *Sports Illustrated* named him Sportsman of the Year in early December, I figured there was no way that he would come. This new honor brought increased demands on his time for public appearances. Nevertheless, Arthur called me on December 15 and said he would accept my invitation. He believed so strongly in the causes that the TLC Clinic was promoting.

However, in January 1993, Arthur caught pneumonia, and his physical condition declined rapidly. His memoir, *Days of Grace*, was nearing completion. Arthur knew that he was going to die soon. He remembered how much he missed his mother, who had died when he was only six. Instead of focusing on his imminent death, Arthur wrote a letter that offered to his six-year-old daughter Camera a blueprint for life's most difficult decisions. That letter became the last chapter of his book, and it ended with the following words of encouragement. "Camera, whenever you feel sick at heart and weary of life, or when you stumble and fall and don't know if you can get up again, think of me. I will be watching and smiling and cheering you on." (*Days of Grace*, pp. 341-342)

Arthur was not consumed by the fear of death as he experienced his final years and days. Instead, there was a confidence residing within him that freed him to act. He attributed this security to God. Arthur did not anticipate a pleasant end. He wrote, "I may linger, or I may die; I may suffer acutely... Nevertheless, God is sufficient: '"I shall not be overcome; God is with me." (*Days of Grace*, p. 327)

Arthur admired Vice-President Hubert Humphrey, who bravely faced death by cancer. Ashe wrote, "In his splendid career as a liberal he taught us how to live...In his magnificent battle with cancer he later taught us how to die." (*Days of Grace*, p. 327)

Arthur wondered if he would be able to approach death with the same dignity as Humphrey. Arthur did emulate Humphrey's example. Similarly, I hope to act as bravely as both men when my time comes.

Wilkinson welcomes Ashe to the 1984 Tennis and Life Clinic, a spring workshop for coaches, players, and the general public. This yearly event attracted more than 1,000 participants annually, was co-sponsored by the Northern Tennis Association, and continued through 1997.

52

BILLIE JEAN KING LEADS GENDER EQUITY

*Professional sports are segregated, except for tennis.
The salaries, audiences, and media attention for
professional women athletes pale in comparison to
men, except at the Grand Slam tennis tournaments.*

At the 2011 Wimbledon tournament, I watched a first round mixed doubles match between Eric Butorac/Olga Govortsova and Mike Bryan/Samantha Stosur. Mike was ranked #1 in men's doubles, and Samantha was the U.S. Open singles champion that year. Nevertheless, Eric and Olga won 6-4, 3-6, 6-4, much to the surprise of the ESPN television commentators.

In this match and Eric/Olga's next two, I was struck by the doubles' skills of all four players. Neither man was holding back or trying to be "nice" to the opposing woman. Prize money and the potential honor of a Grand Slam title motivated each player.

Mixed doubles is played at the four Grand Slam tennis tournaments, where men and women professionals receive equal prize money, audiences, and media attention. This is unique in the professional sporting world. Nowhere else do men and women compete against each other and receive equal compensation. Professional tennis leads the sporting world in gender equality, and mixed doubles is the crown jewel.

As I noted earlier, the torchbearer for gender equality in tennis has been Billie Jean King. She was the primary force behind equal prize money for men and women at the Grand Slam events. Also, she was the founder of World Team Tennis (WTT), a professional summer tennis league that features coed team competition between American cities. The format involves women's singles and doubles, men's singles and doubles, and mixed doubles. Each match is one set. The games won in each set contribute points to their team's total.

Other sports, where both men and women play professionally, could follow suit. Basketball, volleyball, golf, hockey, soccer, cricket, etc. could create innovative formats where men and women compete together for equal pay.

As of 2014, professional sports are gender segregated, except for tennis. The salaries, audiences, and media attention for professional women athletes pale in comparison to men, *except* at the Grand Slam tennis tournaments. Thanks to Billie Jean King, the prize money is equal. Also, through 36 years of World Team Tennis leadership, she has offered another blue print for gender equality.

More than anyone else, Billie Jean King has advanced Title IX goals and created the opportunity for women to compete in sports. Her Women's Sport Foundation, founded in 1974, has contributed millions of dollars "to advance the lives of girls and women through sports and physical activity." *Life* magazine named Billie Jean one of the 100 most important Americans of the 20th century. The world is deeply indebted to this courageous and innovative leader.

Billie Jean King came to Minneapolis in 1991 to honor Steve, Barb, and other Northern Tennis Association award winners

53

GIFT OF WIMBLEDON

The gift of Wimbledon was a manifestation of Eric Butorac's character. Eric has climbed higher in the pro tennis ranks than any previous student of mine. His accomplishments are outstanding, yet he proceeds with humility and thankfulness.

Will you coach me at Wimbledon?

In February of 2011, Eric Butorac called and asked, "Will you come to Wimbledon this year and be my coach? I want you to scout opponents and to offer tactical advice." I deferred, but let him know that I was flattered by his offer. I assured Eric that I would get back to him after I talked to Barb. When I told her about his offer, she grew excited and exclaimed, "Let's go!"

My official coaching relationship with Eric began in 2001, when he transferred from Ball State University to Gustavus for his last three years of college. However, my influence on Eric predated that. His father, Tim, was a collegiate player under me from 1971 until 1975. Many tennis and life lessons got passed on as Tim trained his eldest son.

After Eric graduated in 2003, I continued to help him from St. Peter, Minnesota. We talked every week or two by phone. When I could view his matches on television or by tape, I would offer both tactical and mechanical suggestions.

More frequently, my input centered on mental issues. For example, Eric used to worry about losing sets after being up a break. "It has happened six out of the last eight sets," he lamented. I advised him to stop keeping track of negative statistics. It creates a self-fulfilling prophecy. He did stop, and the problem soon disappeared. I reminded him of the high percentage of Association of Tennis Professionals (ATP) pro tournament finals that he had won. That was a statistic worth remembering.

Sometimes, my advice was personal. For example, he met his future wife by chance on a plane flight. They immediately bonded. "Can I trust my instinct?" Eric wondered. "Should I break off my relationship with someone

I have dated for two years and whom my family adores?" I pointed out that my chance meeting with a beautiful European woman on a ski slope near Mount Baker in Washington had worked out rather well. No one introduced us. We just started talking, and seven months later, we were married. Forty-eight years later we have shared a wonderful life together. "Yes, Eric, you need to follow your instinct."

Wimbledon, what an experience!

Finally the big day arrived. Barb and I were headed to Wimbledon, encouraged by well-wishers. We traveled with Tim and Jan Butorac, Eric's parents, and stayed with them in a private home near the Wimbledon grounds. Each day we walked to the courts and then back to our house via Wimbledon village.

The grounds at Wimbledon were larger than I expected, with numerous gates of entry. But only Gate 14 allowed admittance for coaches and players' guests. We felt privileged as gate keepers scanned our badges and let us straight in, while others waited patiently in line, some since the night before, when they queued up for a ground pass.

Once inside the grounds, we were scanned again and again as we moved into special areas reserved for players, coaches, and their guests. It was common to have Roger Federer, Andy Murray, or other top players sitting at the table next to us in a restaurant area. While we were tempted to introduce ourselves, take pictures, or act enamored by their presence, we knew we should give them personal space. Elsewhere, in areas open to the public, the top stars had adoring hoards pestering them for autographs and pictures.

We loved the players' restaurant that overlooked Show Court #3. From the open-air dining area, we could watch the action on 10 different courts. What a view—beautiful green grass with players dressed in white.

With my coach's badge, I could go virtually anywhere except for Centre Court. If Eric had played there—a privilege generally reserved for singles players and doubles finalists—I would have received a ticket. Otherwise, I would have needed to use the one ticket that each player was given daily. However, even that was not really a ticket. There were approximately 100 seats reserved for players or their guests, but more than twice that number of tickets issued. If I had wanted a seat for a popular match, I would have needed stand in line for hours. After I had a seat I could not have left—even for a short bathroom break. It would be safe to say that access to Centre Court was "bladder" controlled. I think the British loved the idea of everyone having the chance to "queue up" and stand in line.

Instead, I could watch Centre Court on the large screen in front of Henman Hill, the monitors in the restaurants, or the monitors in the locker room areas. As a coach I could accompany Eric everywhere. In the locker room, the screen could be adjusted so that we could watch any court we chose. But the best aspect of the coach's badge was watching Eric interact respectfully with other players and coaches. I could see why he was so popular and why he had been chosen to serve on the ATP Player Council.

Also, I liked going with Eric to the practice courts, where no spectators were allowed, and to the workout room, where Eric would use the exercise equipment, the weights, and the stretching mats. I joined him, riding a stationary bike for a half hour, followed by pushups, crunches, and yoga stretching. Eric later shared the following story with me:

> When you were working out in the corner of the gym one day (doing push-ups), Dmitry Tursunov (a fairly out-spoken player) turned to me and said, "Who is that old guy?" as he pointed in your direction. I said proudly, "That is my coach." As you continued to crank out push-ups, he looked back to me and said with a half-smile. "Pretty good."

These June days in London were the longest of the year. The sun rose at 5 a.m. and set at 10 p.m. Often it rained in the afternoon but not in the morning. Matches started at noon and at 1 p.m. on Centre Court. I wondered why the Wimbledon planners did not take advantage of the morning weather. Would they change? Not a chance.

Tradition is a powerful force at Wimbledon. No matches are played on the middle Sunday in this two-week event, while other tournaments use Sunday as a featured day. All the players dress in white, while other tournaments permit colored clothing. The officials wear long sleeves and distinguished sports jackets. Many of the British spectators come dressed formally. Strict protocol is enforced. By contrast, at the Australian Open many spectators dress in outlandish garb, use body paint, and do loud, choreographed cheers that end just before one of the players serves. That would never be allowed at Wimbledon.

I was inspired and excited to share by daily email these observations of Wimbledon with tennis-loving friends back home. Many told me later that they had the feeling of being there.

The gift of Wimbledon has great meaning for us

The gift of Wimbledon gave us a "once in a lifetime" trip to the tennis Mecca. Wimbledon is recognized as THE tennis event, older and more special than the other three Grand Slams. Major Walter Wingfield invented lawn tennis in February of 1874. Wimbledon Club officials modernized the game with changes in court shape and rules in 1877, just in time for the first Wimbledon tournament.

Wimbledon is still played on grass. Participants only wear traditional white. Proper etiquette and sportsmanship seem to matter more there than elsewhere on the tennis circuit. My emphasis on sportsmanship and trusting one's opponent resonates with Wimbledon priorities. Therefore, our trip there was a pilgrimage to my tennis roots.

Finally, the gift of Wimbledon was a manifestation of Eric's character. Eric has climbed higher in the pro tennis ranks than any previous student of mine. His accomplishments are outstanding, yet he proceeds with humility and thankfulness, serving all of his fellow professionals through his work on the ATP Council and giving back to the tennis public through his support of many fundraising events.

Barb Wilkinson, Gordon Reid, Steve Wilkinson, Eric Butorac, Jean-Julien Roger, Marcia and Mike Busse enjoy a moment together after Butorac-Rojer's 2nd round victory at the 2011 Wimbledon tournament

54

RETIREMENT WITH GRATITUDE

*Tommy Valentini is the new men's tennis coach and
professor of sport ethics. Neal Hagberg heads the Tennis
and Life Camps (TLC) program and Dan McLaughlin
serves as his assistant. Their commitments to servant
leadership are positively impacting many lives.*

Gratitude for Gustavus

At my retirement reception in 2009, I thanked many people. How fortunate
I was to be hired by Gustavus. A 3-2 decision by the religion department
gave me the job. If one more faculty member had voted for the other world
religions candidate, my life path could have been very different.

Now, Tommy Valentini is the new men's tennis coach and professor of sport
ethics. Neal Hagberg heads the TLC program, and Dan McLaughlin serves
as his assistant. Their commitments to servant leadership are positively
impacting many lives.

Tommy Valentini, my coaching successor

My 2002 team had six All-Americans (Nick Crossley, Josh Heiden, Daryn
Collins, Michael Hom, Eric Butorac, and Kevin Whipple), but the team's
real leader was Tommy Valentini, a Rhodes scholar finalist and an Arthur
Ashe Jr. Award recipient.

At the end of practice each day, the guys would gather in a team circle.
Frequently, Tommy spoke up. "You know, guys, how blessed we are to have
each other…to have a place like this in which to practice and to have the
opportunities that we have been given."

As a child Tommy had grown up coming to Tennis and Life Camps
(TLC). It became his family when he himself felt he needed it most. He
immersed himself in the TLC message and lived what he called "the dream."
After his freshman year in college, he seamlessly transitioned into a TLC
instructor who loved the campers, and they loved him.

Following graduation, Tommy spent two years as assistant women's tennis coach at the University of Nebraska and the next two years working on his master's degree in ethics at Emory University's Candler School of Theology. He was drawn to sport ethics, a love that he had discovered in an undergraduate course that I taught.

Tommy Valentini

After graduating from Emory in the spring of 2006, Tommy decided to enroll in a Ph.D. program in sport ethics at the University of Minnesota. His advisor would be Dr. Nicole LaVoi, a national authority on moral behavior in youth sports and a former national tennis champion for Gustavus. In the fall of 2006, Tommy began his Ph.D. studies and simultaneously became my assistant coach.

As I observed the excellence and compassion with which he taught and coached, our futures became clearer. Tommy would succeed me as head tennis coach and teach sport ethics. With this in mind, Barb and I started to endow a sport ethics/men's tennis coach position at Gustavus. The plan was set.

Dan McLaughlin, TLC pedagogical leader

Dan McLaughlin came to TLC in 1991 with a strong recommendation from Dr. Joe Walsh, sport psychologist at Minnesota State University-Mankato. Dan was working on his master's degree in sports psychology. By 1993, he was leading the TLC sports psychology sessions that I had traditionally taught.

Dan McLaughlin

In 1995, after a year of doctoral work in sports psychology at the University of California-Berkeley, Dan went to the University of North Carolina-Greensboro for a Ph.D. program in physical education pedagogy. From August 1999 to May 2006, he taught at Idlewild Elementary School in Charlotte, North Carolina, refined his theories of teaching and learning, and completed his Ph.D.

In 2006, Dan accepted a faculty position at Wingate University near Charlotte, North Carolina, teaching physical education students how to teach. In 2013, the university awarded him the Debra M. O'Neal Excellence in Teaching Award.

Dan's expertise in teaching pedagogy has made a monumental impact on the TLC teaching mission. Clearly written training manuals, intensive pre-camp training programs, supervisory assistance, and frequent professional development sessions led by Dan have molded each summer's staff into a unified team. Instructional consistency is critical—and very difficult to achieve as 36 teachers interact with each individual camper. Dan achieves it.

The excitement for teaching that Dan fosters in the staff is remarkable. They exude energy, happiness, optimism, gratitude, and commitment to service. This, in turn, helps adult and youth campers be transformed by the camp experience.

A ritual that Dan developed illustrates his impact on the staff members. At the beginning of every camp, they gather in a circle and begin to clap. Dan cuts off the clapping and then invites a few of the staff into the middle. Dan presents each with a humorous gift that symbolizes their importance. Smiles and laughter abound as the honored staff members are asked to go down on one knee, and the rest of the staff extend their arms forward above their heads. A group cheer follows, and then an energized staff moves out to meet the new campers. Every staff member receives Dan's special treatment on some occasion in the summer.

Dan's ability to command excellence and accountability from the staff in a non-intimidating manner is a rare gift. His non-judgmental approach to everyone explains why. And it embodies the spirit of TLC.

Neal Hagberg, our TLC successor

In 1981, four years after TLC began, we recognized our lack of an important component that could produce energy and draw the participants together. Also, the missing ingredient could cause them to pause, listen, reflect, and retain what they had heard. That component was music.

Our search for someone to fill this void ended when we met Neal Hagberg, the starting quarterback on the varsity football team and a Rhodes scholarship finalist. He was a singer/song writer, who later married Leandra Peak. They formed the Neal & Leandra duo and toured the United States, playing in venues that ranged from coffeehouses to Carnegie Hall.

Even though school obligations and a music career pulled Neal away from TLC for two separate summers, he always came back, because he believed in the life-changing influence that TLC was making on campers, staff, and himself.

He led drills, taught tennis, shared morning reflections, and used personal stories and music as a way to introduce thought-provoking concepts that stressed compassion and meaningful relationships. His song "Serenity" reinforced the emphasis that TLC put on the Serenity Prayer. Neal's presence put him at the center of every important aspect of TLC.

Neal Hagberg

However, Neal's gratitude trumped everything else. He continually thanked the staff and created opportunities in staff meetings for them to thank each other. At the end of each summer, he wrote thank you notes to every member of the 39-person staff, some as haiku poems, some as limericks, some as essays. During camp, he always thanked the campers and taught them how to do the same for others.

In 2010, Barb and I donated TLC to Gustavus with the hope that Neal would be the new director. This came to pass. The new nonprofit status allowed TLC to seek donations on behalf of youth who could not afford camp, another of Neal's passions. This marked the beginning of a new era for TLC.

Section VIII

WHAT I BELIEVE

*My faith springs naturally from my understanding of
God as Divine Love, a universal force that unites and
unconditionally accepts all people. There is nothing
that anyone must do to earn this acceptance.*

Since 1965, I have taught religion and ethics to college age students. My
areas of special interest have been world religions, religion and culture, and
sport ethics. My students have been Christian, Jewish, Muslim, Buddhist,
Hindu, Baha'i, humanist, agnostic, and atheist.

In each class I taught, I first pushed my students to describe their own faiths.
What did they believe? What made their lives truly count? For what
principles or causes would they risk their lives? How would they like to be
remembered?

Next, I moved my students from self-analysis to understanding other faith
positions empathetically. I wanted my students to "walk a mile in their
shoes." Finally, I encouraged comparison and dialogue. On what points did
my students agree or disagree?

During this process my students sometimes coaxed me to share my faith, but
I resisted. I feared that my beliefs would unduly prejudice and inhibit their
own analysis. But now, in retirement and away from the classroom, I wish to
present what I believe. This is the same challenge that I put before my
students at the beginning of each religion or ethics class.

My faith springs from my understanding of God as Divine Love, a universal
force that unites and unconditionally accepts all people. There is nothing
that anyone must do to earn this acceptance. We must simply accept the fact
that Divine Love has accepted us, just as we are.

What I believe undergirds my Tennis and Life Philosophy (TLP) and how I
have chosen to orient my life. My belief in service led me to create Tennis
and Life Camps (TLC) and to coach varsity tennis. Also, Barb and my
convictions on charity led us to give away TLC and to prioritize full
scholarships for financially challenged youth.

Furthermore, my faith has allowed me to face difficult questions. Why have I
survived three life-threatening car accidents while a dear friend did not
survive even one? Why are some people so blessed while others are not? Is it

logical to believe that only one religion reveals God? These and other thought provoking questions are analyzed in the following chapters.

In the final analysis, I have searched for universal values that inspire me and give meaning to my present life. I feel comfortable having my past before conception and my future after death shrouded in mystery. With the help of the Serenity Prayer and a strong belief in Divine Love, I seek to live fully in the present.

1972 January Term travel class that traveled to Hawaii to study Japanese religion in the Hawaiian culture.

Wilkinson's 1972 religion class being hosted by a Nichiren Buddhist student group in Hawaii

55

WHY WAS I SO LUCKY?

The car slammed down on its side and slid toward the edge
of the road. I was on the bottom side. My right arm was
partially out the window, being dragged along the asphalt.
My seat belt held tight, keeping me from being thrown out
of the car or having my weight push me down on the road.

Saved by luck and seatbelts

In August of 1962, at the age of 21, my life could have ended. My friend and I decided to take a vacation, going west to the Tetons, then north to the Canadian Rockies, west to Vancouver, and then south to Seattle, to visit the World Fair and the newly constructed Space Needle. As a safety precaution, I personally installed seat belts in my newly purchased Volkswagen "bug," even though they were optional at the time.

On the first day, I drove many hours across the flat plains of Nebraska until I started to get sleepy. Near Lusk, Wyoming, I passed off the driving responsibilities to my friend. Shortly thereafter, it happened. Half asleep with my head down, I felt the car go off the right side of the road. I looked up and yelled. My friend, who had dozed off, awakened and cranked the wheel back to correct our course. That sent the car careening back across the middle line. The oncoming traffic was still in the distance. Again, my friend corrected, but the adjustment was too severe.

The car became airborne, making a 180-degree turn; I remember looking back down the road from where we had come. A metal cooler, almost as wide as the entire back seat and filled with food cans, was hurled out through the open sunroof, grazing my head on the way out. When it hit the pavement, the contents flew everywhere. If the cooler had caught the back of my head full force, it could have killed me.

The car slammed down on its side and slid toward the edge of the road. I was on the bottom side. My right arm was partially out the window, being dragged along the asphalt. My seat belt held tight, keeping me from being thrown out of the car or having my weight push me down on the road. My arm could have been ripped off, but it only had lacerations.

The car stopped sliding at the edge of road, next to an incline that descended into a valley. I looked up. My friend was above me, secured in place by a seat belt. An hour later, still shaken, barely able to talk, I related the accident to my parents. My friend and I had escaped major injury, thanks to the seat belts.

Lucky again, just six months later

In February of 1963, I was a senior at the University of Iowa in Iowa City, Iowa, looking forward to my final season of intercollegiate competition. The winter before, I had traveled to Sioux Falls, South Dakota, to play in a challenging indoor tournament at the Sioux Falls Racquet Club. In the finals I upset Wendell Ottum, a legend who had dominated tennis in the upper Midwest for years. This year I hoped to do it again.

Two good friends decided to accompany me to Sioux City, Iowa, where my parents lived. At noon on Friday, we climbed into my rebuilt '62 Volkswagen, the same car that had suffered the previous accident. Five hours later, we arrived in Sioux City, where dinner was waiting. After eating, I continued to Sioux Falls, arriving just in time for my first singles match.

Saturday was a busy day but not so demanding as Sunday. That day all four of my matches lasted three sets. I played 12 sets in 10 hours. I was exhausted.

I took a quick shower, gathered my gear, and headed back to Sioux City. Arriving at 8 p.m. I picked up my two friends and headed back to Iowa City. We anticipated a 1 a.m. arrival, in time to get some sleep before classes and a test on Monday morning. In my exhausted state, I decided that it would be best for one of my friends to drive. Both friends sat in the front, while I curled up in the back seat and immediately fell asleep.

About three hours into the drive, we ran into freezing rain. I was oblivious to the weather until the sensation of a spinning car awakened me. At first I thought I was dreaming. Terrible memories of the summer before came rushing back. I quickly realized that I was not dreaming. There was nothing that I could do to influence what was going to happen next, so I kept my head down, remained silent, and hoped for the best.

The car spun a complete 360 degrees and then 90 degrees more. We headed off the road at a right angle, went down a small incline, and settled into a snow bank. The car was still upright, undamaged, and no one was hurt. Unbelievable! The time was about 11:30 p.m. There was no one else on the road when we took our spin.

We got out of the car and assessed our predicament. Soon, another car stopped to help. Fortunately, it contained a number of strong guys. They helped us work the Volkswagen bug out of the snow and back onto the road. We thanked them profusely, climbed back into the car, and continued on our way after an hour delay. This time I drove. My adrenaline was pumping, and I was wide-awake. We took things slowly, making it back to Iowa City at about 3 a.m. in the morning.

This near brush with death, the second time in six months, made a lasting impression. Never again would I feel comfortable riding while someone else was driving. As my family and tennis teams know, I have always driven, no matter how long the continuous hours.

Lucky again, for a third time

In March 1981, Barb, Stephanie, and Deb accompanied the Gustavus tennis team and me on our annual spring trip. Our first matches were at Millsaps College in Jackson, Mississippi and the last ones at Oral Roberts University in Tulsa, Oklahoma. I drove our Toyota Corolla, while the team and my assistant coaches traveled in vans.

After our final matches, we headed north through Kansas. In Topeka we parted ways. The team continued north on Interstate #35 while my family and I took Highway #75 to Sioux City, Iowa, where we planned to spend Easter with my parents. At 10 p.m. a light rain began to fall. By that time our daughters had fallen asleep in the back seat with their seat belts unbuckled.

All of a sudden, our peaceful trip became chaotic. As we drove over what appeared to be a normal railroad crossing, our front tires suddenly dropped into a hole that had been created by a missing railroad tie. The wheels came out again, but now they were turned at a 45-degree angle. A broken tie-rod pierced our car's floor and came up between my legs. Our car slid down the wet road, following a curved path that covered both sides of the road. We stayed on the pavement and came to a stop upright, facing back down the road from where we had come.

A person in the car behind us saw the accident and set out flares. We quickly climbed out of our car and got to the side of the road, wishing to avoid the possibility of being struck by another car. Eventually the police came. The railroad tie, which may have been flipped out by a passing truck, was replaced. We were driven to a nearby town and left at a bus terminal, where we caught a bus to Sioux City, Iowa, early on Easter morning.

Looking back, I shudder to think what could have happened. What if the road had not been wet? What if we had rolled instead of slid? Would the girls, with no seatbelts, have been tossed from the car? What if a car had been coming from the other direction as we slid out of control? There were so many horrible possibilities that could have happened, but they did not. We were lucky.

A tragic accident

By contrast, consider the story of David and Erik Aasen. David was like a son to Barb and me. His parents, Nita and Paul, are good friends. Paul worked at Gustavus with me and we all attended First Lutheran Church. I helped teach David's confirmation class. Also, I taught him tennis, first through the local recreation program and later through Tennis and Life Camps (TLC). David became the director of the recreation program and then an outstanding teacher at TLC for seven years.

Now, I think back to Thanksgiving Day, 1994. It started with a beautiful sunrise and no snow yet on the ground. My parents had arrived from Sioux City. Barb and daughter Stephanie were there. We were sharing breakfast together, anticipating the arrival of daughter Deb, who was coming from Edina, Minnesota, where she was working as a third grade elementary school teacher. This was going to be a special day, different than most, free from demands to get things done.

At the same time, Paul and Nita Aasen were driving to Chicago to spend Thanksgiving with their son Kevin. Sons David and Erik followed them in a second car. At 10 a.m. came the call that I will never forget. Paul somehow forced out the words,

> David has been killed. My son Erik also, two out of my three sons, gone in an instant! You were like a father to David. He would want you to know. How can this be? It was terrible. I saw everything in my rear view mirror. The car that Erik was driving slipped on black ice on a curve in Highway 14, west of Rochester. I hoped they would slide away from the oncoming semi-truck. Instead, they ended up in front of it. I saw the expressions on their faces! The pain is too much to bear. I ran to the car, but when I got there, it was obvious that David was dead. We still hoped that Erik would live. It took them 45 minutes to get them out of the car.

Making sense out of it all

The contrasting outcomes of my three car accidents and the one of David and Erik are hard to explain. Why did I live while they died? Some people believe that each of us has a guardian angel that protects us in life-threatening situations. However, that explanation does not ring true for me. If a guardian angel was protecting me on three occasions, then where were David and Erik's guardian angels on the day they were killed?

Others have told me that it was God's plan for David and Erik to die young while I lived into my 70s. However, I recoil at the thought that God picks some to die early while others live long or that God chooses some to suffer extreme hardships while others prosper. For me, God is Divine Love, the creator and sustainer of us all.

David Aasen

As the years have passed by, I have thought about these accidents at least a thousand times. What sense can I make out of the contrast between David, Erik, and me? I was lucky, and they were not. Why do some win the lottery, and others do not? The winners were lucky. Why are some people born with genes that facilitate a long and healthy life, and others are not? Some are lucky, and others are not.

I do not blame God (Divine Love) for natural calamities, famine, war, disease, atrocities, suffering or the untimely deaths of David and Erik. For me, God is not all-powerful, and therefore not responsible for bad things. Divine Love (God), by its very nature, stands in opposition to all injustice and cruelty.

Fortunately, the true measure of all lives grows out of choices that lie within our control. What makes our lives count does not depend on luck. It rests on our courage to love, serve, forgive, console, pardon and be joyful. David and Erik modeled these virtues in powerful ways. The outpouring of grief at their funeral and countless stories of how they inspired others point to an impact that transcended their deaths.

56

"ONLY"

*I realized that all images of God inadequately represent
Ultimate Reality. Stories, holy books, revelations,
philosophies, and testimonies are all humankind's attempt
to express the Infinite (God) through finite means.*

Growing up in the *only* true Christian denomination

During my school years in Sioux City, Iowa, I spent many hours at church,
attending Sunday morning services, Sunday school, Wednesday evening
prayer services, church youth group, youth service projects, and congregation
potlucks. I taught Sunday school to younger kids, was president of the
church youth group, led the service projects, and participated in the
presentation of Sunday morning worship. I believed that *only* my Christian
denomination was authentic.

At the University of Iowa, my denominational church house was the center of
my social and religious life. The large living room on the first floor served as
the sanctuary for Sunday morning worship and Wednesday evening prayer
services. Side rooms hosted Sunday school classes. The entire downstairs,
including the kitchen, was the gathering place for a dynamic student
fellowship.

The upstairs of the house had four bedrooms, which accommodated seven or
eight university men. I lived there for four years, until I completed my MBA
studies. My peer group prioritized worship, religious study, community
service, and alcohol-free socializing.

Discovering the truth in other Christian denominations

As an undergraduate I took a literature course where the tools of literary and
historical criticism were applied to the Bible. I began to look at religion in a
new way, and my literalism took a big hit. My "proofs" for belonging to the
only true Christian denomination no longer seemed persuasive.

More importantly, my understanding of the Christian faith expanded through my elective classes in the religion department. I especially liked the ones taught by Dr. George Forell, a Luther scholar. As I studied love, law, gospel, and grace under him, I realized that what I had in common with other Christian denominations was more important than what divided us.

This new perspective had a growing influence on my entire church youth group. Dr. Forell spoke to us on several occasions. Members of other faiths— Jews, Muslims, and Hindus—occasionally attended and found our fellowship environment supportive.

No longer were we stressing our exclusiveness. This produced a liberal/conservative split in our congregation between the college students and the older, more conservative members who still believed that they belonged to the *only* true faith. Nonetheless, even though we disagreed theologically, we affirmed each other personally.

Exploring non-Western religions and cultures

As an undergraduate I had limited exposure to non-Western religions. I saw Christianity professing grace and non-Western religions emphasizing works. Also, Christianity emphasized the self while Eastern religions did the opposite. My Christian denomination alone was no longer the *only* way, but my Christian faith certainly was.

My post-undergraduate perspective changed gradually during my 12 years of teaching students about world religions and leading them to Japan, India and Hawaii. I journeyed to the base of Mt. Fuji with Buddhist pilgrims, slept on a tatami mat in a large meeting hall, practiced daily chanting from Buddhist scripture, and watched Zen masters teach meditation to judo and kendo students. While in India, I visited ashrams and met with devotees who had personally walked and worshipped with Mahatma Gandhi. I came to realize that people received fulfillment through non-Christian paths. My preconception that *only* Christianity emphasized grace proved false.

Eye-opening experience in Hawaii

In Hawaii my students, Barb and I had an eye-opening experience with Bishop Hirai from the Kegon Buddhist sect. After making prearrangements, we arrived at her temple, which had surrounding walls topped with barbwire. An ominous sign on the entrance gate said "Visitors Not Welcome!" Nevertheless, we knocked, and an assistant let us in. We entered a beautifully manicured garden that was filled with fruit trees. Bishop Hirai, a petite, elderly woman, came out to greet us. Her warm smile and gracious manner put us at ease. She took us on a tour of the grounds, which included a waterfall under which she meditated each morning at 5 a.m.

After the tour we asked about the barbwire and the sign on the gate. Bishop Hirai apologized but then explained how vandalism by Honolulu youth had prompted her response. Also, previous visitors had not shown respect. Then why had she responded favorably to my request to visit? She agreed because she had sensed in my letter a genuine interest to learn more about her religion.

Our students were conscientious about showing respect. It meant taking off their shoes before entering the temple, greeting her in Japanese with "konnichiwa" and bowing respectfully in traditional Japanese style. Also, they listened attentively, even when her strong Japanese accent made it difficult for many to understand. Our women students wore muumuus to discreetly cover their knees, and the men shaved neatly, tied back longer hair, and wore long pants, all in keeping with her conservative preferences.

We stayed that first day through the evening meal, which allowed us to meet many of her followers. They told us that Bishop Hirai had amazing healing powers. One devotee, a practicing physician who had graduated from Northwestern University Medical School, confirmed the validity of her healings. Also, it was reported that she could see spirits, events in our past, and things to come. Several of my students expressed surprise when Bishop Hirai told them things about their parents, which she had no discernible way of knowing.

We returned for several visits, and our relationship grew. We learned how to practice reverently the Japanese tea ceremony. Whenever we participated in religious ceremonies, we sat on our heels in traditional Japanese style. Every time that we visited, she showered us with gifts and praise. All of us felt that we had met a true saint, a person who radiated love, generosity, humility, and service.

Gustavus students participating in the Tea Ceremony with Bishop Hirai in 1972.

During our month-long study period in Honolulu, which included visits to many other Japanese religions, we attended a Lutheran worship service in Waikiki. After it was over, we talked with the parishioners. They wanted to

271

know what we were doing in Hawaii. This led to my glowing description of Bishop Hirai and all that she had done for us. A very concerned look crossed over the face of a local woman member. She sternly warned me, "The devil has devious ways of winning your soul." I left the building discouraged, but mindful that the woman could have been me, only 15 years before.

Different ways to conceptualize the Christian faith

Most practitioners of Asian religions accommodate religious diversity well. They view every religion as an accessible pathway to God. For them, all paths go up the mountain to where God resides.

By contrast, many Christians start with the words of Jesus in John 14:6, "I am the way, and the truth, and the life; no one comes to God but through me." This communicates only one "super highway" heading up the mountain with each on-ramp controlled by a Christian minister, demanding acceptance of Jesus Christ as one's savior and repentance for one's sins. The entry gate goes up at the moment of baptism. For millions of Christians, including me, the "super highway" is not a helpful way to conceptualize God and the Christian faith.

Instead, God can be conceived as the sun (love), which freely dispenses its rays of light (grace) upon everyone, regardless of their religion, race, or degree of righteousness. Many people escape the sun's light by choosing to enter dark tunnels. Sometimes, they spend so much time in the dark that they are convinced there is no sun at all. Religious leaders of many different faiths invite people out into the light. Jesus is one messenger of the light, but so are Gautama, Mohammed, Confucius, Isaiah, and the prophets of all great religions.

I realize that all images of God inadequately represent Ultimate Reality. Stories, holy books, revelations, philosophies, and testimonies are all humankind's attempt to express the Infinite (God) through finite means. A few themes seem to appear in all of the great religions—universal brother and sisterhood of all people, the supremacy of love and peace, and the Golden Rule. Other themes may seem to contradict, but perhaps they can be explained by the analogy of the five blind men trying to describe an elephant. They each grab a different part of the elephant and describe what they feel. Even though there is truth in each of their descriptions, the five blind men are not describing the larger reality beyond their experiences.

A respectful approach to other world religions does not make them equally valuable to me. My Christian faith provides the lens through which I see clearly my identity and my responsibility to others. By analogy, I respect the family traditions of others. But for me, my family relationships were special. No other mother or father could have molded me better. Similarly, I deeply respect the values, customs, and national loyalties of people from all over the world. However, for me, my country, with its freedoms and opportunities, is the place where I wish to live.

Barb and Steve join Nichiren Buddhist students for a presentation of their faith at their Hawaii student center.

I am deeply grateful for the many ways in which my Christian faith has been enriched by my international exposure to non-Christian friends, including humanists, agnostics, and atheists. Nevertheless, I see God (Divine Love) primarily through the life of Jesus. He fed the hungry, healed the sick, and visited the prisoners. Jesus washed the feet of the poor, accepted harlots and society's outcasts, and forgave the people who crucified him. He rejected holier-than-thou behavior and reinterpreted the Mosaic Law from the perspective of love. Through Jesus, I understand clearly what Divine Love looks like in everyday life.

How the *only* approach limits God

Christians limit the universality of God (Divine Love) if we proclaim that God is revealed *only* in Jesus Christ. We deny universal grace if we limit it only to adherents of our own faith. The lives and teachings of Mahatma Gandhi (Hindu), Thich Nhat Hanh (Buddhist), Martin Buber (Jewish) and Shaykh-al-Alawi (Muslim) clearly illustrate how God is powerfully manifested in many religions and cultures.

Advocates of the *only* approach have labeled Mother Teresa, who was canonized as a saint by the Roman Catholic Church, a heretic. It is easy to see why. In her book *Everything Starts From Prayer, Mother Teresa's Meditations on Spiritual Life for People of all Faiths,* she writes, "I've always said we should help a Hindu become a better Hindu, a Muslim become a better Muslim, a Catholic become a better Catholic."

For Mother Teresa the dying, the crippled, the hungry, the unwanted, and the unloved are Jesus in disguise. Whatever people do for the least of their brethren, they do for Christ. Mother Teresa and her fellow workers prayed frequently each day. Prayer reinforced their belief and love, motivating them to serve with humility and a spirit of forgiveness. They viewed their own

273

poverty as a freedom to give more. By contrast, people with possessions can be occupied with them and thereby give less.

Becoming Lutheran

Upon coming to Gustavus in 1970, I left the denomination that had commanded my loyalty for almost 30 years and became a Lutheran. I was motivated by Luther's emphasis on God's (Divine Love's) grace. Works were still important, but not as a way to prove oneself or achieve righteousness. Deeds were a response to God's grace, not a way to earn it.

We liked many things about our new church environment. The ministers were well educated and able to deliver sermons that made the Gospel come alive. The choir was professional and committed to classical church music, which motivated Barb immensely, bringing back fond memories of her church choir in Germany. The Sunday school program provided a Christian foundation for our daughters, Stephanie and Deb. Socially concerned committees reinforced our desire to serve Christ through helping others— especially the poor and hungry. Also, we liked worshipping with friends who were connected to us through work and other relationships.

How the *only* approach hurts Christian outreach

Positive and inclusive ministers have led the Lutheran congregation where Barb and I have worshiped for the last 40 years. We have never heard a sermon from our pulpit that touted Christ as the *only* way to God (Divine Love). If we had, we would have sought another congregation.

Nevertheless, we are troubled by the strong presence of an *only* emphasis. Our services are liturgy based. Consequently, *only* references appear frequently as the traditional creeds and Biblical readings are integrated into our services. They state clearly that belief in Christ is the *only* way to God.

I cringe when I hear or am expected to say the word *only*. I have worshiped in many non-Christian settings and always felt welcomed. There was nothing in their services telling me that my Christian beliefs were wrong or inadequate. However, this is precisely what we do in the Lutheran church when we use the word *only*. Consequently, I am reluctant to bring a non-Christian to worship in a Lutheran service.

If we would eliminate our *only* references, I would feel different. When I profess that Jesus is the Son of God (Divine Love), I present my faith in a powerful way. However, if I should say that He is the *only* Son of God, I directly slap the faces of non-Christian believers. I discredit Krishna, Mohammed, Gautama and all the other revealers of God. As a Christian, I find God communicated most powerfully through Jesus. However, as an appreciative student of other religions and a good friend of many non-Christians, I know that God is revealed to them differently. If I do not affirm this, I show lack of respect and sensitivity.

The *only* way of thinking does not need to be part of the Christian message. Indeed, three of the most widely used Christian prayers (Lord's Prayer, Serenity Prayer, and St. Francis Prayer) do not include the *only* way of thinking. I urge that all Christian councils in the 21st century go through the scriptures, creeds, prayers and hymns and strike out the *only* perspective.

I wanted to do that at the Lutheran service that I attended recently. The first three Biblical texts were uplifting. Numbers 21:4-9 described Moses and the experiences of the Israelites in the wilderness. Psalm 107:1-3, 17-22 proclaimed God's mercy and enduring love. Ephesians 2:1-10 explained God's grace. "For by grace you have been saved through faith, and this is not your own doing; it is the gift of God—not the result of works, so that no one may boast." What a beautiful expression of the Christian perspective.

Next came the Gospel from John 3:14-21. "Those who believe in Him (Jesus Christ) are not condemned; but those who do not believe are condemned already, because they have not believed in the name of the *only* Son of God." My heart sank. There again the *only* way of thinking was introduced to an otherwise open and inclusive service. Fortunately, the minister did not interpret or defend the Gospel words quoted above. Nevertheless, I felt relieved that no non-Christian friends had accompanied me that day.

Unfortunately, the exclusive *only* way of thinking in America does not stop with creeds or Bible verses. It creeps into the way that many Christians think about marriage, which in their view should be *only* between a man and a woman, and about sexuality, which should be *only* heterosexual.

As a young student, I was advised never to select a multiple-choice answer that contained the word *only*. I followed that recommendation, and it served me well. Now, I apply this insight to my understanding of God (Divine Love), and still it rings true. God is universal, revealed in all of the world's great religions, and not restricted to only one formulation of Ultimate Truth.

57

MY FAITH EXPLAINED

*Jesus inspired my most admired people. They
include Martin Luther King Jr., Nelson Mandela,
Arthur Ashe Jr., Mother Teresa and Albert Schweitzer.*

What faith is and is not for me

Faith for me is "the courage to be" in the face of doubts. Why live with hope
when evil seems to triumph in so many situations? Why continue to try
when so many people criticize me? Why help others when they do not seem
to appreciate or respect me? These and similar questions can drive some to
cynicism, depression, and sometimes suicide.

Faith is a centered act that includes one's intellect, emotions, and will. It
undergirds all aspects of life—work, play, family, etc. Faith is ultimate
concern, taking into account both the individual who is concerned and the
object of that concern.

From this perspective faith differs from common understandings of it. Faith
is *not* a religious creed, recited in worship services but irrelevant to one's daily
life. Faith is *not* history or science, capable of being proved or disproved by
historical or scientific methods. Nor is it what a religious text or church
authority tells one to believe. Faith is *not* just a strong act of the will, devoid
of logic and reasoning. Nor is it something purely emotional, although one's
emotions play a critical role.

Faith that involves doubt

In my early church years, I was taught that doubts were a sign of a weak faith,
or perhaps no faith at all. I was expected to accept the Bible, church creeds,
and religious teachings without doubts. If something did not make sense, I
was told to pray about it until it did.

On the other hand, my high school and university teachers insisted that I
doubt. Skepticism was part of taking an analytical approach to knowledge.
In the chemistry classroom I tested chemical formulas by running closely

controlled experiments. In the history classroom I learned historical criticism and how to evaluate the reliability of various sources. In the literature classroom I studied literary criticism and discovered what I could learn by analyzing texts. When I studied religion at the University of Iowa in my freshman year, repressing my doubts was no longer a constructive approach.

After reading Paul Tillich's *Dynamics of Faith* and *The Courage To Be*, I came to believe that doubts are a necessary part of faith. However, these doubts transcended the truth of historical facts, scientific formulas, literary texts, or concepts of God. They went to the heart of the human situation, to my "courage to be." How could I believe that Divine Love unites all people when the world experiences so many wars, tragedies, and atrocities? Are cynicism, depression, and suicide valid responses to the human condition? These are the doubts that my faith must confront and take seriously.

God as Divine Love but not omnipotent

If God is omnipotent, then God is responsible for both good and evil. Many people feel comfortable giving God credit for their blessings, but they wonder how tragedies, senseless deaths, and unfortunate situations can be the will of God. This can leave them in a quandary, wondering why bad things happen to good people, or taking it a step further, denying the existence of God.

For me, God is Divine Love, but not all-powerful. This view preserves human free will and makes it possible to understand why people's poor choices or evil intent can produce terrible tragedies. Also, natural catastrophes can be horrendous. If God is Divine Love rather than omnipotent, then God is not responsible for disasters. With this understanding, I do not harbor resentments toward God. It puts me in a position where I can relax and embrace the Serenity Prayer sincerely.

How faith is conveyed by myths

If myths are not taken literally, they can be a powerful way to convey the "truths" of faith. For example, in the Book of Genesis there are two creation myths. Historically and scientifically, they contradict each other. One myth puts the creation of man and woman first, followed by the creation of animals. A second one reverses the order. However, both myths affirm a purposeful creation, rooted in a Divine Love that unites all life. This is the truth that was critical to the Biblical writers, not historical or scientific consistency.

If myths are to express our faiths, they must resonate with us, engaging our minds, emotions and wills. They must make sense to us at every level. Myths expressing faith help us understand why there is so much pain and suffering in the world; why things often don't work out the way that we intended them to; why we need to practice forgiveness and be forgiven; how we need to love and be loved in return; and how we need to conduct our lives with family, friends, colleagues, fellow citizens, and the international community.

Stories containing myths are all around us. Novels, plays, short stories, fairy tales, superhero comics, legends, songs, musicals, cultural celebrations, etc. can all include myths. We know that they are not true from an historical or scientific perspective. But that does not matter. They either speak to us or leave us flat, depending on how they address our lives personally. If they cut to the core of who we are or want to be, then they are myths of faith. If the myths do not express our bedrock values, they are just stories.

Consider the myth of Santa Claus. Everyone over the age of nine knows that this myth is not true historically or scientifically, but that does not detract from its power. Francis Church, a *New York Sun* editor in 1897, wrote the myth's most famous interpretation. His editorial responded to 8-year-old Virginia O'Hanlon, who asked, "Is there really a Santa Claus?" Church wrote, "Yes, Virginia, there is a Santa Claus. He exists as certainly as love and generosity and devotion exist, and you know that they abound and give to your life its highest beauty and joy." Church went on to explain other truths in the myth but stopped short of saying that there was no literal Santa Claus. If he had, his response would never have become so famous.

In spite of Church's noble attempt to find meaning, the current Santa Claus myth rings hollow for me. It perpetuates the idea that Christmas is about receiving material gifts, based on good behavior during the past year. It promotes commercialism, associates love with material gifts, and encourages people to spend extravagantly for presents they cannot afford and which recipients often don't appreciate.

On the other hand, the *Christmas Carol* by Charles Dickens does resonate with me. It tells the story of Scrooge, a miserly workaholic, who has ignored the personal life of his dedicated employee and the needs of the poor, including the crippled Tiny Tim. The supernatural spirits of Christmas past, present, and future confront Scrooge, force him to reflect, and prompt him to become more caring. Thereby, he discovers the importance of loving relationships, compassion for the poor, and the true meaning of Christmas.

Jesus, the authoritative center of my faith

Teaching world religions to college students in both India and the United States exposed me to many faith traditions. So did my time in Japan, leading a student group and doing research on Nichiren Shoshu Sokagakkai, a modern Buddhist sect. I learned to appreciate many religious faiths and personal philosophies, including those of agnostics and atheists.

However, Jesus embodies my understanding of Divine Love. He embraced the poor and societal outcasts, rejected the hypocrisy and false pride of church officials, turned the other cheek when wronged, accepted sinners who repented, and substituted love for strict legalism under the Mosaic Law.

When confronted with his own unjust execution, he counseled forgiveness. The story of Jesus presented by the Gospel writers touches my heart and motivates me to be the type of person that I know I want to be.

Predictably, Jesus also inspired the people whom I admire the most. They include Martin Luther King Jr., Nelson Mandela, Arthur Ashe Jr., Mother Teresa, and Albert Schweitzer. All are Christians who faithfully applied the life and ministry of Jesus to the most important issues of their day. Also, Mahatma Gandhi, my most admired religious and political leader of the 20th century, respected Jesus immensely. Even though Gandhi was a Hindu, the only icon that he allowed in his ashram was a crucifix.

Heaven

Many people view heaven as a post-death existence, where they will maintain their present life identity and will be reunited with people they knew and loved. It is a place where justice reigns, suffering is eliminated, and discrimination does not exist. Isaiah described it as a place where the wolf lies down with the lamb. In short, heaven is a paradise that satisfies the dreams and longings of each person contemplating an afterlife.

However, when heaven is conceived as a place where people go with their physical and mental identities intact, logical problems are created for me. Tragedies, diseases, and aging change the appearances and personalities of loved ones. Which version of them would go to heaven? Would it be the daughter, before or after disabling brain injuries completely changed her personality? Would it be the veteran, before or after wartime experiences sent him into depression and suicide? Would it be the grandfather, before or after, Alzheimer's robbed his personality and memory? Would it be the person that a stillborn fetus might have become?

I believe that our souls, but not our bodies, minds, or selves, continue after death. Souls are pure essence, present in us before we were born and still with us after we die. Our souls unite us with Divine Love and all of humanity.

Self and soul

The terms "I" and "me" refer to the self, which is tied to specific thoughts, actions, and memories. This identity shapes my personhood and makes me different from even an identical twin. Physical characteristics and ways of thinking can change during a lifetime, but there is one self that connects the experiences until death.

By contrast, the soul is the eternal within each of us, the bond that connects us to all humanity and Divine Love. The soul's existence and continuation after death can be affirmed only by faith. The soul is not our thoughts, memory, or sense of individual identity. These are elements of the self and tied inescapably to our physical bodies.

Me-centered selves perpetuate unspeakable horrors in the names of my family, my friends, my religious group, my country or myself. The fact that Jesus would not resist execution and would forgive his executioners runs counter to a me-centered orientation.

We are born selfish, which can be observed in children and adults alike. Teaching unselfishness and empathy is a continuing responsibility for parents, teachers, ministers, and people of faith. The Christian sacrament of infant baptism acknowledges this natural human condition, which is called original sin (selfishness). At the same time, the Christian Gospel proclaims the good news that Divine Love's grace has freed all people from having to worry about original sin. In spite of it, ALL are accepted!

For non-Christians grace is symbolized in other ways. However, whatever the form, Divine Love's grace is the key to living freely. We know that we will never be perfect. We give love our best effort, but when we fall short, as everyone does, we know that Divine Love forgives us and empowers us to try again.

Meditation and prayer

When alone and unrushed, I start with listening (meditation) and follow it with talk (prayer). When together with others, attending a church service or sharing table grace, we start with prayer. I appreciate the communal aspect of public prayer and the introspective depth of private meditation/prayer.

My need for meditation and prayer becomes apparent when I am confronted with undesirable events outside my control. For athletes, it may be losing, playing poorly, or being cheated. For students, not being able to solve a problem or flunking an exam may be the culprit. For anyone, being rejected by a friend, becoming sick or injured, having a loved one die, being bullied, or experiencing a devastating natural disaster may be the trigger. When these things occur, it is common for us to experience negative emotions such as fear, nervousness, anger, despair, and anxiety.

When I experience negative thoughts, I close my eyes and begin to follow my breathing. I breathe in slowly through my nostrils, feeling my stomach and lower lungs expand until they can go no further. Then I breathe out slowly through my mouth, taking twice the time that it took me to breathe in. I breathe in and out, following the movement of the air with my mind. All other thoughts are let go, and an automatic relaxation response comes over me. All negative emotions drift away, my breathing and heart rate slows, and my blood pressure drops. I become detached from what was bothering me. I begin to look at myself in the third person.

With a sense of supreme calm, I begin to repeat the Serenity Prayer. Often, I will repeat the prayer frequently, one time after the other. I collect the things that are bothering me and put them in a red balloon that is tied and hovering just above my forehead. After I have filled that balloon with my problems, I cut the balloon free. I watch it drift higher and higher until it disappears out of sight. Then my attention returns to my breathing and the calming effect that it produces.

Another prayer that I use frequently is the Peace Prayer of St. Francis:

> Lord, make me an instrument of your peace; where there is hatred, let me sow love; where there is injury, pardon; where there is doubt, faith; where there is despair, hope; where there is darkness, light; and where there is sadness, joy. O Divine Master, grant that I may not seek so much to be consoled as to console; to be understood as to understand; and to be loved as to love; for it is in giving that we receive; it is in pardoning that we are pardoned; and it is in dying that we are born to eternal life.

These words convey the peaceful, loving manner in which I want to serve others. I like the way the prayer incorporates the wisdom of the Serenity Prayer, emphasizing what I have control over (e.g. to love), rather than what I do not (e.g. to be loved).

Meditation or prayer resonates with me when its purpose is thanksgiving, confession, praise or listening. On the other hand, I feel uncomfortable when prayer becomes a petition for a special benefit or favor. Even in the immediate face of death, Arthur Ashe Jr. could write:

> Prayer is a medium through which I ask God to show me God's will, and to give me strength to carry out that will ... When I played tennis, I never prayed for victory in a match. I will not pray now to be cured of heart disease or AIDS. (*Days of Grace*, p. 326)

To Divine Love, I can only say thanks, not petition for still more. I have a wonderful wife, grateful children and grandchildren, capable successors to Tennis and Life Camps and Gustavus tennis, and many supportive friends. I am a fortunate, blessed man with so many reasons to give thanks.

Concluding thoughts on faith

Many influences have enriched my faith—worshiping in Christian churches my entire life, studying religions in a Ph.D. program, teaching world religions, traveling worldwide with college students, appreciating worship experiences within many religious traditions, enjoying discussions with agnostics and atheists, and applying ethics to sports participation.

My understanding of Divine Love is universalistic. The accepting grace revealed in Jesus applies to everyone. We have all been freed, regardless of where we were born or what religion we practice.

Yet, we often fear that we have not done enough or that we are not good enough. If only we could believe at our deepest level that we are free, accepted by Divine Love, how differently we might act.

58

VALUES THAT MATTER

*Charity lies at the center of what it means for me to
be Christian. Jesus could not have been clearer.
"Whatsoever you do to the least of my people,
that you do unto me." (Matthew 25:40)*

Values are judgments of what is most important in life. Mine are represented clearly in the life of Jesus and evident in the commitments of Martin Luther King Jr., Nelson Mandela, Mother Teresa, Albert Schweitzer, and Mahatma Gandhi. Also, my values often are reflected in the mission statements of the organizations that serve humanitarian, environmental, world peace, inner peace, and anti-poverty goals.

The following 16 values pull together my interpretation of life. I expect my cherished values to apply relevantly to society's vexing challenges.

Love

The supreme power in the universe is Divine Love, the force that gives meaning to all human life. The New Testament calls this power God, Love, and Father. All these labels (and others found in non-Christian religions) have positive aspects. The unconditional acceptance present in Divine Love is closely paralleled in human experience by the devoted commitment of a mother or father to their child, regardless of their behavior.

Unfortunately, the words God or Father can be misleading. They convey the idea of a literal person, who exists in a place above the earth called Heaven. This view violates what we know scientifically about the universe.

Consequently, Divine Love is a better label for me to describe the supreme power in the universe. Divine Love is universal, present in all religions, cultures, and human lives. The term encourages everyone to be more open and accepting. Divine Love is Mother as easily as Father, Allah as easily as Jehovah, and Tao as easily as Amida Buddha. Even atheists, who by definition reject God, are often open to love as a universal force.

Love is evident in this mother and daughter relationship at TLC

Grace

Our daughter Deb sang "Amazing Grace, How Sweet the Sound" so beautifully at my father's funeral. My mother's middle name was Grace. So are the middle names of our granddaughters Caroline and Audrey. The emphasis on grace led me to the Lutheran Church, where I have worshipped most of my adult life.

Grace is at the center of the important "Three Gs" message that I have taught to Tennis and Life campers. The first "G" is gifts. All of us have been given so many incredible gifts. The second "G" is grace. We have done nothing to deserve these gifts, yet we have received them. The third "G" is gratitude. The only proper response to gifts that we do not deserve is profound gratitude.

Grace affirms my worthiness, no matter how short of perfection I may fall. Paradoxically, my service to others gives meaning to my life; but it does not determine my self-worth. That was established by the grace of Divine Love.

Serenity

The Serenity Prayer offers a blueprint for living life fully. "God, grant me the Serenity to accept the things I cannot change; the Courage to change the things I can; and the Wisdom to know the difference."

It is easy to focus on the things outside our control, which we cannot change, instead of things within our control, which we can change. If we worry about disrespectful people, we may lose motivation to show respect to others. If we worry about winning or playing well, we may stop giving full effort with a positive attitude. If we worry about not getting an "A", we may not apply ourselves to mastering the subject matter. Finally, if we worry about death, we may not live our days to the fullest.

The wisdom to know what we can change and what we cannot is critical. Frustration and stress beset those who do not possess this wisdom. Serenity and courage mark the lives of those who do.

Trust

If we treat others with trust, they will become trustworthy. If instead, we convey suspicion and distrust, others will act accordingly.

My journey from distrust to trust was influenced by a 1965 conversation with Arthur Ashe Jr., who believed that tennis line calls should never be challenged. Previously, I had shown distrust by staring at opponents and smiling when I disagreed. I used this ploy because I thought it was a discreet way of pressuring them to make better calls. Since my conversation with Arthur, I have communicated trust instead. The results have surprised me. Opponents, even those with reputations for cheating, have treated me fairly.

Trust is an important aspect of every important relationship. For children to act trustworthily, their parents must trust them. For marriages to succeed, both partners must communicate trust. Also, for businesses to prosper, management and employees must trust each other.

Do there need to be standards to which both parties agree? Yes. Will people fall short of what they have promised? Certainly. Do offenders need to apologize and pledge to do better? That is crucial. Moving forward, must the betrayed forgive and trust again? No question. The alternative is distrust, a dysfunctional relationship that bleeds the potential out of partnerships.

Forgiveness

Forgiveness is trumpeted in the teachings of all the world's great religions. Medical research confirms the health benefits for people offering forgiveness and those being forgiven. Psychological studies show that forgiving people are more positive, self-confident, optimistic, and compassionate. Forgiveness sets in motion a dynamic process that is capable of transforming all human relationships.

Forgiveness is unique and powerful. Consider the inspirational lives of Mahatma Gandhi, Martin Luther King Jr., and Nelson Mandela, who responded to injustice, prejudice, and persecution with a call for reconciliation and forgiveness. So did Jesus, who forgave the people who crucified him.

Gratitude

Gratitude is an appreciative state of being that leads me to be aware of my blessings. I was born to caring parents who surrounded me with love. Barb, our daughters, Stephanie and Deb, our sons-in-law, Scott and Jon, and our grandchildren, Caroline, Eloise, Stephen, and Audrey, are sources of great joy. Besides family, I have received countless other blessings.

Marcus Cicero claimed, "Gratitude is not only the greatest of virtues, but the parent of all the others." Charles Swindoll said something similar about positive attitude, which he extolled as being more important than anything else. He concluded, "I am convinced that life is 10% what happens to me and 90% how I react to it." Gratitude and positive attitude point to the same reality…a choice that I can make regardless of any negative situation.

Gratitude, positive attitude, and saying "thank you" to others are all within my control. When I live in a state of gratitude, I am upbeat, have a ready smile on my face, and convey a sense of serenity that puts others at ease. When I choose to be positive, I let go of the negatives and express the best possible interpretation of every predicament. When I interact with others, whether by direct conversation, email, or letters, I look for specific ways to express thanks.

When I find myself not measuring up to these standards, I meditate on the nature of Divine Love and picture myself doing better.

Compassion

Compassion includes more than the Golden Rule, sympathy, or empathy. The Golden Rule can lack sympathy, for example, in the case of rich people who rationalize that they would decline help if they were poor. Sympathy demands feeling sorry for people in a tough predicament. Empathy requires more than sympathy—the ability to "walk a mile in another person's shoes" and to suffer with them. Finally, compassion includes something more than empathy—action to help alleviate another person's suffering.

Compassion is prioritized by all of the world's great religions. In Hinduism, compassion (*daya*) is one of the three central virtues. In Judaism, God is invoked as the Father of Compassion. In Buddhism, compassion (*karuna*) is central. The Dalai Lama has said, "If you want others to be happy, practice compassion. If you want to be happy, practice compassion." In Islam, every chapter of the *Quran* except one begins with the words, "In the name of God the Compassionate, the Merciful." In Christianity, the life, teachings, and death of Jesus embody compassion. He taught, "Whatever you do for the least of these, you do for me."

In spite of a universal emphasis on compassion, compassionate approaches by the U.S. government have been vilified as "socialism." The poor are blamed for their predicament, characterized as dependent "takers," and challenged to "pick themselves up by their own bootstraps." Given this attitude, the income gap between the rich and poor has been widening in American society every year since 1979. No wonder there is widespread opposition to universal health care, even though the United States is ranked 31st in the world in infant mortality—worse than virtually every industrialized economy.

Compassion is the missing virtue that America desperately needs. Volunteer charity alone is not sufficient to meet the social needs of society. Many problems are too big for charities, cities, or states to solve alone. We need a national government with a compassionate commitment to its entire people. Compassion does not create dependency. Instead, it lifts people up, gives them strength, and encourages them to serve others.

Service

"Whoever desires to become great among you shall be your servant." This quote from the Gospel of Matthew has close parallels in the Gospels of Mark and Luke. Hindu, Buddhist, Muslim, and Jewish scriptures emphasize service as well. It rewards both the server and the recipient.

A powerful example of a service orientation is the Center for Servant Leadership at Gustavus Adolphus College. The Center tries to instill in all students the importance of service, through which they "make their lives count." By recognizing their gifts and passions, they can serve "where deep gladness and the world's deep hunger meet." The Center publishes its own newsletter and brings together career counseling, job placement, church relations, community service and vocational reflection.

2012 TLC instructor Natalie Prittinen practicing servant
leadership by sharing her gift for teaching tennis with appreciative
students who seek a better understanding of the game.

The servant leadership approach emphasizes collaboration, cooperation and empowerment. Instead of a top-down hierarchal method, servant leadership emphasizes delegated and shared responsibility. It prioritizes the growth of students, players, and employees, hoping to build environments where humility, trust, compassion, listening, and good stewardship prevail.

Apology

The Center for Conflict Resolution claims: "A sincere apology is one of the most powerful tools to bring peace, stop arguments, and restore broken relationships. It can bring solace and comfort to the offended, relief to the wrongdoer, and healing to their relationship. A genuine, effective apology is an act of honesty, humility, and generosity."

Counselors universally tout the power of an apology. For example, Beverly Engel, author of *The Power of Apology: Healing Steps to Transform All Your Relationships*, shows that apologizing can prevent divorces, lawsuits, family estrangements, and even atrocities. Failing to admit error and express regret shows disrespect.

The famous South African Truth and Reconciliation Commission realized that prosecution and punishment of apartheid crimes would prolong the pain, not end it. Therefore, it encouraged perpetrators of violence to admit their guilt, apologize and ask for forgiveness, with the understanding that they would be granted amnesty. It aided the transition from apartheid to racial equality in South Africa.

All religious traditions emphasize repentance, contrition, and regret for sins of commission and omission. C.S. Lewis, in *The Screwtape Letters* and *Into the Wardrobe,* shows that pride leads to every other vice. Prideful people do not consider apologizing. From their perspective, they have not done anything wrong. They view an apology as a sign of weakness, betrayal, and "caving in."

Unfortunately, many Americans believe that any apology for their country's actions is a sign of weakness. During the presidential campaign of 2012, President Obama was maligned for conducting "An Apology Tour" of foreign nations. In his defense, Obama and fact checkers confirmed that he had not apologized. How ironical, given American foreign policy mistakes, that apologizing would be viewed as unacceptable behavior by our president.

Apologies are powerful and life changing. Nelson Mandela created amnesty for perpetrators of apartheid crimes in South Africa. Why is amnesty for illegal aliens in America such a difficult step? Could apologies and the promise of amnesty end one of the vexing social problems of our time? I believe so. However, not only the illegal aliens need to apologize. We, as a country, should apologize to the entire Latino population for the prejudicial way that our country has treated them.

Justice

When a woman committed adultery at the time of Jesus, the Mosaic Law prescribed death by stoning. This was considered justice. Yet, Jesus questioned the law with reasoning that Pharisees found subversive. (John 8: 3-11) He told the potential stone throwers that anyone without sin should throw the first stone. When no one stepped forward, Jesus told the woman, "Neither do I condemn you; go and sin no more." By freeing the woman, Jesus disregarded the law of the land in the name of Divine Love.

Could Divine Love also have an important role on the issue of illegal immigrants In America? Many have been in the United States for years, performing vital work for employers who needed their skills. Others came as young children. For them, the United States is the only country they have known. Now, they are subject to deportation. Sometimes, one member of a family is a legal citizen, but other family members are not. Deportation can be a cruel and disruptive punishment for separated families. If Jesus lived today, I believe he would summon us to follow Divine Love, not current immigration law.

Restorative justice has become the pathway to reconcile law and love. Wikipedia defines restorative justice as an approach that "focuses on the needs of the victims and the offenders, as well as the involved community, instead of satisfying abstract legal principles or punishing the offender." It worked in South Africa after apartheid ended. Also, my former student Maureen Farrell has used restorative justice to improve the legal system in her Minneapolis community. She has brought victims and teenage offenders together, focused on both of their needs, and produced outstanding rates of victim satisfaction and offender accountability.

Traditional criminal justice centers on broken laws, the offenders, and their punishment. In the case of illegal immigration, this approach leads too many Americans to oppose amnesty. On the other hand, restorative justice centers on the needs of the victims and offender accountability. Could restorative justice, honoring the demands of both law and love, be the best way to solve a vexing American problem like the immigration issue?

Acceptance

Unconditional acceptance is learned best as a child. I was fortunate. No matter how many times I failed or misbehaved, my parents and teachers were in my corner, giving me support. Granted, there were times that I did not feel accepted. I was crushed when my 3rd grade classmates laughed at me because of my religious beliefs. Later, in the 7th grade, some classmates bullied me as I returned home from school. However, these experiences helped me form my views on how I wanted to treat others.

Later, in my university years, I read *The Shaking of the Foundations*, a book of Christian sermons by Paul Tillich. His description of Divine Love and grace resonated with me. It reinforced the acceptance I had experienced as a child.

> You are accepted. You are accepted by that which is greater than you, and the name of which you do not know. Do not ask for the name now; perhaps you will find it later. Do not try to do anything now; perhaps later you will do much. Do not seek for anything; do not perform anything; do not intend anything. Simply accept the fact that you are accepted! (*The Shaking of the Foundations*, p. 162)

Regrettably, many children of the world are less fortunate than I. They grow up in dangerous war zones, where death and brutality surround them; in uncaring cities, where homeless young girls are forced into prostitution; in churches and youth groups, where young boys are sexually abused; in broken homes, where children are beaten and ignored; in evangelical communities, where gay and lesbian children are forced to view their sexual orientation as sinful; or in any home, where children are made to feel that acceptance depends on athletic or academic success, good looks, etc.

The spirits of many children have been crushed. For them, Tillich's message, "Simply accept the fact that you are accepted," does not mesh with their childhood experiences. For these words to ever ring true, abused children need to build bonds with adults who can accept them unconditionally.

Hope

Dr. Martin Luther King Jr. delivered his "I Have a Dream" speech to two hundred thousand people on the Washington Mall in August of 1963. It was a powerful expression of hope in the face of prejudice and brutal oppression. In spite of every discouraging fact, Reverend King hoped:

> I have a dream that one day, down in Alabama, with its vicious racists, with its governor having his lips dripping with the words of interposition and nullification; one day right there in Alabama, little black boys and black girls will be able to join hands with little white boys and white girls as sisters and brothers.
>
> I have a dream today.
>
> I have a dream that one day every valley shall be exalted, every hill and mountain shall be made low, the rough places will be made plain, and the crooked places will be made straight, and the glory of the Lord shall be revealed, and all flesh shall see it together.

> This is our hope. This is the faith that I go back to the South with. With this faith we will be able to hew out of the mountain of despair a stone of hope.

Reverend King was an inspiring conveyor of hope. He chose to be optimistic and trusting in the face of violence and prejudice. His persuasive and buoyant oratory lifted the spirits of his audience and encouraged them to continue their fight for social, political, and economic equality.

However, convincing hope needs to be based on reality. It must be more than wishful thinking, or as some might say, "pie in the sky." Most importantly, Reverend King's hope was based on his biblical faith in God, expressed eloquently in the words and actions of the Old Testament prophets and reinforced powerfully by the love and sacrifice of Jesus.

Other factors fueled Reverend King's hope. Mahatma Gandhi's successful use of nonviolent resistance to accomplish Indian independence was an inspiration. King knew that his nonviolent approach, if applied correctly, could work to end desegregation. Also, King cited a legal tradition that supported his words. The Declaration of Independence, the Constitution, the Emancipation Proclamation, and the "Brown vs. Board of Education" Supreme Court decision all enshrined King's hope for desegregation.

Finally, Reverend King's message of hope was built on the courageous actions of Freedom Riders. Two years before King spoke, the first Freedom Riders had left Washington, D.C. on May 4, 1961. Their bus contained black and white civil rights activists who were committed to nonviolence. They hoped to peacefully integrate bus stops across the South, where Jim Crow laws still preserved segregation. The riders were almost killed when a mob set their bus on fire and the doors were locked. They did escape the bus, but then the mob savagely beat them. Yet, they continued to work with hope.

Other Freedom Riders followed, sponsored by the Congress of Racial Equality (CORE) and the Student Nonviolent Coordinating Committee (SNCC). The federal government was reluctantly pulled into the violence, which pitted Ku Klux Klan activists and local police against federal militia. In the summer of 1961, approximately 60 busses and hundreds of Freedom Riders bravely faced frenzied mobs, baseball bats, and jails. One of the bravest was Bernard Lafayette, a student at the American Baptist Theological Seminary in Nashville. Twenty-seven times he was beaten and jailed, narrowly escaping death in Montgomery, Alabama.

In 1962, Lafayette accepted a position with SNCC to do organizing work in Selma, Alabama. Eleven years later, he became the first director of the Peace Education Program at Gustavus Adolphus College. Through all of his civil rights work, Lafayette continued to believe and hope.

When Dr. Martin Luther King Jr. delivered his "I Have a Dream" speech in 1963, he was expressing the hope of the American Civil Rights Movement. He departed from his prepared text after Mahalia Jackson cried, "Tell them about the dream, Martin." King's dreams of freedom and equality, arising from slavery and hatred, excited the world and gave hope a foundation.

Charity

Charity encompasses not just our possessions, but also time, actions, and love. Everything that we have, including life itself, is on loan from Divine Love. We are stewards of our possessions, not owners. We are obligated to be charitable—to sacrifice everything that exceeds our needs for a modest lifestyle. No one illustrated this better than Mother Teresa.

However, many wealthy people believe they are entitled to their riches. They oppose tax increases that could help feed the hungry, heal the sick, or care for the poor. Wealth redistribution and socialism are negative concepts for them. "Charity or handouts create dependency and stifle initiative," they claim.

However, that need not be the case. In the Great Depression of the 1930s, proud individuals did not want handouts, even though they were without work and their families were starving. The federal government met both their physical and dignity needs by creating the Civilian Conservation Corps (CCC), which provided work when the unemployment rate exceeded 25% and jobs were not available.

Both private charity and governmental programs for the needy can be based on the universally accepted maxim, "Give people a fish and you feed them for a day. Teach people to fish and you feed them for a lifetime." This is being modeled in Denmark, where all unemployment benefits depend on workers entering government sponsored job-retraining programs.

Our stewardship approach to charity was strongly advocated by 18th century, Protestant reformer John Wesley. He inspired the revival that created the Methodist Church. For Wesley, the industry and frugality that resulted from a religious approach to life naturally produced an increase in wealth. Unfortunately, as riches increased, so did pride, anger, and love for worldly goods. The only way to avoid this conundrum was continual stewardship, based on giving and a modest lifestyle.

Drawing upon Martin Luther's emphasis on grace, Wesley emphasized that God owned everything. Out of God's grace, everything that anyone possessed came as a gift. It was God's wish that all gifts were shared, especially with the poor. For Wesley, charity was more than tithing, where a tenth of income was given to God. Stewardship-based living acknowledged that the other nine-tenths was not ours either.

The disparity between the rich and the poor was always a source of anguish for Wesley. He believed that it was not right for him to enjoy comforts, while others did not have the necessities of life. Nor did he believe that parents should shower their children with gifts. To do so would only create more lust, vanity, false pride, and hurtful desires.

Wesley modeled what he preached. Even though he earned from 30 to 120 pounds a year, he lived on 28 pounds and gave away the rest. When he died, he had only 10 pounds to his name.

In the modern world, Warren Buffet exemplifies a stewardship approach to charity. Although one of the richest men in the world, Buffet still lives in the same home that he bought in 1957 for $31,500. In 2006, after pledging to give away 99% of his wealth, Buffet contributed $37 billion to the Bill and Melinda Gates Foundation. In 2010, Buffet and Gates persuaded 92 of the richest individuals to sign a pledge committing the majority of their wealth to philanthropy.

Furthermore, I admire Buffet when he pushes our country to establish justice and to provide for the citizen welfare goals that Thomas Jefferson wrote into the preamble of the United States Constitution. Stewardship-based charity is not only the responsibility of individuals and the private organizations that they support. It is also the obligation of the organization formed to represent all the people—the U.S. federal government.

Charity lies at the center of what it means for me to be Christian. Jesus could not have been clearer. "Whatsoever you do to the least of my people, that you do unto me." (Matthew 25:40) "Peter was grieved because Jesus said unto him the third time, 'Do you love me?' And he said to Him, 'Lord, You know all things. You know that I love you.' Jesus said to him, 'Feed my sheep.'" (John 21:17)

Peace

Jesus is called the "Prince of Peace." A common greeting between Christians is "Peace be with you." This "peace" is a personal, inner peace that is celebrated by every great religion. For example, the famous Oglala Sioux holy man Black Elk, who died in 1950, wrote this beautiful description of inner peace.

> The first peace, which is the most important, is that which comes within the souls of people when they realize their relationship, their oneness with the universe and all its powers, and when they realize that at the center of the universe dwells the Great Spirit, and that this center is really everywhere, it is within each of us. (*Black Elk Speaks*, p. 25)

Most world leaders strive to create a world where inner peace is more likely to be experienced. Yet, even in areas of the world where no wars are being waged, obstacles to inner peace stand in the way. The 14th Dalai Lama poignantly wrote:

> Peace, in the sense of the absence of war, is of little value to someone who is dying of hunger or cold. It will not remove the pain of torture inflicted on a prisoner of conscience. It does not comfort those who have lost their loved ones in floods caused by

senseless deforestation in a neighboring country. Peace can only last where human rights are respected, where people are fed, and where individuals and nations are free. (*Dalai Lama: A Policy of Kindness,* "The Nobel Peace Prize Lecture," p. 17)

However, in many places, human rights are not respected; people are not fed; individuals are not free; tyrants slaughter the innocent; and invading armies overrun free states. What is the appropriate response? Most world leaders agree with the Dalai Lama, that both individual and world peace depend on human rights. Do leaders prioritize social, economic and humanitarian reforms with non-violent means? Or do they commit overwhelmingly to military solutions?

The current path of the United States is clear. A fact sheet from the humanitarian organization Care shows that the American government spends 19.1% of its federal budget on military spending, and .39% on poverty-focused development programs. The contrast is startling. It reflects a popular American belief that peace and national security are promoted best through violence or the threat of it.

Peace at the individual level is achievable through many religions and philosophies if two conditions are present. First, people need to live in areas where basic human needs are met. *Bloomberg Businessweek* estimated that if 5% of the U.S. budget would be spent each year on the world's poor in targeted programs with measurable outcomes, we could eliminate absolute poverty in the world.

Second, people need basic human rights and personal security. Because of oppressive regimes, wars, and intolerance, these are more difficult and expensive challenges, but ones that could be met with 14.1% of the budget spent on the military instead of 19.1%.

By waging two simultaneous ground wars for the first 13 years of the 21st century and using preemptive drone strikes that kill innocent people, America continues to move away from peace and national security. The following critique by Dr. Martin Luther King Jr. gives reason to reflect.

> One day we must come to see that peace is not merely a distant goal that we seek, but that it is a means by which we arrive at that goal. We must pursue peaceful ends through peaceful means. ("The Casualties of the War in Viet Nam," speech delivered on February 25, 1967)

Nonviolence

Nonviolence, for me, was possibly innate. As a child, I would not fight back, even when smaller children bullied me. Consequently, I was harassed more than most kids. To avoid confrontations, I depended on strategic routes and my running speed.

When I was a freshman in high school, my basketball coach forced me to go out for football, thinking it would make me a tougher basketball rebounder. All season, I hated the contact, violence, and continual putdowns. When it was over, I promised myself I would never play football again.

During basketball season, my coach always pushed me to be more aggressive. In practice, he encouraged teammates to use dirty tactics against me, so I would become tougher. He expected me to create extra rebounding space with my elbows. I tolerated practice and enjoyed games, where referees would penalize unsportsmanlike play.

I have a nonviolent reverence for life. When my friends used slingshots to kill birds, I was repulsed. I have never owned a gun or wanted one for self-defense. Serving in the military was not an option for me. If I had been drafted for service in Vietnam, I would have sought civilian service alternatives. If they were not an option, I would have gone to prison.

Jesus inspired me. "Turning the other cheek" was not cowardice, but a symbol of strength. Jesus did not violently oppose his killers. Instead he forgave them, and in the process became a lasting symbol of Divine Love.

Mahatma Gandhi energized me. In the 1970s, I taught a college seminar on his religious beliefs and politics and took students to India to meet his followers and to visit his ashrams. Gandhi showed that nonviolence could be used as a method for social change. By combining *ahimsa* (nonviolence) and *satyagraha* (truth force), he developed a nonviolent approach to politics and life that persuaded the British to leave India. Dr. Martin Luther King Jr. wrote:

> If humanity is to progress, Gandhi is inescapable. He lived, thought, acted and was inspired by the vision of humanity evolving toward a world of peace and harmony…Gandhi was probably the first person in history to lift the love ethic of Jesus above mere interaction between individuals to a powerful and effective social force on a large scale. (*The Words of Martin Luther King Jr. Jr*, p. 71)

Gandhi's influence stretched across the world. Martin Luther King Jr., Nelson Mandela, Cesar Chavez, and Aung San Suu Kyi have credited Gandhi. Also, his approach encouraged movements that toppled Ferdinand Marcos in the Philippines in 1986, Augusto Pinochet in Chile in 1989, and Slobodan Milosevic in Yugoslavia in 2000.

Gandhi's method of *satyagraha* includes the following eight principles.

1) There are causes for which to die, but none to kill for.
2) People and nations need to be the change that they wish to see in the world.
3) Power built on love is more lasting than power built on violence and fear.

4) Retaliation is unacceptable. "An eye for an eye" leaves both opponents blind.
5) Everyone has a "higher self," one that honors truth and justice.
6) Love and respect for everyone needs to include enemies.
7) The willingness to sacrifice self-centered desires sways others.
8) Boycotts and non-cooperation put economic pressure on perpetrators of injustice.

Satyagraha remains a powerful force for human rights and social change. Faith in others, courage, optimism and trust lead countries to prioritize peaceful solutions. On the other hand, lack of faith in others, fear, pessimism, and distrust encourage nations to use military solutions. The future of the world depends on the principles of *satyagraha*.

Humility

Humility is another virtue extolled by all of the world's great religions. Commonly it is defined as the quality of being modest and respectful. The opposite quality is being prideful and self-absorbed.

Some people try to project humility by being self-effacing. For example, I once responded to a compliment saying, "I should have done better." My mother immediately pulled me aside and said, "When you are complimented, look the person in the eyes, smile, and say 'thank you.' Otherwise, you are unintentionally 'fishing' for more praise."

As I grew older, I learned another lesson. After saying "thank you," I found an appropriate way to praise the person who had complimented me. It can begin with the simple words, "How thoughtful of you to say that."

Brilliant women and handsome men sometimes put themselves down dishonestly, thinking that this conveys humility. C.S. Lewis, author of *The Screwtape Letters*, captured the irony of this misunderstanding in letters from senior devil Screwtape to his junior devil Wormwood. In the following passage, Screwtape explained to Wormwood their strategy for undermining true humility in the person they were trying to corrupt.

> Fix in his mind the idea that humility consists in trying to believe his talents to be less valuable than he believes them to be. No doubt, they are in fact less valuable than he believes, but that is not the point. The great thing is to make him value an opinion for some quality other than truth, thus introducing an element of dishonesty and make-believe into the heart of what otherwise threatens to become a virtue. (*The Screwtape Letters*, p. 65)

True humility is achieved when people no longer focus on themselves, but instead prioritize others. The Golden Rule says, "Do unto others as you would have them do unto you." Similarly, the Bible's Second Great

Commandment is "Love your neighbor as yourself." In both cases, the laws emphasize someone else, but they circle back to include the self.

When "it's all about me," the consequence is selfishness and arrogance. When "it's all about you," the result is selflessness and humility. The paradox is this: An emphasis on "me" undermines my self-worth, and an emphasis on "you" elevates my self-worth.

One of the persons we most commonly associate with humility is Mother Teresa. She wrote:

> Humility is the mother of all virtues.... It is in being humble that our love becomes real, devoted and ardent. If you are humble nothing will touch you, neither praise nor disgrace, because you know what you are. If you are blamed you will not be discouraged. If they call you a saint you will not put yourself on a pedestal. (*In the Heart of the World: Thoughts, Stories and Prayers*, p. 65)

Mother Teresa's Humility list, followed by the Sisters of St. Francis, includes simple recommendations that are worth incorporating into everyday living. They include:

1) Speak as little as possible about yourself.
2) Keep busy with your own affairs and not those of others.
3) Do not interfere in the affairs of others.
4) Accept small irritations with good humor.
5) Do not dwell on the faults of others.
6) Accept censures, even if unmerited.
7) Accept insults and injuries.
8) Accept contempt, being forgotten and disregarded.
9) Be courteous and delicate, even when provoked by someone.
10) Do not seek to be admired and loved.
11) Give in, in discussions, even when you are right.
12) Choose always the more difficult task.

This simple advice for humility provides a guide to living that reinforces all of my admired values. The list includes love, grace, serenity, trust, forgiveness, gratitude, compassion, service, apology, justice, acceptance, hope, charity, peace, nonviolence, and humility. These are the values in which I truly believe. They are my guiding lights, inextricably connected to this life, and open to whatever may lie beyond.

EPILOGUE

Both Karen and Arthur modeled the wisdom of the Serenity Prayer. They showed me how powerful it is, even in the face of death. Now it is my time to follow their lead.

Take my kidney out!

On the evening of July 2, 2008, the emergency room doctor who discovered my cancer made an appointment for me in Mankato with an oncologist. However, I knew that I wanted to be treated at the Mayo Clinic in Rochester. At 10:15 p.m. I called our TLC friend Dr. Charles Loprinzi, a medical oncologist at Mayo. By 11:00 p.m. he had me scheduled for an appointment the next morning at 8:00 a.m.

By July 7, Mayo physicians determined that there was no evidence that the cancer had spread. It appeared to be confined to a large tumor (9 x 7 x 7 cm) in my right kidney. The tumor was larger than the kidney itself. The right approach seemed simple. Take my kidney out! There was no point in trying to save it. My surgery was on Tuesday, July 15, and I planned to be back teaching at TLC on Thursday, July 17. Before the operation I wrote:

> I'm very comfortable with the idea of losing a kidney. It's something that I have been contemplating ever since Barb and I met an amazing man at the Gift of Life Transplant House in Rochester over five years ago. He had traveled all the way from Australia to donate a kidney. He did this as part of his service commitment to mankind. Australia did not permit kidney donations to strangers (only family members or close friends), so he had traveled half way around the world to fulfill his mission. We only need one kidney (unless you get kidney cancer), so given the number of people who need kidneys, donation strikes me as a noble commitment to others.

> Now I won't be able to donate a kidney to someone else, but Neal Hagberg told me "Consider this a donation to cancer. And remember, you are being extra nice, because cancer does not have many friends."

The news following the surgery was encouraging. My cancer was determined to be of the chromophobe variety, which occurs in only 5% of kidney cancer cases. It was considered to be slow growing and commonly cured with surgery. I wrote:

> The doctors called this a "wimpy" cancer. Yeah! Eighty percent of kidney cancer cases are "clear cell", or a more aggressive form of cancer. As a competitor, I usually like tougher competition, but guess what? Competing against a "wimp" sounds really good to me at this point!

On Thursday, July 17, I did return home…just in time to greet family campers arriving at TLC late that afternoon. I was on a reduced activity schedule for a month, but I did not miss any teaching responsibilities at TLC. I made periodic visits to Mayo over the next six months for checkups, but no chemotherapy or radiation was necessary. At the end of December, I was confident that I had met the cancer challenge and won—just like my wife, Barb.

I drew inspiration from my wife.

In 2002, Barb faced an incurable but treatable cancer named multiple myeloma. She discovered it after her hip broke for no apparent reason. Soon we learned how a cancer of certain white blood cells called plasma cells could produce lesions in the bones. To stop this cancer growth, we decided to follow a two-pronged approach. First, Barb received four months of chemotherapy to thwart the multiple myeloma growth. Second, we pursued an aggressive strategy labeled an "autologous stem cell transplant." By doing this, we hoped to eliminate the need for ongoing treatment.

The second strategy required that Barb's own stem cells (remarkable master cells that have the ability to continuously divide and form new cells) be collected from her blood stream over a five-day period, then frozen, and later reintroduced into her blood stream after her bone marrow was destroyed by high-intensity radiation.

The reintroduction of stem cells marked the beginning of engraftment, which for Barb occurred on February 6, 2003. The stem cells moved to the bone marrow and began to produce new white and red blood cells and platelets, which were necessary for clotting. During this time, Barb had virtually no defense mechanism against disease, so she received daily transfusions to keep up her blood count up until her body could replenish on its own. Barb successfully handled the treatment, but others at the Transplant House with us suffered frustrating setbacks.

The doctors, nurses, and staff at the Mayo Clinic were impressive—both compassionate and extremely skilled. The loving environment at the Transplant House brought us in contact with many inspiring people. They included a young woman who gave 70% of her liver to her father and then ran in a marathon four months later. Two other kidney donors gave a kidney to people they barely knew—one, a fellow church member, and the other, a post office worker acquaintance.

Barb returned home from the Transplant House in early March. As she got stronger, she handled TLC registrations and baby-sat our granddaughter Caroline. By the summer of 2003, she was again working full time. Her recovery was and continues to be amazing.

More bad news, my cancer metastasized.

On January 16, 2009, I had my first CT scan after the operation. As my surgeon and I looked at the screen together, I could see shock come over his face. This was not what we were expecting. He was almost speechless. My cancer had gone from Stage Two to Stage Four, and my 10-year survival expectation of 80% was out the window. Now the average survival rate was only nine months, although I would not be told that until later.

I was placed in a trial for patients with various forms of *advanced* cancer. I received the highest doses of RAD001 and PTK787 that previous trial groups had been able to tolerate. I was put on four-week cycles that would continue as long as the cancer did not get worse, and I avoided serious side effects. At the time, I wrote:

> When my oncologist described the pathway ahead, he emphasized that attitude was the key thing that separated those who did well from those who did not. My daughter Stephanie responded, "Then we know that Dad will be successful!"
>
> She is right! I will be successful, no matter what happens. I am doing well, with the strong support from wonderful friends, a gracious God, and loving family members.

I took the chemotherapy in pill form, three times a day. Through the summer of 2009, I continued to feel strong, play tennis, coach the team, and do all the other things that were part of my normal life. Certainly, there were unpleasant side effects to the chemo, but they were tolerable and manageable. Subsequent CT scans, every two months, revealed that the cancer did not appear to be growing. Again, I was feeling more confident.

Surprise! I have prostate cancer as well.

In June 2009, a rise in my prostate specific antigen (PSA) from 4 to 10 over a two-year period caused my oncologist to recommend a biopsy of my prostate. The procedure confirmed cancer in three out of four sections of my prostate. My Gleason Score was 6, midway between the least and most aggressive forms of prostate cancer.

What should I do? After discussing "watchful waiting" and surgery with a physician assistant in urology, we agreed that surgery was the right choice. I returned several weeks later for my pre-operative appointment. The possible complications were discussed, and the date and time for my surgery was set.

In October, I finally met my urology surgeon. He came into the room, apparently having read my medical history only a few minutes before. His first words were, "I am not going to operate". I was shocked. How could this be? My complete medical history had been available to him for almost two months. I had met with his urology department colleagues three times in the preceding months. If this was the outcome, why did we schedule a biopsy in the first place?

I pressed the surgeon for an explanation. "Would you perform surgery for someone my age with a Gleason score of 6 and a 10-year life expectancy?" He answered "yes." I countered, "That means you believe my life expectancy is *less than* ten years." He agreed, and left the room as abruptly as he had arrived, leaving his surprised physician assistant the task of helping me make sense out of this turn of events.

Perhaps this was the wakeup call that no one else was willing to deliver so directly. I had terminal cancer. Until this point, I had not had a discussion with the Mayo doctors and staff about life expectancy. My serious situation had been clothed in optimism. My medical oncologist had emphasized, "Life expectancy is connected to attitude. Every individual is different." He was right. I remain pleased that he had taken that approach with me. However, it had fueled an optimism that crashed head-on with this doctor's decision not to do surgery.

In November 2009, with surgery no longer an option, my oncologist recommended a hormone depressant drug named Casodex. Unfortunately, my body reacted strongly. There were many negative side effects, but the worst was pain that kept me from sleeping. I lay awake at night, pleading for an end to my suffering. Painkillers did not work; they only constipated me, ruined my liver test results, and almost got me eliminated from the kidney cancer trial.

In December, I stopped taking Casodex because the side effects were too severe. Since then, I have watched and waited, not knowing what my prostate cancer will do. One Mayo oncologist explained to me that the chance that the prostate cancer would cause major problems was less than 5%, given that I already had the metastatic kidney cancer. Living with my cancers, rather than eradicating them, became my *modus operandi*.

I was removed from the kidney cancer trial.

In January 2010, after my liver recovered from the Casodex debacle, I was allowed to remain on the kidney cancer trial. However, my period of grace proved short lived. Seven months later, I was removed. Thereby, I lost access to the chemotherapy drugs that had kept my cancer from further metastasizing for 18 months.

In part, I had myself to blame. With my oncologist's permission, I stopped taking the chemo, hoping to end the neuropathy in my feet. He valued both my quality of life and my quantity of life. Every step I took was painful. I had tried more comfortable shoes, but they did not help. However, two weeks without chemo made the difference. The feet were feeling good; I was enjoying my tennis again; and I was hoping that I no longer needed the drugs that were reducing my quality of life. As the two weeks ended, I discovered that I needed oral surgery two weeks later. Protocol demanded that I not take chemo prior to surgery, so my oncologist agreed to two more weeks without it.

A month off chemo proved unfortunate. The next CT-scan revealed a slight advancement in the cancer. The physician assistant who showed me the scan thought I would *not* be eliminated from the trial. However, my oncologist, who saw the scan later, judged otherwise, because of the rules written into the experimental kidney cancer trial.

Leaving the trial had at least two advantages. One was my ability to avoid its strict protocol, which required a CT scan, a blood draw, and a trip to Mayo every two months. I worried about my frequent exposure to high dosage radiation. The other was my freedom to take one chemo drug instead of two. Perhaps that would lessen my neuropathy problems and decrease the amount of poison that I was pouring into my body.

I remained convinced that either of the two drugs I was receiving, RAD001 or PTK787, had worked, and was continuing to do so. However, I dismissed both as possible options when I was taken off the trial. Neither of these drugs had Federal Drug Administration (FDA) approval. My situation illustrated the problem of conducting a trial with two drugs—one an mTOR inhibitor (RAD001) that targeted one cancer pathway, and the other, a VEGF inhibitor (PTK787) that targeted another one. After 18 months of using both, my oncologist did not know which one had been helping me. He suspected that it was the VEGF inhibitor, so he chose Pazopanib, an FDA approved drug that targeted the same pathway.

Within nine months, I had ten tumors and three operations.

From September 2010 until June 2011, my oncologist gave credit to Pazopanib for preventing tumors in my lungs and liver. That was a tough line of reasoning for me to accept. I had never experienced tumors there, although CT-scans sometimes produced false cancer alarms. Suspicious cysts sometimes appeared to grow, but subsequent tests proved the opposite.

However, this was a time when seven large tumors grew in my spine, two in my ribs, and one in my left femur. Cryoablation procedures in December and April froze eight tumors and filled my larger skeletal holes with cement.

In early June, high-intensity, stereotactic radiation eradicated two more large tumors that had spread beyond the spine into the surrounding soft tissue.

All three procedures required extreme precision from highly skilled specialists. Any miscalculation or slip could have left me permanently disabled. My recoveries were challenging. I longed for nights when I would be able to sleep lying down again, rather than sitting in a chair or walking until exhausted in order to relieve the pain.

For me, this was not a prudent or sustainable path. I became convinced that Pazopanib, a VEGF inhibitor, was not working. This medication was supposed to block blood vessel growth around the cancer. I had gone through three operations in six months, each involving my spine. Through these experiences, an important fact became clear to me. It must have been the mTOR inhibitor that kept my kidney cancer from metastasizing while I was on the trial. I was convinced that was what we needed to try next. If RAD001 was not available, then we needed to try another mTOR inhibitor.

My oncologist was not convinced. He continued to doubt that an mTOR inhibitor was the way to go. Instead, he proposed another VEGF inhibitor. At that time, the literature suggested that VEGF inhibitors were more promising than mTOR inhibitors for stopping kidney cancer metastasis.

"Please give me an mTOR inhibitor," I insisted. Finally, he agreed. "RAD001, the mTOR inhibitor that you took on the trial, is now FDA approved. It is called Everolimus, and I will prescribe it for you." I was elated. Leaving his office, I was convinced that life was going to get better.

I moved forward with hope.

For the remainder of 2011, life was good. I could teach each day at TLC, be a volunteer assistant coach for the Gustavus varsity, and enjoy trips and long hikes. Barb and I traveled to Wimbledon as guests of Eric Butorac, and later to Newport, Rhode Island for his wedding. Challenging hikes included a high peak in the White Mountains of Arizona and a seaside cliff in Puerto Rico.

There were no more surgical procedures or excessive side effects from chemo. An August CT-scan showed that the cancer was not advancing. This was the best I had felt since the cancer began to metastasize. My conditioning came back, thanks to daily bicycle rides. When I pedaled, I was aware of no physical limitations. The same was true when I would do my daily pushups, stomach crunches, and yoga stretching.

I chose not to worry.

On January 4, 2012, a hip x-ray revealed that the tumor on the top of my left femur had expanded. The doctor analyzing the x-ray insisted that I be placed in a wheelchair. My oncologist was immediately informed. He, in turn, contacted an orthopedic surgeon, setting in motion the plan for an immediate hip replacement.

I resisted. Why operate when I was still able to ride bikes, hike mountains, and play tennis—all without discomfort? The orthopedic surgeon agreed that the surgery could wait, provided I used a cane. On the way home, I picked up a cane, which remained in the closet for over a year.

My January CT-scan was encouraging. The cancer had not metastasized further in my spine and ribs. My chemo seemed to be working everywhere except my hip. How could this be? To me the answer seemed simple. No hip x-ray had been taken the previous June after nine months of rapidly metastasizing cancer, so the deterioration went undetected. In a way I was grateful. A surgery then would have stopped my trip to Wimbledon.

Subsequent CT-scans and x-rays in 2012 and early 2013 did not show any further metastasizing in the bones. Walks, bicycle rides, coaching, and restricted tennis playing had not bothered my hip, confirming to me that my approach to chemotherapy and hip replacement was correct.

I continued to hope, even though my oncologist had told me that all chemotherapies only work for a while, and then they are ineffective. So be it. If there would be another proven chemotherapy that I could use if my present one fails, I was open to trying it.

So far, my kidney cancer had metastasized only to my skeletal system. Only one thing—Everolimus—had limited the tumor growth, since my metastasis began in July 2008. I had gone without it for six months in 2008, and nine months in 2010 and 2011, during which times my skeletal system was decimated.

However, Everolimus caused my body to pay a demanding price. My triglycerides and cholesterol were elevated. Different parts of my body bled for no apparent reason; my lower legs swelled and itched; my nose ran continuously; my digestive track was affected; and my body stiffened, stooped, and lost strength, changing my run into a slow and labored walk.

Why have I accepted these consequences? Instead, why did I not use natural cures, anti-cancer diets, exercise, and meditation as an alternative to chemotherapy? I wish any of these practices offered to me an effective, cancer elimination choice. They have aided the quality of my life—before I contracted cancer and ever since. However, they have not been effective in limiting my cancer metastasis.

Living without worry became more difficult.

Living without worry became harder on May 1, 2013. Pain in my left femur took away my ability to walk. Pre-operation x-rays of my entire left femur showed startling cancer growth. These tumors dwarfed the ones revealed previously in x-rays of the femur head. The cancer had completely destroyed my left femur, making a titanium femur and hip replacement necessary. The abductor muscle was cut, but could not be reattached, causing me to walk permanently with a cane and a limp. After recovery, bicycle riding and walks were still part of my daily regimen, but tennis and rigorous wilderness hikes/climbs were part of my past.

How was this possible? The CT-scans in early January had shown no cancer growth in the chest, spine, pelvis, and hip. Those positive tests left me with the continuing hope that my chemotherapy was checking cancer growth everywhere in my body. That hope ended on May 1. My path forward will involve frequent CT-scans and x-rays of my entire body, followed by early interventions with intensive, stereotactic radiation.

As the summer progressed, the cancer continued to metastasize in my skeletal system. It was obvious that my chemotherapy had lost some of its effectiveness. The progression has been relatively slow, and six troublesome tumors in the ribs, right hip, and spine were eliminated by stereotactic radiation in June, August, and November.

In July, a relatively minor leg wound below my left calf did not heal because of the chemotherapy. I let it go too long. An e-coli infection almost reached my bone, prompting eight days in the hospital during early September. Surgery, a wound vacuum, and four more months of supervised care were necessary. I was taken off chemotherapy to promote healing.

In late November, after going back on chemotherapy, I suspected that it was creating new problems—pain throughout my midsection, loss of appetite, and vomiting. However, when sores broke out after two weeks, I was comforted to know that I had shingles. It was a disease with an end point.

January 15, 2014, was a day for celebration. I was temporarily over the shingles and feeling much better. Also, it was the 48th anniversary of the day that Barb and I had met on a mountaintop. We "celebrated" by going to the Mayo Clinic for my two-month checkup, a full day of tests and physician consultations.

Two positive results encouraged us. First, my plastic surgeon thought my leg wound had healed beautifully. No further checkups were necessary. Second, my radiation oncologist confirmed that my chemotherapy was having a positive effect. There was no further metastasis in my skeletal system, a welcome change from the cancer advancement that had occurred during the months that I had been off chemotherapy because of leg wound issues.

However, my PET-scan revealed an ominous development, one that my kidney cancer oncologist had anticipated and one that I had hoped would never occur. He thought the cancer had metastasized to three spots in my right lung, marking the first time that it had attacked soft tissue. On the other hand, my radiation oncologist was not convinced. She thought that we might be looking at fluid buildup in the lungs caused by the chemotherapy, not cancer growth. Each explanation had challenging implications, but I hoped that my radiation oncologist was right. CT-scans two months later would provide a more definitive answer.

On March 12, 2014, I returned to Mayo Clinic in a weakened state. I was so tired that even standing caused me to breathe hard. Pain in my back left me convinced that the cancer had spread to new spots in my ribs that would require stereotactic radiation.

The CT-scans and blood work revealed both good and challenging news. I was pleased to learn that the cancer had not spread to the lungs. Nevertheless, fluid buildup and cloudiness in the lungs were troubling. Secondly, there was no further cancer metastasis anywhere in the skeletal system, marking four months of chemotherapy protection. Then what was causing my pain? My radiation oncologist detected that I was experiencing a relapse of shingles and prescribed medicine to alleviate the pain.

However, my blood work revealed a troublesome development. My red blood cell count had dropped to eight, leaving me anemic and very tired. My oncologists took me off chemotherapy, speculating that it was affecting my bone marrow's ability to produce red blood cells. Also, they ordered two units of blood. Subsequently, my energy level increased.

Through all of these challenges, I have continued to coach, write, and travel. In early March, I flew to Phoenix, rode a bicycle each day with my brother John, drove with him to Indian Wells, California, watched Eric Butorac compete, and visited friends. At the end of March, Barb and I traveled to Florida for a Caribbean cruise with our family. I may not be as strong and mobile as I used to be, but I am determined to live out my remaining days and years as vigorously as my body permits.

Will I continue to avoid chemotherapy, given the fluid buildup in my lungs and the anemia it apparently produces? I don't know. What if these conditions do not improve while I am off chemotherapy, and my cancer lesions multiply? Will I go back on chemotherapy? I don't know. Will reduced levels of chemotherapy be the right compromise? I wonder. What will cure my recurring cases of shingles that have challenged me for the last five months? That remains to be seen.

These questions do not dominate my thinking. What will be will be. Instead, I focus on the important activities that I can still pursue, thanks to the loving support that Barb gives me every day. "Let Love Serve" is our motto, and we feel enriched and empowered by this approach.

Living with cancer is my goal. I used to see it as something to be defeated or eradicated, but now I prefer to view cancer as a gift that adds immeasurable quality to my life.

Terminal cancer has become a gift.

Seeing terminal cancer as a gift requires a unique perspective. Before kidney cancer metastasized to my bones in 2008, I knew that I should live each day as my last, but I found this challenging at a time when death seemed to be so far away. I pictured myself playing tennis into my 90s. After my life expectancy was reduced to less than a year, it became easier. With everything that I do or say, with every person that I see or say goodbye to, I am conscious of how special this present moment is. Yes, terminal cancer can be a gift. Let me enumerate the ways that my cancers have blessed me.

1) **Cancer prompted my family and friends to reach out with support, love, and appreciation.** Without the incentive that terminal kidney cancer has provided, many thoughtful notes would not have been written, numerous calls would not have been made, and visits would have been postponed. It is human nature to put off kind gestures, if we think there is time in the future to express how we feel. My death warning has put family and friends on alert, pushing them to express sooner, rather than later, how they feel. What a blessing!

2) **Cancer encouraged people to share their personal stories with me.** They feel comfortable doing so because they trust that I will empathize and understand. Often they tell me about cancer battles involving them or their loved ones. We connect immediately on a deep level that often focuses on the meaning of life. These contacts are very fulfilling for me, and I look forward to them.

3) **Cancer promoted reflection within me.** My longstanding interest in religion and ethics has made this an ongoing focus throughout my life. However, professional demands had interfered with the time I devoted to introspection. Cancer changed that. It put me back in touch with my inner self, what really matters, and how I want to spend the limited time that I have.

4) **Cancer activated a support system that has me covered.** I am indebted to Barb, who has accompanied me to every operation and Mayo appointment. Daughters, Stephanie and Deb, joined us at 4:30 a.m. for each surgery preparation and then stayed with us all day. Good friends Jan and Tim Butorac met us after most Mayo visits and hosted us for overnight stays. Dr. Charles and Margie Loprinzi counseled us whenever we asked. Also, Neal Hagberg and Tommy Valentini, my successors at Gustavus, held us in the light and carried on the causes to which I have committed my life. I feel so blessed.

5) **Cancer helped motivate us to donate TLC to Gustavus.** TLC has always functioned like a nonprofit, donating its profits to youth who could not afford camp and to Gustavus for tennis facilities and sport ethics projects. The best way to move forward was to make TLC officially nonprofit, which facilitated better cooperation with other nonprofits serving low-income youth.

6) **Cancer provided the time and impetus to write this memoir.** I learned much from Arthur Ashe Jr.'s memoir, *Days of Grace*. Similarly, I would like to leave behind a written record of my struggles, values, and insights on life.

My life has come full circle.

Karen Gibbs prepared me for my cancer challenges. When Barb and I started Tennis and Life Camps (TLC) in 1977, Karen's struggle with cancer communicated the philosophy and values of our camp. She modeled positive attitude, full effort, and good sportsmanship in the face of great adversity. I internalized her struggle as I told her story to thousands of campers over a 34-year period. I knew that I wanted to act similarly, should cancer confront me. I never dreamed that it would, but then it happened.

Arthur Ashe Jr. prepared me as well. His memoir, *Days of Grace*, presented a calm approach to death. The last chapter, a letter to his daughter, Camera, was written two weeks before he died. Arthur focused on the advice he wanted to give to his daughter and let go of the fact that he would die soon.

Both Karen and Arthur modeled the wisdom of the Serenity Prayer. They showed me how powerful it is, especially in the face of death. Now it is my time to follow their lead.

Wilkinson family in 2009: Caroline Sundal , Jon Sundal (son-in-law), Mike Wilkinson (brother), Steve, Ann Wilkinson (sister), Eloise Sundal, Deb Sundal (daughter), Stephen Reddington, Stephanie Wilkinson-Reddington (daughter), John Wilkinson (brother), Barb, Scott Reddington (son-in-law), and Audrey Reddington.

Wilkinson grandchildren in 2010: Audrey Reddington, Caroline Sundal,
Eloise Sundal, Steve, Barb, and Stephen Reddington

BIBLIOGRAPHY

Ashe Jr., Arthur and Arnold Rampersad. *Days of Grace*. New York: Ballantine Books, 1994.

Fromm, Erich. *Art of Loving*. New York: Harper Perennial Modern Classics, 2006.

Gallwey, Tim. *Inner Game of Tennis*. New York: Random House Trade Paperbacks, Revised Edition, 1997.

King Jr., Martin Luther. "The Casualties of the War in Viet Nam," speech delivered in Los Angeles on February 25, 1967.

    The Words of Martin Luther King Jr. New York: Edited by Coretta Scott and Martin Luther III King, William Morrow Paperbacks, Second Edition, 2001.

Lewis, C.S., *The Screwtape Letters*. New York: Harper One, Harper Collins Edition, 2001.

Mother Teresa. *In the Heart of the World: Thoughts, Stories and Prayers*. Novato, CA: New World Library, 2010.

    Everything Starts from Prayer, Mother Teresa's Meditations on Spiritual Life for People of all Faiths. Ignacio, CO: White Cloud Press, Second Edition, 2009.

Niehardt, John. *Black Elk Speaks*. Albany, NY: State University of New York Press, 1932.

Piburn, Sidney. *The Dalai Lama: A Policy of Kindness*. Delhi: Motilal Banarsidass, 2002.

Tillich, Paul. *Courage to Be*. New Haven, CT: Yale University Press, 2 Sub edition, 2000.

    The Shaking of the Foundations. Eugene, OR: Wipf & Stock Pub; Reprint edition, 2012.

ABOUT THE AUTHOR

Steve Wilkinson, Ph.D.

- Recipient of the International Tennis Hall of Fame Education Award.
- Member of the Intercollegiate Tennis Hall of Fame and the United States Professional Tennis Association Hall of Fame.
- Founder and co-director of Tennis and Life Camps, which has taught tennis, life values, and sportsmanship to over 50,000 students since 1977.
- Head tennis coach at Gustavus Adolphus College for 39 years. Compiled more wins than any other tennis coach in collegiate history.
- Inducted into the Gustavus Athletic Hall of Fame.
- National executive committee member of the U.S. Professional Tennis Association (USPTA) for 17 years and the Intercollegiate Tennis Association (ITA) for 13 years.
- United States top ranked player in the 45, 50, 55, and 60-and-over senior divisions, and winner of seven consecutive USPTA singles titles in the 45-and-over division.
- Earned a BA degree in accounting, an MBA in international finance, and a Ph.D. in ethics, world religions, and Japanese studies, all from the University of Iowa.
- College professor of accounting for 3 years, world religions for 10 years, and sport ethics for 30 years.
- Recipient of the University of Iowa "I" Club Lifetime Achievement Award.